Union-Free
America

Union-Free America

Workers and Antiunion Culture

LAWRENCE RICHARDS

UNIVERSITY OF ILLINOIS PRESS
Urbana and Chicago

Contents

Preface

This study was motivated by my experience of trying to organize computer programmers for collective action in the mid-1990s. Although not an effort to form a union, even my more limited ambition of getting programmers to join a political action committee that would lobby on their behalf received a very cool reception. As an acquaintance of mine noted at the time, trying to organize programmers was like trying to herd cats.

Two experiences during this time were especially memorable. In one instance, I attended a programmers' meeting that was called independently of my own efforts. At this meeting the principals complained of worsening job prospects and decreasing pay. They expressed an interest in forming a "software guild" and possibly creating a hiring hall (though they did not use the term *hiring hall* and probably would not have known what one was). To these workers, who were clearly thinking in the direction of collective organization, the term *union* was anathema. Instead, they looked to an older form of organization that reflected their artisan self-perception, even though the difference between a guild and a union seems more semantic than practical.

In the other instance, I attempted to have several organizations join together to form a united front on a piece of legislation that concerned us. One of these organizations, the Institute for Electrical and Electronic Engineers (IEEE, the main professional association representing software programmers), although totally behind this effort, proved very hesitant to associate itself with the American Federation of Labor–Committee for Industrial Organization (AFL-CIO). At one point the organizations involved in our drive put together a handout for legislators, which was to include the letterheads of all the organizations represented. The IEEE, however, backed out rather than have their letterhead on the same piece of paper with an AFL-CIO letterhead. Although the IEEE lobbyist was willing to accompany us, along with a representative of the AFL-CIO, he insisted on bringing his own material rather than risk exposing his organization to the charge that it was turning into a labor union.

This aversion to labor unions among programmers might not seem that remarkable. Yet even among blue-collar workers I have known, there has been a general distrust of organized labor. Horror stories about the bad things unions do abound in the folklore of American workers. Even workers who undoubtedly would benefit from a union have discussed at length the reasons they feel unions are bad.

Where did these stereotypes come from? How did organized labor come to be held in such ill repute by so many people? These were the questions I wanted to explore. Although this study cannot provide a complete answer, it does provide a start by summarizing and cataloging the views of antiunion workers in the postwar period. It lays out the lines of discourse that have had the most effect in making workers wary of unions.

In writing this book I have had the help of many people. Most especially, I would like to thank Nelson Lichtenstein for his many insightful comments, suggestions, direction, and for his constant push to improve and deepen this study. To the extent that this book is successful, much of that success can be attributed to Nelson. (To the extent it is unsuccessful, I, naturally, accept full responsibility.) Timothy Minchin generously provided many helpful suggestions and reviewed a number of my revisions. The manuscript has benefitted tremendously from his insightfulness. I also wish to thank Mark Thomas, who was very generous with his time in helping me with the statistical work embedded in chapter 4. Joseph McCartin and Robert Zieger also provided excellent comments and suggestions. I want to thank them for their input and apologize in advance for any shortcomings that still remain. Thanks also go to my editor, Laurie Matheson, who provided many useful comments. I also wish to thank William McDonald, Charles McCurdy, and Grace Hale for reading a draft of this work. The Bankard Fellowship at the University of Virginia helped fund a portion of the research and writing for this manuscript. I also wish to thank Dawn McIlvain for her meticulous copy editing.

Finally, I wish to thank my parents, without whose support and faith this book would never have been possible.

Workers' Role in Postwar Union Decline

In August 1989, the United Automobile Workers (UAW) suffered a humiliating defeat at the Nissan auto plant in Smyrna, Tennessee. After an eighteen-month campaign to convince Nissan employees that they needed a union, and despite spending hundreds of thousands of dollars and employing 30 of the union's organizers, the 2,400 workers at Nissan voted against being represented by the UAW by a 2–to-1 margin. To add insult to injury, after the results of the election were announced, antiunion workers celebrated their victory by waving American flags and donning shirts and hoisting banners that read "Union Free and Proud."[1]

Why were these workers so opposed to organized labor? What was it they thought unionization would mean that made them so hostile to the UAW? From reading the works of most historians of American labor one would barely suspect that such workers even existed. Rather, in the most familiar picture of employees celebrating victory and waving flags, the workers are wearing buttons proclaiming their allegiance to the CIO (Committee for Industrial Organization), not their employer.

Understandably, historians of U.S. labor have tended to focus their efforts on studying those workers who did organize, or, at least, attempted to. They have been motivated by a desire to uncover the sources of worker solidarity and discover how workers overcame the many obstacles that stood in the way on their path to unionization. Thus, for instance, numerous historians have studied divisions within the workforce, such as race, ethnicity, and skill, and how these divisions were (or, in some cases, were not) overcome.[2] Although such studies acknowledge that class consciousness and class solidarity have often been subordinated to racial, ethnic, and other solidarities, they generally assume that when workers' action is motivated by class interests they will move in the direction of unionization. Another growing body of literature has focused on the obstacles thrown up by both employers and the state that have either hindered worker organization or limited unions' power.[3] In this case, obstacles to unionization lie outside the working class rather than within it. The most forceful examples of this trend are reflected in the recent works of Stephen Norwood and Robert Michael Smith who detail the history of commercialized strike breaking and union busting.[4]

Only occasionally do we find mention of workers who were opposed to unions as such. For instance, several historians have noted the opposition of African American workers to unions during the 1920s and '30s because of the American Federation of Labor's (AFL's) overt racism.[5] Stephen Meyer notes the divisions among workers at Allis-Chalmers, many of whom were bitterly opposed to the UAW local.[6] Jacquelyn Hall also provides some analysis of antiunion textile workers during the early '30s, whom she characterizes as either related to management or as newcomers to the mills as opposed to the long-time residents of the mill villages.[7] (As will be seen in chapter 4, these factors were still at work in 1980.) Immigrant workers before World War I, according to David Brody and John Bodnar, were largely apathetic about unionization because of their intention to only remain in the United States for a short while before returning to their home countries.[8] Only Timothy Minchin, however, devotes much effort to examining the attitudes of antiunion workers during the postwar period. Yet his argument, that Southern textile workers either felt no need to join the Textile Union because they were already making union wages, or feared for their jobs, only partially illuminates the phenomenon and cannot explain the level of hostility to organized labor displayed by the workers at Nissan.[9]

What, if anything, had changed in the fifty years since the great organizing drives of the 1930s that could explain such antagonism? Had worker consciousness undergone a transformation since the dramatic rise of the CIO? These questions become ever more pressing as unions continue their steady descent into oblivion that began in the mid-1950s. From a high of 35 percent in 1955, unions now represent only 15 percent of the total workforce, and less than 10 percent of the private sector workforce.[10] Whereas unions in the 1950s won between 65 and 75 percent of representation elections, by the 1980s they were winning only 50 percent of the elections that they themselves had called. Likewise, the number of elections, and, most especially, the number of workers involved in such elections fell dramatically.[11]

In analyzing the reasons for this downward spiral, scholars have identified a number of factors, some of which do point to a change in worker consciousness. Many students of labor relations explain the decline of organized labor by pointing to an increase in employer opposition to unions.[12] For instance, the number of unfair labor practice charges filed with the National Labor Relations Board (NLRB) exploded after 1970 even though the number of elections actually declined.[13] More broadly, observers such as Michael Goldfield and Gary Fink have postulated a general shift in class power since the 1940s, which has allowed employers to successfully fight off unions both in the work place and in the legislative arena.[14] Not all such opposition takes the overt form most familiar during organizing drives. Both Jack Fiorito and Sanford Jacoby, for instance, point to welfare capitalist measures as well as human resource management techniques which provide a substitute for unionization and prevent union drives from ever starting.[15]

Employers' ability to resist unionization, of course, is conditioned by the legal environment, which establishes the rules within which businesses must operate when dealing with unions. Thus, many scholars have pointed to the role of the state in accounting for union decline. Legal scholars, such as Craig Becker and Paul Weiler, social scientists, such as Joel Rogers and Kate Bronfenbrenner, and labor historian David Brody, for instance, have examined how labor relations law allows employers to engage in certain practices, particularly during organizing drives, that have a tendency to discourage unionization.[16] Other analysts point to the role of the NLRB and its decisions which, in their view, grew increasingly hostile to organized labor.[17]

Building on the New Left's critique of the AFL-CIO, developed during the 1960s and '70s, another group of analysts has blamed organized labor's decline on the unions themselves. According to Mike Davis and Kim Moody, the devolution of the CIO from a social movement into mere business unionism was responsible for labor's stagnation and eventual decay. In this interpretation, unions became narrowly focused on wages and working conditions, ignoring the broader needs of workers.[18] According to Nelson Lichtenstein, this narrowing in focus resulted in both a decline in organized labor's political clout and a lessening of its appeal to workers in general.[19] Related to this critique is the charge that unions failed to maintain an organizing pace that would have allowed them to keep up with the expansion in the workforce, much less that would have allowed them to grow.[20]

A fourth explanation for union decline, one that points indirectly at a change in worker consciousness, has to do with structural changes within the economy and demographic changes within the workforce. Several observers have pointed to the shift from a manufacturing-based economy to a service economy to explain union decline. Although unions were strong in manufacturing, they failed to gain much of a foothold in white-collar fields. Thus, the change in the relative sizes of these fields led to an overall loss in union membership in relation to the total size of the workforce.[21] The increased participation of women in the workforce, according to Henry Farber and Edward Potter, also tended to lower demand for unions. This shift, however, was partially offset by the growing number of immigrants and nonwhites within the workforce who were more receptive to organization than native-born whites.[22]

Finally, some analysts point directly to a change in worker attitudes to explain the decline of organized labor. Seymour Martin Lipset, for instance, argues that the traditional American value of individualism, which was briefly eclipsed during the Depression, experienced a resurgence, making workers less inclined to join unions by the 1970s.[23] Charles Craver, echoing C. Wright Mills, notes that many white-collar workers rejected unions because they feared a loss of status.[24] And Richard Freeman's argument about the "bottom up" nature of union growth during the 1930s also implies a change in worker consciousness, for if it were workers themselves who "made a New Deal" during the '30s, then one may legitimately assume that it was also workers who were, to some degree, responsible for the decline in union density since the '50s.[25] Indeed, it is rather ironic that labor historians who focus on worker self-organization during the '30s have not extended this analysis to include worker responsibility for union decline in the postwar period. Since the 1970s the idea that subaltern groups, including slaves, women, immigrants, and the working class, have not simply been pawns in the hands of their oppressors, but have been able to shape the world in which they live, many times in opposition to the ruling class, has gained in popularity among historians. Yet this focus on "agency" has not been extended to explanations of union decline.

All of these factors have contributed to union decline. This book, however, will focus on just one: worker opposition. This does not mean I view this factor as the most important. But, so far, it has received far less attention than the other explanations. Also, we should recognize that these elements interacted with each other in a synergistic way. In examining the methods management used to fend off union-organizing drives, for instance, one finds that its principal tool was a direct appeal to workers designed to heighten the opposition many employees already had towards organized labor. Likewise, welfare capitalist measures and human resource management techniques were geared to providing workers with many of the perceived benefits of unionism without the costs—both economic and psychological—of actually joining a union. At the same time, the ways in which employers oppose unions are conditioned by the laws governing labor relations. Yet these laws are passed by a democratic legislature. Thus, presumably, if workers cared deeply enough about changing the sorry state of labor relations law in the United States, they could do so by electing representatives who would be more sympathetic to organized labor. Conversely, as critical legal theorists have argued, the law can have a powerful effect in shaping the way people think about a particular issue.[26] For example, the government's policy of encouraging union growth during the 1930s not only provided many new legal protections for workers seeking to organize, it also "raised the prestige value of unions," as C. Wright Mills noted in 1951.[27] Likewise, several historians have argued that the Taft-Hartley Act was detrimental to organized labor, not because of any specific provisions in the act itself, but because of the message it conveyed about the place of unions in American society.[28] And the idea that structural and demographic changes were responsible for union decline depends directly on the notion that some workers—that is, women and white-collar employees—were disinclined to join unions.

Central to this study will be the effort to explain why, by a two to one margin, workers in the 1970s and '80s told pollsters that they would vote against a union if a secret ballot election were held at their place of work.[29] What was the source of these workers' antipathy toward organized labor? What was it they saw in unions that they did not like? These are the questions this study seeks to answer. For, in order for us to gain a fuller understanding of the history of American workers in the postwar period, we need to take into account not only those who sought to form unions, but also those who opposed this movement.

I believe the negative attitudes towards organized labor can be attributed to a pervasive antiunion culture that existed in the United States. Although this culture was, in some respects, contradictory—holding, for instance, that unions both benefited workers and, at the same time, exploited and oppressed them—its general tenor was one of suspicion and derision. Polling data, studies by sociologists, and media representations of unions clearly attest to the extent to which the place of unions in American culture was almost wholly negative. Indeed, labor leaders ruefully acknowledged that the word *union* had become a derogatory term for many people, calling it the "u-word".[30] Part I of this volume details the content of this antiunion culture—why unions became the "u-word."

From there, the study examines how this antiunion culture operated to thwart the growth of organized labor. A number of case studies of organizing drives are presented to show how employers, and, in a few cases, even unions themselves, exploited images of organized labor derived from the antiunion culture to sow doubt in workers' minds about the relative merit of being represented by a union. The goal here is not to detail employers' successful antiunion strategies, however. Rather, by examining the campaign literature put out by employers *and* unions during these organizing drives, I believe it is possible to gain insight into the concerns workers themselves had about unions, and why many of them opposed unionization. Both parties to these contests understood that there was a deep-seated suspicion of unions among many workers and sought to either reinforce or bring into question their preconceived ideas about organized labor. Thus, whereas employers used the negative images of organized labor prevalent in the general culture to bolster their case, unions found it necessary to spend considerable time and effort to convince workers that these images were either not true, or not applicable to them.

Rather than assuming that workers were always and inevitably desirous of joining a union, then, this study starts from the premise, stated by Thomas Kochan in 1979, that "[u]nions are seen by a large number of workers as a strategy of last resort rather than as a natural or preferred means of improving job conditions."[31] Why this situation came about is the subject of the chapters that follow.

PART I

America's
Antiunion Culture

Since its origins in the early nineteenth century, organized labor in the United States has operated under a cloud. The dominant Anglo culture, although prepared to tolerate their existence, has nevertheless held a generally negative view of unions. Indeed, it would be no exaggeration to say that an antiunion culture has existed within the United States. This section explicates the shape and content of this culture. Having established such a foundation, it will then be possible to show in the next section how this culture worked to thwart the growth of unions when they tried to reach out to unorganized workers in the late twentieth century.

What I am particularly concerned with here is establishing the cultural image of unions in the United States during the twentieth century. By "cultural image" I mean those associations and ideas that immediately came to mind when the average American heard the term *union*. A cultural image, in other words, can be thought of as the common knowledge or the common understanding a society has about a particular subject. This is most readily seen in jokes that assume a prior understanding of the culture. To give just one example, consider the comedic staple of lawyers as sharks and ambulance chasers.[1]

This is not to say that there was a monolithic image of unions that all Americans shared, although I do believe there was a hegemonic image.[2] Many people's views of organized labor would have differed based on their experiences with unions and their particular backgrounds. Workers on an assembly line might have pictured unions as an impersonal and distant bureaucracy, whereas workers in some skilled craft, such as plumbers, might have seen unions as a job trust. Additionally, simply because people are raised in a particular culture does not mean that they will accept all the tenets of that culture. For instance, Seymour Martin Lipset found that workers whose political ideology leaned in a social democratic direction had a more positive view of unions than workers who held to more individualistic ideologies.[3] Rejecting elements of the culture is not the same as being unaware of them, however. In the union I belonged to while in graduate school, joking about mobsters, "enforcers," and the "union boss" (a female graduate student) was quite common at union meetings. These jokes both confirmed our familiarity with the cultural image of unions and demonstrated our conscious rejection of it (at least with respect to our own union). Nevertheless, even among unionized workers, attitudes about unions from the 1960s through the '80s were mostly in agreement with those of the rest of the populace.[4]

To reconstruct the place of unions in the public imagination during these years, I examine the ways in which a number of people discussed unions, in particular, the words, images, phrases, and tropes common to people of opposed political and social ideologies. The goal here is not to evaluate the veracity of any particular claim about the make-up or behavior of unions, but simply to understand what society generally believed was true in regards to organized labor. To accomplish this, I considered a number of different sources.

Polling data, where and when available, are highly useful in revealing how people felt about a particular subject. Rather than simply relying on the responses to survey questions, however, it is also important to realize that the *questions* themselves are important clues to how people thought about unions. As an example, consider the following statement: "When unions were first started they were needed because workers were being exploited by low wages, long hours, and bad working conditions." That 96 percent of those surveyed agreed with this statement simply confirms that the person doing the survey had a feel for what the average American thought concerning the origins of organized labor. On the other hand, even though only 35 percent of those surveyed in 1981 agreed with the statement that "[u]nions served a useful purpose once, but they've outgrown their usefulness," the question reflects the impression that was gaining ground among many intellectuals during the 1970s and '80s that unions had become obsolete.[5] The formulation of poll questions, then, is based on a presumption that the surveyor already has some knowledge about the range of answers his respondents might give for a particular question; the surveyor and those surveyed share the same cultural milieu.

The work of sociologists and industrial relations specialist forms another important source for understanding the place of unions in American culture. Studies of various groups of workers often posed questions about how people viewed unions. Although not as comprehensive as polling data, because such studies were generally confined both geographically and occupationally, they allow a more in-depth understanding of how particular groups of workers thought about organized labor.

Because polling data and sociological studies have left gaps in understanding how people felt about unions, and because polls, especially, have not provided the kind of depth desirable for a study of this nature, portrayals of organized labor in the media have also been examined as yet another source for understanding the cultural image of unions. At its height, organized labor could claim to represent just one-third of the working population. Hence, the majority of Americans had no direct involvement with unions. They may have had relatives in unions, or worked alongside union members, and these experiences no doubt shaped their opinions about organized labor. For many Americans, however, their only contact with the labor movement was when they were inconvenienced by some strike or through the mass media. In addition, even those Americans who belonged to unions in the 1960s, '70s, and '80s did not display attitudes towards organized labor that varied significantly from the general public. Although supportive of their own unions, they were as skeptical as nonmembers about the labor movement as a whole.[6] This no doubt reflected the importance of the media in shaping even union members' attitudes towards organized labor.

The media, of course, not only shape but reflect popular prejudices. Script writers, columnists, and journalists, for instance, all are raised within the same cultural milieu as their audience and thus share many of its same preconceptions. Indeed, communication would be much more difficult, if not impossible, if this were not the case. Knowing and catering to one's audience is as much a part of the media as it is of any other enterprise. The question of whether the media are more a reflection or shaper of popular culture, however, is not a question that needs to be settled here, and is not an issue that I wish to address. Rather, it is enough to assert that the way the media treat any particular topic influences, at least to some extent, how people view that issue; at the same time, it also provides a valuable source for understanding how society thinks about that subject.[7]

This use of the phrase "the media" is, of course, an oversimplification. There is no single entity that can be labeled "the media." Thus, it cannot be said that there is a single, universal, "media portrayal" of unions, or any other subject. Rather, each different medium has its own particular point of view and conception of the audience it is speaking to that is reflected in its choice of and treatment of content. It is not the differences among various media, however, but the commonalities among them that are important here. The premise of this study is that by examining what a variety of media, especially those with a wide audience, had to say about unions, it is possible to reconstruct the place of organized labor in American culture.

In this regard, magazines proved to be especially useful because of the large number of articles and the breadth of their coverage. *Ladies Home Journal, Reader's Digest, Life* magazine, and *Saturday Evening Post* were chosen for study because of their wide circulations. *Reader's Digest,* for example, had a readership that went from four million in 1946 to ten million in 1954. By 1960, "the magazine was going to one out of every four households in the United States and Canada and being read, according to pass-along polls, by half the population of both countries."[8] In 1947, *Life* had a circulation of over five million, *Ladies Home Journal* was delivered to over four million subscribers each month in 1942, and the *Saturday Evening Post's* circulation went from about four million in 1946 to six million in 1959.[9] Although not explicitly political in nature—in fact *Reader's Digest* went to some lengths to preserve its air of neutrality by occasionally condensing articles from liberal publications—all of these magazines were either edited or owned by deeply conservative publishers.[10] For instance, in 1941 a committee of the National Council of English Teachers labeled *Reader's Digest* a "fascist publication."[11] And although Henry Luce, the owner of *Time, Life,* and *Fortune,* may have employed several notable leftists such as Dwight Macdonald and Daniel Bell, his own politics, which were reflected in the editorial position of his magazines, were very conservative. For a contrasting point of view to that of these generally conservative mass circulation magazines, the *New Republic* was also consulted to see what a liberal publication was saying about unions during the same period. Though *New Republic* never reached a mass audience the way *Reader's Digest* or *Life* did, it did tend to reflect the thinking of liberals during this period. *National Review* was also included in this study to examine how an explicitly conservative magazine treated unions. It needs to be repeated, however, that the point here is not to trace the political debate about the place of unions in American society, but to try to reconstruct the image of unions in the public mind by examining how a variety of different sources talked about organized labor.

Movies and television programs were also considered, but in this case unions were most notable for their absence. Very few movies had unions as their subject. Unions might be mentioned in passing, as in the 1996 movie

Ransom, where the hero Mel Gibson admits to paying off a union leader to avoid having his company struck, or the 1947 classic *Miracle on 34th Street,* where the political power of the AFL and CIO is mentioned. On the whole, however, Hollywood has seen fit to largely ignore organized labor. For instance, Tom Zaniello lists 147 movies in his 1996 guide to films dealing with labor, *Working Stiffs, Union Maids, Reds and Riffraff.* Yet, of these 147, 29 are foreign films and 33 are documentaries (most of which had a very limited circulation). Of the remaining 85, a large number, such as *Golddiggers of 1933, Spartacus, Raisin in the Sun,* and *9 to 5,* deal with labor issues, but fail to address unions at all.[12] Depictions of unions on television, either in dramatic or comedic series, were also rare.[13] C. Wright Mills noted in 1948 that "[i]n radio soap operas, in the comic strips, movies, and pulp fiction, labor unions and labor leaders are almost never brought into the picture in any way."[14] This state of affairs, like most aspects of America's antiunion culture, did not change in the half-century since that time.

This selection of sources may strike some readers as being overly focused on middle-class attitudes towards labor. There are a number of reasons for this. First, as just indicated, many of the sources selected were chosen precisely because they had such a wide circulation. This, of course, meant focusing on middle-class publications. Second, it is my intention to document the dominant or hegemonic view of unions, the union image that was most widespread and influential. Although this may appear to have little relation to working-class or minority attitudes towards unions, it is precisely the hegemonic function of middle-class culture and its influence on the rest of society that is at issue here.

Ever since the publication of E. P. Thompson's *Making of the English Working Class* and the rise of the new labor history, labor historians have been concerned with reconstructing the world view and culture of the working class, not as a mere derivative of middle-class and bourgeois culture, but as an autonomous entity.[15] This research has contributed greatly to our understanding of the working class and the process of industrialization. But for the most part, these studies have focused on the nineteenth and first half of the twentieth centuries. Much less work has been done on working-class culture in the postwar era, particularly in regards to workers' attitudes about organized labor. In fact, such evidence as does exist for the postwar period indicates that unionized workers' views of trade unions did not vary significantly from those of the general public from the 1960s through the 1980s.[16] Thus, by the late twentieth century, whatever working-class culture had existed prior to World War II had experienced a good deal of erosion, at least with respect to attitudes towards unions.

"Installment buying, television, and suburbanization," as George Lipsitz has noted, "functioned as powerful agents for the nationalization and homogenization of U.S. culture," during the 1950s and '60s.[17] Although this process could work in both directions—for instance, as with the popularity of rock and roll, which had its roots in African American culture and then spread to the white middle class—a good deal of this "homogenized" culture was based on middle-class, Anglo-Saxon, Protestant values. In addition, prior to World War II America's blue-collar working class had been largely composed of immigrants, who, to a large degree, lived in a cultural milieu separate from that of the middle class. After immigration was cut by the National Origins Act of 1924, however, the cultural diversity of the United States decreased significantly from the 1930s through the 1970s. As white ethnic groups increasingly assimilated to the dominant Anglo culture, the antiunion bias in that culture began to influence even many blue-collar workers. It is also significant that the one major group that by the 1970s remained mostly supportive of unions was African Americans, who continued to reside in a separate cultural universe from that of whites.[18] As a result, the cultural image of unions laid out in this section, though in many ways derived from middle-class sources, greatly influenced the way that even many blue-collar workers came to view organized labor by the 1970s.

One of the most remarkable aspects of this image has been its consistency. During the course of the twentieth century—through good economic times and bad, through periods of war and peace, domestic tranquility and upheaval—many of the ideas Americans harbored about organized labor were remarkably constant. As one example, Americans long believed that unions were particularly prone to corruption.[19] As another, the idea that unions were organized primarily to foment strikes had an equally long pedigree.[20] In part, this stability in the union image was an artifact of organized labor's structural position in the capitalist system. For instance, Frank Morrison, secretary-treasurer of the AFL, observed in 1920 that the interests of "labor" and "the community" were "structurally and historically antagonistic." Whereas workers were interested in higher wages and better working conditions, the community's interest was in uninterrupted production. Therefore, when workers struck to improve their situation (thus stopping production), they came into conflict with the community's interest in securing the product of their labor. This conflict, then, tended to paint organized labor as a special interest whose every gain could only come at the expense of society.[21] In part, the unchanging aspects of organized labor's image were a reflection of the manner in which information about unions was disseminated. For instance, Walter Lippmann noted in the early 1920s that the public was under the impression that unions were constantly on strike because newspapers tended to classify events, rather than process, as news. Thus, strikes qualified as "news" because they were "events," whereas the process of negotiation and the accumulation of grievances that led to strikes went unreported because they were not "events."[22] Whatever the cause, many features of the union image remained virtually unchanged from 1900 to 1990.

In spite of the stable nature of many of the specifics of the union image, the general level of sympathy Americans have had for organized labor as a whole has varied greatly from one era to another. Prior to the Great Depression, labor was viewed with a good deal of suspicion, if not alarm. Often referred to as the "labor question" or the "social question," the impression that unions were subversive, potentially insurrectionary, organizations was widespread. Dating from the Great Depression and lasting through the 1960s, the level of approval for organized labor was considerably higher. Instead of being regarded as potential seedbeds of revolution, unions came to be seen as champions of the "underdog," fighting to achieve justice for low-paid and mistreated workers. Beginning in the 1960s, organized labor again fell out of favor with many Americans. Unions' seeming success in raising their members into the ranks of the middle class eroded the idea that unions spoke for the underprivileged. Organized labor was now believed to represent the "haves" rather than the "have-nots."

Key to this changing level of approval for organized labor was the changing perception native, white, middle-class Americans had of the members, real or potential, of unions. To rephrase this, what many Americans thought about unions depended on what they thought about union members, and, particularly in the earlier period, of the working class. When, as prior to the Depression and from the 1960s through the 1980s, Americans looked on union members with either suspicion or impatience, they were less likely to approve of unions. When, as during the 1930s, Americans looked on the working class more sympathetically, their acceptance of organized labor was generally higher.

Part I will trace this changing level of support for organized labor and show how it was related to Americans' shifting perceptions of union members and the working class. More important, it will also lay out the many aspects of Americans' image of unions that came to dominate their thinking about organized labor by the 1970s. In other words, part I describes the cultural milieu in which workers operated when faced with the choice of supporting a union or not. Part II will then show how this cultural milieu worked to dissuade many workers from supporting unionization during the 1970s and '80s.

1

The Union Image in the
Age of Industrialization

Un-American Workers; Un-American Unions

From 1886 through the first third of the twentieth century, middle-class Americans viewed the working class as both alien and subversive. The proletariat, in this view, was un-American in every sense of that word: it was composed largely of immigrants and their children; and it was wedded to radical and foreign ideologies. Eric Hobsbawn has observed that the middle and upper classes of every industrial society viewed the working classes as "barbarians" during the nineteenth century.[1] If this was true for such (generally) ethnically homogenous countries as England, France, and Germany, it was even more applicable to the United States where much of the working class truly was "foreign." Although Americans' level of anxiety about the threat posed by the working class may have varied in intensity, waxing in certain periods, waning in others, the image of the unruly, dangerous, even revolutionary nature of the proletariat remained a constant throughout this era. This perception of the working class would in turn influence Americans' ideas about the institutions—generally trade unions, but also political parties—that represented it.

From the early years of the nineteenth century, Americans had worried about the creation of a permanent class of wage earners in the United States and the threat this development posed for the maintenance of its republican institutions. After the Civil War, as the Second Industrial Revolution gained momentum, and the realization sunk in that wage work was no longer a temporary phase through which workers passed on their way to becoming independent, self-supporting citizens, but had become a permanent condition, this anxiety increased. The formation of various Working-Men's parties and the National Labor Union during the era of Reconstruction, in conjunction with the example of the Paris Commune in 1870, seemed to confirm the fear that the existence and spread of a permanent wage-labor class presented a danger to the republic.[2] The Great Railroad Strike of 1877 proved to be a dramatic confirmation of these fears. To many Americans, this strike represented an incipient revolution. In response, many cities built formidable armories and militias underwent training to suppress urban rioting.[3]

Labor and the anarchist. *Los Angeles Times,* Sept. 10, 1910.

It was the Haymarket "riot" of 1886, however, that was to prove decisive in shaping middle-class Americans' image of the working class and its institutions.[4] The picture of the bomb-throwing, knife-wielding, bewhiskered and foreign-looking anarchist, poised for both individual and collective rebellion, formed an important strand in Americans' perception of the proletariat, a strand of thought that would persist through the 1920s. Edward Bellamy's popular utopian novel, *Looking Backward,* written one year after Haymarket, captured this sense of foreboding among middle-class Americans. As Bellamy's protagonist Julian West phrases it in his conversation with Dr. Leete, the "labor question . . . was the Sphinx's riddle of the nineteenth century, and when I dropped out of it the Sphinx was threatening to devour society. . . . We felt that society was dragging anchor and in danger of going adrift. Whither it would drift nobody could say, but all feared the rocks. . . . I should not have been surprised had I looked down from your housetop today on a heap of charred and moss-grown ruins."[5] Likewise, Jacob Riis, in his generally sympathetic treatment of the tenement dwellers of New York, *How the Other Half Lives* (1890), provided a cautionary tale on the threat posed by the working classes if their conditions were not ameliorated. In his chapter "The Man with the Knife," Riis recounts the story of one worker who has gone mad (both mentally and emotionally) as a result of his poverty and the plight of his starving children. He stands on Fifth Avenue watching the wealthy shoppers going in and out of the expensive stores and lashes out at the injustice of his situation, wildly stabbing at the passersby. As Riis warned, "the man and his knife . . . represented one solution of the problem of ignorant poverty *versus* ignorant wealth that has come down to us unsolved, the danger-cry of which we have lately heard in the shout that never should have been raised on American soil—the shout of 'the masses against the classes'—the solution of violence."[6]

Whereas an image of the working class as potentially insurrectionary could coexist with more sympathetic views of workers as *individuals,* this was much less true of the organizations that represented them *collectively.* Bellamy's Julian West, for example, in the course of his conversation with Dr. Leete, expressed the concern many Americans harbored that labor unions had grown dangerously large and powerful:

> "What should you name as the most prominent feature of the labor troubles of your day?"
> "Why, the strikes, of course," . . .
> "Exactly; but what made the strikes so formidable?"
> "The great labor organizations."[7]

"COME, BROTHERS, YOU HAVE GROWN SO BIG YOU CANNOT AFFORD TO QUARREL"

The war between capital and labor. *Harpers Weekly,* June 1, 1901.

William Rogers, an illustrator for *Harper's Weekly,* both reflected and reenforced this concern in several of his cartoons. In one illustration from 1901, for
instance, Capital and Labor are equally powerful and the war between them
threatens the existence of the nation. What is evident from these examples,
at least in hindsight, is that Americans greatly exaggerated the size, power,
and potential danger of organized labor during most of this era.

The fear of working-class radicalism that Haymarket inspired was powerfully reinforced by the arrival of the "new" immigrants. These "new" immigrants came from southern and eastern Europe in increasingly large numbers
beginning in the 1890s. As early as 1891, a strike by Slavic and Magyar coke

workers in eastern Pennsylvania against Henry Clary Frick's coal company was "interpreted as an uprising of the 'Huns.'" Three years later, a similar strike, according to the Pittsburgh *Times* had "the whole region . . . 'trembling on the brink of an insurrection.'"[8] The examples of Alexander Berkman, companion of "Red" Emma Goldman, who attempted to assassinate Henry Frick during the Homestead Strike of 1892, and of Leon Czolgosz, who was the son of Polish immigrants and a self-proclaimed anarchist who assassinated President McKinley in 1901, would only further strengthen the image of the immigrant working class as radical and dangerous. By 1919 during the first great Red Scare, as Frederick Lewis Allen wrote about the American businessman, but as could be said of the middle class in general, "he had come to distrust anything and everything that was foreign, and this radicalism he saw as the spawn of long-haired Slavs and unwashed East-Side Jews. . . . he was ready to believe that a struggle of American laboring-men for better wages was the beginning of an armed rebellion directed by Lenin and Trotsky, and that behind every innocent professor who taught that there were arguments for as well as against socialism there was a bearded rascal from eastern Europe with a money bag in one hand and a smoking bomb in the other."[9]

Even at the height of the Progressive era, a period during which, according to John Higham, Americans regained much of the confidence they had lost in the 1890s, and when, as Michael Kazin argues, many middle-class reformers ceased to view workers as a "rebellious, alien force," most Americans continued to see the working-class as radical and foreign, albeit without same degree of fear so evident in the '90s.[10] Indeed, one motive for reform during this period was the hope that by improving workers' conditions, they would be less susceptible to appeals for revolutionary action.[11] For instance, Herbert Croly, the quintessential Progressive political thinker, pointed to a disturbing trend within organized labor towards insurrection as one reason the U.S. political and economic system needed to be reformed: "The most serious danger to the American democratic future which may issue from aggressive and unscrupulous unionism consists in the state of mind of which mob-violence is only one expression. The militant unionists are beginning to talk and believe as if they were at war with the existing social and political order. . . . the literature popular among the unionists is a literature, not merely of discontent, but sometimes of revolt."[12]

Other evidence points to the continued vitality of this image as well. Walter Lippmann, writing in 1914 in defense of the right of workers to organize, for example, felt it necessary to deny that unions posed a threat to society. The "effort of wage-earners to achieve power," he claimed, did not point to "insurrection." Rather, it was the denial of this right that led to talk of revolution. "It is the weak unions, the unorganized and shifting workers, who talk sabotage and flare up into a hundred little popgun rebellions." The railroad brotherhoods, by way of contrast, were "so powerful that they don't have to flirt with insurrection." They had already "won the very things the lack of which makes rebellion necessary." According to Lippmann, it was "the paradox of the labor movement, that those who can't overthrow society dream of doing it, while those who could, don't want to." And he chided his middle-class readers for not being more understanding of the labor movement: "To expect unionists then to talk with velvet language, and act with the deliberation of a college faculty is to be a tenderfoot, a victim of your class tradition."[13] Even so prominent a reformer as Edith Abbott referred in 1905 to unskilled laborers as "a dangerous class: inadequately fed, clothed, and housed, they threaten the health of the community, and, like all the weak and ignorant, they often become misguided followers of unscrupulous men."[14]

Two developments during this period were especially worrisome to middle-class Americans. The first was the growing vote for the Socialist Party, which, as Jack London observed in 1905, convinced many Americans that socialism "was a very live and growing revolutionary force."[15] The other development, also in 1905, was the founding of the Industrial Workers of the World (IWW), commonly referred to as the wobblies. With its openly revolutionary philosophy of the general strike and its militant activism, the IWW came to personify many Americans' vision of the revolutionary potential of the working class and its organizations.

One particularly infamous incident from this era might also be mentioned for its effect in shaping Americans' image of organized labor: the bombing of the Los Angeles *Times* building on October 1, 1910. Even before the bombs went off, the *Times* had run an editorial cartoon equating unions with the classic image of the anarchist bomb-thrower. When James and Joseph McNamara of the International Association of Bridge and Structural Iron Workers eventually confessed to conspiring to plant the bomb, it had the effect of painting even "respectable" unions (i.e. those associated with the American Federation of Labor) as dangerous, even subversive.[16]

The period stretching from 1917 through the mid-1920s, of course, marked the height of Americans' fears about the foreign and revolutionary nature of the working class. The wartime drive for "100% Americanism," coupled with the specter of Communist Revolutions in Russia, Hungary, and Bavaria, spilled over into the antiunion, antiradical, and anti-immigration movements of the postwar period. The great strike wave of 1919 was accompanied by a huge Red Scare. During the steel strike of that year, for instance, the strikers (most of whom were immigrants, a large portion of whom were Slavic) were portrayed by the management of the steel companies as anarchists and Bolsheviks.[17] The IWW was forcibly suppressed, with much of its top leadership sent to prison. Even Eugene Debs, the perennial candidate for President on the Socialist Party ticket, was locked up in a federal penitentiary (from where he won over 900,000 votes in the 1920 election). The Palmer Raids of 1920–1 rounded up large numbers of foreigners as suspected radicals, many of whom, including Emma Goldman, were later deported.[18]

This hysteria would continue into the 1920s. The second Ku Klux Klan, which was founded in 1915, grew to encompass a membership of, by some estimates, almost five million in 1924. In addition to its more familiar anti-black, anti-Catholic, anti-Semitic, and anti-immigrant biases, the Klan also reflected the petite bourgeois animus against all expressions of class-based divisions in society, particularly those of the working class, that was a common feature of fascist movements throughout the industrial world during the '20s.[19] On August 23, 1927, Nicola Sacco and Bartolomeo Vanzetti, Italian immigrants and anarchists, were executed for the murder of a paymaster in Baintree, Massachusetts, in spite of many legitimate doubts about their guilt. When immigration soared back to its prewar levels in 1920, Congress quickly moved to cut off the flood of foreigners and their supposedly radical ideologies. A stop-gap immigration restriction law was enacted in 1921, followed by the more comprehensive National Origins Act of 1924. The act of 1924 was designed to keep out the undesirable "new" immigrants by tying the immigration quotas to the percentage of each country's nationals present in the United States in the census of 1890, that is, before the "new" immigrants had begun to arrive in significant numbers.

Finally, employers launched the "American Plan" to regain the control of their workers they seemed to have lost during the war. Where unions had not yet gained a foothold, company unions and employee representation plans were created to keep out "outside" unions. Various welfare capitalist measures, such as pensions, employee stock ownership plans, and recreational facilities, were instituted to inspire company loyalty. Where unions did exist, employers engaged in various union-busting strategies, such as strikebreaking and blacklisting, to evict them from their shops. Union membership dwindled from a high of five million in 1919 to three million in 1932. In addition to its antiunion premises, the American Plan also represented an attempt to, as Louis Adamic put it, "'Americanize' the American worker."[20] Classes to teach immigrants English and the virtues of the American political and economic system were created, and pressure was applied on immigrant workers to attend.

Although greatly diminished, this fear of the radical and foreign nature of the working class would persist through the late 1920s and the early years of the Great Depression. Adamic's book, *Dynamite: The Story of Class Violence in America,* published in 1931, forms an excellent bookend to this period. Although sympathetic to the working class (Adamic was not formally a member of the Communist Party but was clearly a fellow traveler), his book was premised on the reality of class struggle and the inevitable outbreaks of violence that were a result of this conflict. Despite the fact that he was writing from a Leftist perspective, Adamic painted a picture of the class struggle that most Americans could readily agree with—and fear. As late as the summer of 1932, shortly after the massacre of the hunger marchers in Dearborn, Michigan, but—significantly—before the Bonus Army's eviction from Washington, D.C., a spate of articles were written for some of the leading opinion magazines of the time that openly discussed the prospects of a revolution. Many Americans, both on the Left and Right, the former with hopeful anticipation, the latter with a sense of dread, clearly expected that the suffering of the Depression would result in a spontaneous and widespread rebellion.[21]

Domesticating the Working Class

Although World War I inspired one of the greatest outbreaks of xenophobia and antiradical hysteria in the history of the United States, it also set in motion a train of events that would, by the mid-1930s, fundamentally reshape Americans' image of the working class and of organized labor. Rather than seeing them as foreign and revolutionary, Americans increasingly came to look on blue-collar workers as essentially "American." The combination of immigration restriction and the Americanization programs of the 1920s restored their confidence in the ability of the melting pot to absorb and assimilate immigrants. The example of the Bonus Army in 1932 also helped alter their understanding of the makeup of the working class. Because of the severity of the Depression and, especially, because of its effect on "American" workers, blue-collar workers, instead of being primarily seen as enemies of the capitalist system, came to be viewed, first and foremost, as its victims. At the same time, businessmen, who had practically achieved the status of sainthood during the 1920s, came to be viewed as venal and corrupt war profiteers by the mid-1930s. No longer would the plight of the working class be understood as the outcome of the natural and impersonal operation of the capitalist system—though, to the extent it was, this was taken as an indictment of capitalism, not workers—but, rather, it was seen as the fault of greedy and tyrannical capitalists who exploited workers for their own personal profit. Efforts to ameliorate the conditions of these victims, then, could be imagined as coming at the expense of business, and not society as a whole. As a result of these changes, unions, as the representatives of this victimized class, were reinterpreted to be the champions of the downtrodden, the "underdog," in contrast to their previous portrayal as subversive and revolutionary organizations.

Even before the war, Progressives had done much to legitimize the principle of collective bargaining. The idea of bringing "democracy into industry," of giving workers a voice in their working conditions, increasingly gained currency during this period, especially following the 1915 report of the U.S. Commission on Industrial Relations.[22] Already by 1916, for example, anti-union employers in San Francisco were claiming that they were not "opposed to labor organizations *per se*."[23] It was the AFL's support for the war, however, that proved to be key to establishing the legitimacy of organized labor. Its patriotism and Americanism were now "beyond reproach." The force of President Wilson's rhetoric in calling for a "War for Democracy" abroad spilled over into calls for spreading democracy at home, in particular for "industrial democracy." Moreover, by endorsing the principle of collective bargaining, and by bringing the AFL into the government to help tame industrial unrest and keep war-related production running smoothly, the Wilson administration had put the imprimatur of the federal government behind organized labor. These developments, as Joseph McCartin has written, persuaded employers by the end of the war that they now had "a moral 'duty to bargain'" with their employees. As demonstrated by the American Plan, this did not necessarily imply the need to bargain with "outside" unions. Nevertheless, "labor now seemed . . . to have achieved 'a moral and political strengthening' that would leave it 'more entrenched in American life than it ha[d] ever been before.'"[24]

Whereas the AFL benefited from the war, temporarily in terms of numbers and permanently in terms of legitimacy, radical organizations were a big loser. The IWW was virtually crushed by a combination of state and vigilante action. After the 1920 elections, the vote total for, and membership in, the Socialist Party also dropped precipitously. As Barry Cushman puts it, "the years following World War I saw the relationship between the Socialist

Party and the nation's workers grow increasingly attenuated. . . . the party became 'increasingly an organization of ministers and intellectuals rather than industrial workers.'"[25] The newly formed Communist Party, meanwhile, had a minuscule membership. As Frederick Lewis Allen recalled in 1931, Attorney General Mitchell Palmer's "inquisitorial methods . . . had at least had the practical effect of scaring many Reds into a pale pinkness."[26] In a similar vein, Adamic felt that many immigrants, during the early part of the Depression, were cowed by their fear of exposing themselves to government repression.[27] Whatever the cause, the threat of radicalism seemed much less credible by the end of the 1920s than it had in 1919. This fact, more than any other, probably explains the disintegration of the Klan after 1925. Whereas fascist organizations in Germany and Italy had very real and large enemies against which to rally—the Socialist and Communist parties—radicalism in the United States was practically nonexistent.

The wartime inspired drive for immigration restriction and pressure on immigrants to enroll in Americanization programs also contributed to relieving Americans' worries about a working-class revolution. With the flow of new arrivals reduced to a trickle, confidence in the country's ability to assimilate foreigners was restored. For example, Whiting Williams, who made a living posing as a blue-collar worker so that he could report on their attitudes, wrote an article for the *Saturday Evening Post* in 1933 that claimed that it was only the most recent immigrants, the "latest comers," that were attracted to the Communist Party. In talking about soap-box orators he had observed, he claimed that, "It is bad enough that their language is usually broken English; one pair of ears is enough to prove the great majority of the agitators completely foreign born, and one pair of eyes and ears soon learn that most of the hearers are Europeans who have come here *too recently to get a satisfactory toehold.*" The great mass of workers, by contrast, had "been giving an amazing demonstration of calmness, courage and confidence under the thoroughly distressing circumstances of the past few years." They were "just perverse enough to consider themselves not as Have-nots, but, instead, as Have-hads."[28] Similarly, in a speech to mark the fiftieth anniversary of the Statue of Liberty in 1936, President Roosevelt praised immigrants' contribution to the nation and claimed that they had become loyal citizens. "In Americanization classes and at night schools they have burned the midnight oil in order to be worthy of their new allegiance." As Gary Gerstle has argued, the success of "the disciplinary project" of the 1920s greatly reduced Americans' anxieties about the new immigrants during the Great Depression.[29]

By cutting off European immigration at the very moment that the demand for new industrial workers was at its greatest, World War I also triggered the start of the Great Migration of African Americans from the South to the North. As these job seekers crowded into Northern cities, racial tensions greatly increased, leading to several race riots in 1919. During the Progressive Era, the "race question" in the North had not been primarily one of black versus white, but rather one of "natives" versus "not-quite-white" new immigrants. With tens of thousands of African Americans pouring into cities such as Detroit, Chicago, and New York, each year, the traditional white American preoccupation with white-versus-black issues gained in importance while concern about the new immigrants began to lose its saliency. As Matthew Frye Jacobson and David Roediger have argued, the Great Migration played an important role in "whitening" the new immigrants.[30] This process of "whitening" would greatly contribute to "Americanizing" the working class in the eyes of middle-class Americans. "Whiteness" was central to the concept of Americanism; to be an "American" at this time was to be white. And even though most African Americans were obviously part of the working class, this did not present a problem at the time because Americans had not yet assimilated African Americans to the image of the "worker," who was white and male.

World War I would have one final, crucial, though long-delayed and totally unexpected, effect in shaping Americans' perception of the working class: the example of the Bonus March in the summer of 1932. When these out-of-work veterans gathered in Washington to lobby for the early payment of the bonus that had been promised them but was not due until 1945, they put a new face on the problem of unemployment. Roy Rosenzweig has credited the unemployed councils and various hunger marches of the early Depression with dramatizing the problem of unemployment.[31] But, because most of these activities were organized by the Communist and Socialist parties, this dramatization was more likely to lead to a reaction of fear than it was of sympathy. Not that fear could not be an effective spur to reform. Charles Walker, writing about the prospects for revolution in *Forum* magazine in the summer of 1932, made this connection explicit. After a large, communist-led hunger march in Chicago during the winter of 1931/32, he noted that Illinois politicians quickly acted to appropriate $20 million for relief, or, as Mayor Cermak of Chicago called it, "civic fire insurance." Similarly, he credited the passage of a $2 billion appropriation for the Reconstruction Finance Corporation to two causes: "hunger and fear; hunger on the part of the unemployed and fear on the part of the government."[32] The communist-led unemployed councils and hunger marches, then, tended to reenforce the long tradition of seeing the working class as separate from, and threatening to, the rest of American society.

The Bonus Army, on the other hand, made Americans see the unemployed as no different from themselves; it evoked a sense of identification rather than distinction. This was because their understanding of the Bonus Army melded together two, somewhat contradictory, images. First, thanks to their status as veterans, the Bonus marchers were treated much more sympathetically than any other group of unemployed workers would have been. As men who had fought for their country, they could not be communists who, by the commonly accepted definition, were "disloyal" and intent on revolution. As one of the veterans put it, "We're loyal—get that straight buddy—we're not Reds."[33] In spite of their special status, however, the marchers were also portrayed as being representative of *all* the unemployed and of Americans in general. Here is how Floyd Gibbons, a correspondent for the Hearst press, put it, "They were just folks—American folks—homeless—jobless—foodless American citizens—just a few stray bewildered, puzzled thousands of the millions of jobless who with their wives and kids and dependents now number so great a percentage of our population."[34]

Rosenzweig has argued that "In the 30s, for the first time, unemployment was an experience shared by both the middle and working classes; but, it was the middle-class unemployed who experienced the greatest shock and attitude changes as a result of the Depression."[35] With its outwardly middle-class appearance, the Bonus Army helped dramatize this reality even for the many middle-class Americans who had not themselves experienced unemployment.[36] It made it possible for them to empathize with the plight of the blue-collar jobless. For example, Gibbons described the men as "steel workers, coal miners, structural iron workers, cowboys, stenographers, newspaper reporters, dairymen, shopkeepers without shops, clerks, farmers—well, they are just American people like you and me."[37] As this list of occupations makes clear, both blue- and white-collar workers could now be considered equally "American" (even though other status distinctions between the two groups would remain).

The rout of the Bonus Army at the end of July 1932 would mark the last gasp of the old association of the working-class with revolutionary intentions. As mentioned above, as late as the summer of 1932 a spate of articles appeared in the major opinion magazines that examined the prospects for revolution. Although all but one came to the conclusion that there was nothing to worry about, they did reflect a widespread fear, particularly evident after the massacre at Dearborn in March. The Bonus Army itself would initially inspire similar concerns. "Serious alarm is voiced by newspapers all over the country. Washington officialdom is on tenderhooks. The gravity, the menace of the situation is discust [sic] everywhere," reported *Literary Digest*.[38] Likewise, after seeing Bonus Army marchers stone the car of his grandfather, Senator Gore, Gore Vidal recalled thinking "my god, it [a revolution] could happen here."[39] George Sokolsky went so far as to predict the fate of the marchers: "These demobilized soldiers constitute the only articulate revolutionary group in the United States. . . . It may become necessary to shoot [them] down some day. . . . the army is likely to shoot [them] down as it would shoot down Communists or striking miners."[40] Even after this prediction became reality, some commentators were still prepared to see it in a positive light. "The incident at Anacostia Flats will become a tradition," wrote the *Memphis Evening Appeal*. "At a time when grubs of revolution and degenerative social upheaval are gnawing at the very foundations of the American governmental order it may have a salutary effect."[41]

This reaction was limited, however, both in time and scope. As Rexford Tugwell recalled in his memoirs:

> In other circumstances Hoover's calling out of the troops and their savage repression of the marchers might have brought him acclaim. . . . In 1932, however, there seemed to be some evil magic at work against Hoover. Even actions that citizens might have heralded as saving the nation from revolution brought him little but criticism. When the more conservative newspapers tried to present the rout of the bonus army as a heroic exploit, their editorials stuttered off into apologetics. . . . Americans were uneasy, but they were not ready to believe that their government had been in imminent danger of being overthrown by a few thousand indigents who, not so long before, had been praised as its heroic defenders.[42]

Very quickly it became apparent that the rout of the Bonus Army was "one of the deadliest boomerangs in political history."[43] A scene from the movie *Golddiggers of 1933* perfectly captured this change in opinion. During the "Ballad of the Forgotten Man," a musical number that is at the climax of the movie and is centered on the example of the Bonus Army, a police officer rousts a man sitting on the sidewalk by the side of a building. By all appearances, the man is a "bum." When the officer grabs the man by his coat lapel, however, he reveals a service medal that the man is wearing on his shirt. After the officer sees this medal, he realizes he has made a mistake and lets the man go.[44] Like the cop, middle-class Americans quickly realized their fears of revolution were mistaken. They came to agree with the editors of the Scripps-Howard papers who saw a direct equation between the Bonus Marchers and the other unemployed: "We protest against the use of guns against these citizens and ex-soldiers. We protest against the Cossack methods of local officials in many parts of the country against the unemployed."[45]

The seeming lack of revolutionary sentiment among the unemployed, even in the face of such great suffering, would further reenforce the obsolescence of the older view of the working class. Most observers were more impressed by the absence of radicalism than its occasional appearances. For example, Jay Franklin wrote a piece for *Current History* (a weekly magazine put out by the New York *Times*) entitled "Why This Political Apathy?" in late May 1932. According to Franklin, "Neither a birdseye view of American politics nor the ear close to the ground can detect anything more radical than the possibility that the Democratic vote may be vastly enlarged." (Rather ironically, he also claimed that, "You can scan the American horizon and you cannot find a single . . . Coxey's Army," just as the Bonus Army was about to descend on Washington.[46]) Frederick Lewis Allen wrote in 1931 that, "The public attitude during the depression of 1930–31 presented an instructive contrast with that during previous depressions. The radical on the soapbox was far less terrifying than in the days of the Big Red Scare. Communist propaganda made amazingly little headway, all things considered, and attracted amazingly little attention."[47] Franklin Roosevelt himself thought that, "It was really a wonder that there hadn't been more resentment, more radicalism," according to Tugwell.[48]

The election of 1932 proved to be a dramatic confirmation of this lack of radicalism for many people. As one "solid citizen" reportedly remarked, "there is something wrong with the Reds in this country if that's the best they can do in a depression like this."[49] Whiting Williams, in his article "The Hopeful American Worker," also remarked on the very small vote totals of the Communist and Socialist parties to buttress his argument about the nonrevolutionary nature of the working class.[50]

From 1933 on, discussion about the "social revolution" largely disappeared, replaced by talk about the "Roosevelt Revolution." According to Lillian Symes, "To a large number of persons no doubt any serious consideration of the former in these still optimistic days of the latter is altogether irrelevant and immaterial." As an "elderly conservative" told her, "This fellow Roosevelt may not be sound, but he has certainly taken the wind out of the radicals' sails."[51] Liberal commentators agreed. Archibald MacLeish, for instance, attributed "the failure of the revolutionary movement in America," in part, to Roosevelt's charisma. "Men's minds are fired by Mr. Roosevelt," he argued in 1934, "because they are sick to nausea of the rich bankers and their economists upon the one side and the great revolutionaries and their economists upon the other."[52] Strikes might be "blazing on a dozen fronts," as Symes wrote, but Americans had overcome their fear that they might be the prelude to revolution.[53] Even the provocation of the massive strike wave of 1934 failed to ignite a Red Scare. Although some citizens, such as Eric Sevareid's father during the Teamsters' strike in Minneapolis, may have been convinced that a revolution was at hand, these fears were fleeting.[54] The communists' turn to the Popular Front strategy merely confirmed a trend that was already in place.

Red baiting, of course, would continue right through the 30s and beyond. Antiunion propagandists continued to portray union leaders as foreign radicals.[55] For instance, here is part of the statement of purpose of a southern California antilabor group, founded during the Depression: "You shall not cast over our churches the shadow of the anti-Christ. You shall not debauch our schools with your false propaganda of hate and fratricidal strife of the Class Struggle of an alien and untenable philosophy."[56] The old charge of disloyalty could also still be heard. Most of the pre-World War II strikes, for instance, were, in the main, blamed on the Communists. "All of us have had the experience of encountering people who, . . . because in a few instances there have been Communists in the unions, argue that the defense strikes are Communist plots," reported Max Lerner in the *New Republic* in 1941.[57] And during the early 1950s, the communist leadership of some unions became a much discussed issue as it related to national security. Articles with titles such as "Communist-Led Unions and US Security," "Red Pipe Line into Our Defense Plants," and "We Are Protecting Spies in Defense Plants!" were typical.[58]

That such propaganda still had some bite is demonstrated by the extent to which unions went to demonstrate their Americanism. For example, in 1943, Max Zaritsky, president of the Hatters Union, found it necessary to argue that "The American trade-union movement is not a foreign growth, but is as native as Thanksgiving and pumpkin pie."[59] Even in the late 1940s, Philip Murray was still constantly reaffirming the Americanism of himself and the union movement. The following is from an article he wrote in 1947: "The six million members of the CIO are Americans first and union men second. Not one of the CIO's forty affiliated organizations has ever advocated that we change our political and economic institutions through importation of any foreign ideology."[60] And here are the first two sentences from an article he wrote in 1948: "I am a trades unionist and a labor organizer. But above all else I am an American."[61] Labor's effort to equate unionism with Americanism also explains the prominence of American flags seen on every picket line and at every union rally during the 1930s and '40s.[62]

Unlike the earlier period, however, this new form of red-baiting focused on union leaders, not on the rank and file. The contrast between the first and second red scares is particularly revealing in this regard. In 1919, many Americans were convinced that a large-scale revolution was imminent. During the 1950s, on the other hand, Senator McCarthy focused on the treason of elites, not the disloyalty of the masses.[63] "The enemy" was no longer scruffy, bedraggled immigrants. Rather, "when hounded into the light, [he] looked just like your neighbor."[64] The impression conveyed by most writers dealing with this issue in the postwar period was not that communism was inherent in unionism. No one, for instance, argued that unions should be abolished because they were a breeding ground for subversive politics. Rather, communism was portrayed as a foreign growth that had invaded the body of organized labor that could be driven out with the introduction of the proper cure, mostly by ensuring that unions followed democratic procedures in selecting their leaders. During the late 1940s and early '50s, most of the articles in popular magazines that discussed communism in unions were about how communist leaders had been expelled from one union or the other.[65]

By the end of the 1950s, except perhaps in the South, the old association between unions and communism had completely disappeared. Indeed, by the 1970s the picture of union workers in hard hats assaulting long-haired antiwar demonstrators had come to supplant any lingering feeling that unions were somehow un-American.[66] The AFL-CIO's support of the war in Vietnam, in fact, made unions appear to be one of the bastions of the old order and caused the New Left to begin labeling its opposition the "liberal-labor establishment."[67] The unexpectedly strong show of support George Wallace received from Northern blue-collar workers caused both liberals and conservatives to reevaluate the place of unions in politics. During the 1970s, for instance, Robert Novak, in the pages of *National Review,* was urging Republicans to call off their war against unions to bring blue-collar workers into their fold, while the TV sitcom *All in the Family,* which satirized the ultra-conservative unionist, became a hit series.[68]

If Americans had overcome their fear of the potentially revolutionary nature of the working class, they had also ceased to view blue-collar workers as essentially foreign. Because these two images had been counterparts of each other, the disappearance of the one would inevitably lead to the fading of the other. As Gary Gerstle has argued, discussions about the "new" immigrant were noticeably muted during the Depression decade. New Dealers privileged images of suffering, rural, white natives, not urban, ethnic workers, to justify their programs. Even this focus on the "Okies," however, made it possible, as with the Bonus Army, for middle-class Americans to identify, by extension, with the plight of blue-collar workers. Leaders of the newly resurgent labor movement and members of the Communist Party went along with this tendency to "erase" the image of the "new" immigrant. Many ethnic members of the Communist Party "Americanized" their names, while the public face of the CIO, whose constituency was predominantly "new" immigrant, was largely that of native-born Americans and those of "old" immigrant stock: John L. Lewis, Philip Murray, Walter Reuther, John Brophy, etc.[69] Two books about the steel industry are especially illustrative of this change. The Interchurch *Report on the Steel Strike of 1919* is full of references to the ethnicities of the steel workers.[70] Contrast this with Robert Brooks's book *As Steel Goes,* which traced the rise of the Steel Workers Organizing Committee (SWOC) in the 1930s and was published in 1940.[71] Even though fewer than twenty years had passed since the great steel strike of 1919, and despite the fact that SWOC paid a great deal of attention to ethnic and racial issues, Brooks completely ignored this issue.

This is not to say that all of the old associations between unions and aliens had instantly disappeared. In 1945, for instance, *Life* magazine found it necessary to argue that "labor leaders, contrary to popular belief, are neither foreign born agitators nor superannuated thugs."[72] (The reference to "superannuated thugs" was due to the widespread association of the AFL with labor racketeering.) C. Wright Mills, writing in 1945, also felt the need to comment on the fact that his research results had shown that "the cry of 'foreign born agitators' . . . has lost whatever relevance it may have ever had."[73] In the South, in particular, much of the antiunion literature through the 1950s conveyed the impression that most CIO leaders were Jewish.[74] (The prominence of Sydney Hillman, president of the Amalgamated Clothing Workers Union and a Jewish immigrant, in the Roosevelt administration no doubt had much to do with this misimpression.[75]) As with the communist issue, however, this focus on the "foreignness" of unions was concerned with the leaders and not the membership.

This does not mean that prejudice against the "new" immigrant did not persist. Status distinctions based on ethnicity would continue through the 1940s. The image of the working-class, and it's identity with the "new" immigrant, however, was attenuated. Rather than being seen as potential revolutionaries, "foreigners" now posed the threat of racketeering. Italians, especially, would be identified with the figure of the gangster. Movies such as *Scarface, Public Enemy,* and *Little Caesar* dramatized this new image, and newspapers portrayed gangsters as a bigger threat to democratic government than the communists.

This logic is played out in the early 1933 movie *Gabriel over the White House.* In one of the opening scenes, the newly elected president denounces the "army of the unemployed" (a reference to the Bonus Army) as anarchists and revolutionaries intent on overthrowing the government. Following a conversion experience (resulting from a car accident), however, the president rejects the idea, supported by his secretary of war, that the marchers are revolutionaries. When he goes to meet them, he is respectfully received by the men, and he promises to provide them with work, which is all they want. Having dispelled the threat of social revolution by the working class, the movie turns instead to the threat posed to the nation by mobsters in the form of Nick Diamond, a Jewish immigrant. In an effort to end this menace and put Diamond and his ilk out of business, prohibition is repealed and government-owned liquor stores are opened. Diamond retaliates by blowing up the stores and sending his henchmen to machine gun the White House in one of those classic scenes of a drive-by shooting from 1930s mobster movies. The president then sends in the army to capture Diamond, after which he and his henchmen are executed by a firing squad in the shadow of the Statue of Liberty.

If this lesson is not clear enough, the movie also includes a meeting between Diamond and John Bronson, the leader of the "army of the unemployed," to emphasize where the real threat lies. Diamond does not want the men, who are encamped in various Hoovervilles throughout the city, to leave for Washington. He claims that his business has never been better because the police are spending more time monitoring these out-of-work men, lest they foment a revolution, than they are with cracking down on Diamond's various enterprises. When Bronson refuses to bow to Diamond's threats and bribes, Diamond sends his men to murder Bronson in another drive-by machine-gunning. Workers, the movie practically shouts, are victims of the current system, not threats to it.[76]

Workers as Victims

At the same time Americans were rethinking their image of the working class, they were also reconsidering their prior veneration of businessmen. As Frederick Lewis Allen wrote, during the 1920s, "the association of business with religion was one of the most significant phenomena of the day."

Bruce Barton, owner of one of the top advertising firms during the 1920s, for instance, wrote a book entitled *The Man Nobody Knows,* that painted Jesus Christ as a smart CEO who enlisted and trained twelve salesmen to create the most powerful and successful enterprise of all time, the Christian church.[77] By 1933, that "carefully constructed image of the divine businessman ha[d] toppled over without a push," as a writer for *Scribners* claimed.[78] "For three and a half years, now," according to Edward Aswell, "the inexorable forces of depression have been chiseling away at him [the businessman] undermining his status and his stature. . . . all of them [leading businessmen] have become so very, very quiet."[79] Both C. Wright Mills and John Kenneth Galbraith would later remark on the efforts by the rich to downplay their status during the 1930s.[80]

Whereas they had once been portrayed as divine, the picture of businessmen as war profiteers quickly gained acceptance in the early years of the Depression. During the Bonus March, for example, the marchers' defenders claimed that "[t]he veterans offered their lives to the country during the war while profiteers at home piled up fabulous fortunes."[81] Even so conservative an organization as the American Legion could editorialize that "[i]t is no coincidence that the very men who now call veterans racketeers because they seek justice for themselves, their comrades, and widows and orphans, were profiteers when the country was at war and in need of defenders."[82]

This fall from grace was greatly reenforced by a number of well-publicized Congressional investigations during the 1930s. The Pecora inquiry, for instance, investigated the banking industry during the winter of 1932/33 and uncovered a slew of questionable and unethical practices. In 1935 the Nye Committee investigated the munitions industry in an attempt to find an international conspiracy of arms makers. Although it did not achieve this goal, it did reenforce a picture of businessmen as venal "merchants of death." Also in 1935, though less well remembered, Hugo Black led an inquiry into the attempt by utility industry lobbyists to prevent the passage of the Wheeler-Rayburn bill, which would have imposed a "death sentence" on utility holding companies.[83]

The most important of these investigations, in regards to the new image of the working class, of course, was that of the La Follette Committee. The committee's investigations helped expose the many methods employers used to break strikes and thwart organizing drives. Its effectiveness was manifest in several different ways. In early 1937, for example, the Senate rejected an amendment introduced by Senator Byrnes condemning the sit-down tactics of the CIO because it did not similarly decry the refusal of employers to negotiate with their employees as provided for in the Wagner Act. A simi-lar amendment was passed only after language was added that upbraided employers for their refusal to bargain. Employers themselves quickly came to abjure the use of industrial spies and professional strikebreakers. As a prospective employee of a detective agency was told, "You, of course, real-ize with the La Follette investigating committee functioning, that we are not putting any men to work on investigations that would have anything to do with labor difficulties or labor unions."[84]

One of the spurs to the formation of the La Follette committee had been the publication of the book *I Break Strikes* by Edward Levinson in late 1935. Levinson's book detailed the career of Pearl Bergof, self-proclaimed "king of the strikebreakers," and, more generally, of the strikebreaking and indus-trial espionage business. According to James Auerbach, "Levinson['s book] stripped the veneer of respectability from strikebreaking and exposed it as a thoroughly sordid business. In fact, Levinson nearly did for strikebreaking what Upton Sinclair had done for the meat-packing industry by publishing *The Jungle* thirty years earlier."[85]

Unions as Defenders of the Underdog

As the old image of a foreign and radical working class faded, therefore, it came to be replaced by an image of workers as the victims of exploitative and unethical capitalists. This picture of workers as the underdog was not new. It dated back at least to the turn of the century. For example, both Jacob Riis's *How the Other Half Lives* (1890) and, even more emphatically, Upton Sinclair's *The Jungle* (1906) had been sympathetic to the plight of poor and exploited workers. This view of the working class, however, had been overshadowed by the anxiety and dislike most Americans harbored toward immigrant workers. As this anxiety abated, the image of workers as the underdog gained wider acceptance. Adamic's book *Dynamite* was a clear marker for this transition. Even as he detailed the numerous instances of class violence in the United States, his favorite description of workers was as the underdog.[86]

As the representative of these downtrodden workers, organized labor came to be viewed in a much more sympathetic light. During the second New Deal, in particular, the government itself turned to unions as an es-sential partner in ending the Depression. By securing for workers the right to organize (the Wagner Act), New Dealers hoped to raise the purchasing power of the working class and thus stimulate the economy. In effect, the government had endorsed the idea that workers were the underpaid and exploited victims of capitalism contained in the underdog image. The New Deal's official stamp of approval sent a powerful cultural message about the legitimacy of the labor movement. For instance, as Clete Daniels points out, many employers (with the notable exception of those in the South) became demoralized into accepting unions as something inevitable.[87] *Business Week* noted in 1954, in a retrospective look back at the Depression, that businessmen suffered a "failure of nerve." "On the labor front, business seemed to be suffering a paralysis of will as well. Its resistance to the new unionism was sporadic, thoughtless, and panicky. It shifted violently from aggressiveness to abject resignation."[88] Consider, for instance, the two great breakthroughs of 1937: General Motors and U.S. Steel. In neither case was resort made to the mechanisms of the Wagner Act to achieve victory. Rather, an aroused workforce, coupled with a management discouraged by its lack of political support led to success for organized labor. As C. Wright Mills put it in 1951, "The New Deal, and especially the personality of President Roosevelt, did more for unions than create an encouraging legal framework; it raised the prestige value of unions."[89] Whereas Wilson's endorsement of organized labor during World War I was rapidly followed by the onset of a Red Scare and the establishment of the American Plan, trade unions during the 1930s, especially those associated with the CIO, were able to build on this legitimization and turn it into a powerful organizing drive that would eventually encompass one third of the workforce.

The New Deal, therefore, powerfully established the idea that unions were supposed to be the champions of the underdog. Although this image was not new, it had previously been downplayed or even denied by the leaders of AFL. Instead, Samuel Gompers and other trade union spokesmen had emphasized the masculine independence that collective bargaining was meant to provide workers. As Alice Kessler-Harris argues, their conception of "volunteerism presumed that wage earners had the courage, independence, and economic power to protect their own interests" without government intervention. Because this pro-union argument was based "on the unified strength of skilled workers," however, its proponents "freely excluded those who might undermine labor's power, including the unskilled, most people of color, and women."[90] Such a picture of union members was directly counterposed to that of the more feminine conception implied in the underdog image.

The image of unions as the champions of the underdog also prevailed over that of its other competitor. As Michael Kazin argues, the leaders of the CIO, employing the tropes of populism, tried to portray organized labor as the representative of the "common people."[91] They denied that the interests of labor and of society were different. As Walter Reuther repeatedly intoned, "We are part of the community. We intend to make progress with the community and not at the expense of the community."[92] This picture of organized labor, however, was never widely accepted. Most Americans did view the interests of labor and of society as distinct, a belief that was perfectly compatible with—indeed, implicit in—their feeling that unions represented the underdog.

The demonization of businessmen and the attention given to organized labor's martyrdom in the 1930s, then, would form the basis for the labor movement's legitimization myth in the postwar epoch.[93] According to this myth, unions, at their best, were not simply economic institutions, but "humanitarian"[94] ones as well. They were formed to protect workers from the "exploitation," "oppression," and "coercion" of "terroristic" and "greedy" employers.[95] They were the working man's response to the Dickensesque world of industrial capitalism where "armies of men sweat in huge, smoke blackened factories, amid a roar of belts and steam" and "every boss carries a whip and every laborer has hunger pangs."[96] They fought against "starvation wages and subhuman conditions" and "to compel a hearing of their [members'] grievances."[97] Or as two questions in a 1976 survey by Lou Harris put it: "When unions were first started they were needed because workers were being exploited by low wages, long hours, and bad working conditions" (96 percent of those surveyed agreed with this statement); and "In many industries, unions are needed so the legitimate complaints and grievances of workers can be heard and action taken on them" (85 percent agreed).[98] This was the image of unions as portrayed in the movie *Norma Rae,* which centered on the Textile Union's attempts to organize a Southern cotton mill.[99]

More than just benefitting its own members, however, organized labor was, at its best, seen to benefit society as a whole. Unions were expected to take "seriously their stated broad objectives for ameliorating human social ills."[100] Thus, unions might be praised for "help[ing] end child labor, [and] the 72 hour week."[101] Or as a 1976 survey by Lou Harris put it, "Labor unions in the U.S. have been good forces, working for such things as national health insurance, higher employment compensation, better Social Security, minimum wage laws, and other desirable social needs" (76 percent of those surveyed agreed).[102] To paraphrase a 1960 editorial in *Fortune,* ideally the labor movement was a force for "reforming our society" and "speaking for the underprivileged."[103]

Not only were unions supposed to fight for the underdog, according to this myth, they themselves had at one time been the underdog when it came to battling "against the greater wealth and power of the corporations."[104] Even so conservative a publication as the *Saturday Evening Post* might mention "the bad old days . . . when strikers were beaten up in the streets," or find it necessary to argue that labor leaders were "no longer helpless and persecuted toilers but big operators."[105] Or as *Life* recalled in one editorial, "martyrs have died for labor in the bloody sieges of countless organizing strikes in an era when the thugs were in the pay of industry."[106]

So powerful was this image that it would continue to shape Americans' attitude towards organized labor for the rest of the twentieth century. Thus, despite the low union density in America, polls done by the Gallup organization since 1937 have shown consistent support for the existence of unions. When asked, "do you approve or disapprove of unions?", a majority throughout this period consistently registered approval.[107] Likewise, when confronted with ballot measures perceived as being antiunion, such as the many referenda on "right to work" laws during the 1950s, unions generally garnered the support of the public.[108] Indeed, even the harshest critics of unions would find it necessary to claim they were not antiunion.[109]

* * *

The 1930s marked not just an institutional and legal watershed for organized labor, but a cultural one as well. Prior to the New Deal, middle-class Americans had been suspicious of, if not alarmed by, organized labor. They may have been prepared, because of their belief in freedom of association, to concede unions' right to exist, but this was about the extent of their tolerance. Many of the problems they saw with unions will be mentioned in the next two chapters. But at heart, the antipathy in the last third of the nineteenth and first third of the twentieth centuries was rooted in their dislike and distrust of the working class. When, through such processes as immigration restriction, the Great Migration, the marginalization of radical organizations in the early 1920s, and the example of the Bonus March, their image of the working class was transformed, their acceptance of organized labor greatly increased. Many of the images of organized labor that existed at the turn of the twentieth century would continue to inform their thinking about unions into the postwar period. But a decisive shift had occurred: no longer were workers seen as threats to the American system. Instead, they were re-imagined as fellow citizens and victims of an unjust system. As a result, unions came to be seen as champions of the underdog. This image would form the basis of labor's legitimization myth for the rest of the twentieth century. As we shall see, however, although American's may have lost their fear of organized labor, they continued to harbor many doubts about unions, doubts that would reach a peak in the 1970s and '80s.

2

The Postwar Offensive
against Organized Labor

During the 1930s Americans came to view unions much more positively than they had during the first third of the twentieth century. In large
part, this newfound acceptance was based on their changed perception of
the working class. Whereas Americans once viewed blue-collar workers as
foreign and radical, they now saw them as native victims of greedy and exploitative capitalists. This changed perception in turn altered their view of
organized labor, the representative of the working class. Both unions and
workers were now seen as the underdogs, and the labor movement was believed to be, ideally, the champion of the underdog.

Unfortunately for organized labor, this newfound legitimacy rested on
a very shaky foundation. As William Puette, a student of organized labor's
presentation in the media, has noted, "as long as labor could be viewed as
an underprivileged, generally helpless and disenfranchised object of pity, the
media were glad to take up its banner. But . . . the motive was always self-
serving, and it turned around when these same workers' unions were sufficiently organized to begin exerting the very power the media had formerly
advocated." He points to the following lines from *Citizen Kane* as a perfect
summation of this attitude:

> As long as I can remember, you've [Kane] talked about giving people their
> rights; as if you could make them a present of liberty . . . as a reward for ser-
> vices rendered. . . . You used to write an awful lot about the working man. But
> he's turning into something called organized labor. You're not going to like
> that one little bit when you find out it means that your working man expects
> something as his right, not as your gift. When your precious underprivileged

really get together . . . Oh boy! That's going to add up to something bigger than your privilege.[1]

It was precisely this transformation that opened unions to a vigorous counteroffensive following World War II. Conservative politicians and business interests launched a well-funded and wide-ranging attack on organized labor in the 1940s and '50s.[2] Central to this offensive was an attempt to convince Americans that unions were no longer the underdogs they had been during the 1930s, and that they were failing to live up to "their stated broad objectives for ameliorating human social ills" and "speaking for the underprivileged."[3] Rather than attacking union members, criticism now focused on union leaders in an attempt to show that "instead of being one of the most important agencies for the betterment of the laboring man," unions had become the "most powerful means of his oppression."[4] Though no one directly questioned unions' legitimacy, this line of attack was meant to undermine labor's legitimization myth established in the 1930s. By showing the divergence between the way unions were supposed to behave, as postulated in the underdog myth, and the way they operated in the "real world," labor's enemies hoped to turn Americans against unions.

This offensive was only partially successful. Union approval, for instance, would continue at a high level until the 1960s. Nevertheless, many of the criticisms leveled at organized labor during this period would continue to shape Americans' image of unions into the 1980s. (And, in fact, many of these critiques simply recycled criticisms that had been leveled at unions at the beginning of the twentieth century.) Especially important in this regard was the debate over the Taft-Hartley Act in 1947. As Melvyn Dubofsky has argued, there is a good deal of evidence "for seeing the Taft-Hartley Act as a continuation of New Deal labor policy in a slightly diluted form." He notes the success of those unions that should have suffered most under this act and points out that union density reached its peak "in the era of the Korean War, four to six years after the passage of Taft-Hartley." In light of this evidence, he goes on to ask:

> That being the case, how do we explain the apoplectic reaction of the leaders of both national labor federations, dedicated New Dealers, the vast majority of the academic and legal practitioners of "industrial pluralism," and most historians who have studied the subject? The answer, I believe, is plain enough. We should consider more carefully the *language* used by the sponsors and advocates of amending the Wagner Act, whether in the ranks of the Republican party, the business community, or the media.[5]

Precisely. It was not so much the actual provisions of the Taft-Hartley Act that would work to eviscerate unions, but the fact that this act withdrew the government's sanction of one part of labor's legitimizing myth. The Wagner Act had implicitly endorsed the idea that *both* unions and workers were "helpless and persecuted toilers."[6] The Taft-Hartley Act, on the other hand, sanctioned the idea that unions, at least, were no longer "the underdogs, whose officials were jailed regularly, tarred and feathered, blacklisted and even murdered."[7] Instead, they had now achieved a "hard won equality" with employers and no longer deserved special treatment.[8] Employers were emboldened to resist unions, and workers heard a clear message "associating unions with coercion, intimidation, violence, corruption, and crime, and their leaders with greed, tyranny, and communism."[9] Instead of providing a counterweight to America's antiunion culture, the federal government had declared itself neutral in the war between capital and labor.

This chapter will focus on this postwar offensive. In particular, it will trace the various ways in which unions were seen as failing to live up to their role as the champion of the underdog. Despite the fact that most of the sources cited here are from the 1940s and '50s, however, it needs to be stressed that many of the images of organized labor that were invoked during this period would continue to inform Americans' thinking about unions into the 1980s. (Conversely, many of these same ideas dated back to the beginning of the century.) So, for instance, polling data from the 1970s and '80s will be presented to demonstrate the widespread acceptance of many of these antiunion ideas. As with many aspects of Americans' ideas about organized labor, these images had a remarkably timeless quality about them.

Unions as Topdog

The greatly increased size of labor unions in the postwar period, combined with their increased political and economic clout, helped undermine one part of labor's legitimization myth. As Seymour Martin Lipset put it in 1986, "Most Americans who are normally sympathetic to the needs of the weak and the underprivileged [no longer] classify labor organizations among the oppressed. Rather, like big business, they are seen as powerful and essentially self-serving."[10]

By the end of World War II, it was commonly acknowledged that the days when unions were "helpless and persecuted"were over.[11] From the left mention could be found of "the hard won equality [with employers] which labor ha[s] achieved in the last 20 years."[12] Philip Murray, president of the CIO, for instance, conceded in 1948 that "the professional strikebreaker has faded from the scene; the day when labor's just demands could be met by gunfire and police clubs has gone forever."[13] C. Wright Mills labeled union leaders "the new men of power" in 1948, and in 1951 the economist John Kenneth Galbraith portrayed organized labor as one of the "countervailing powers" that had arisen to offset the monopolistic position of big businesses.[14] By 1963, even Max Lerner, a former radical and strong supporter of organized labor, was conceding that, "The strong corporation is matched by the strong union, and the welfare corporation by the welfare union."[15]

From the Right, the message was not just that unions were no longer the underdog, but that their power now exceeded that of employers. Beginning in 1937, that is, from the time of the CIO's major successes and the widespread use of the sitdown tactic, and reaching a crescendo in 1947, the year the Taft-Hartley law was enacted, the refrain, repeated over and over, was that the Wagner Act had unbalanced bargaining power in favor of unions.[16] Typical of such sentiment is the following statement by a senator who voted in favor of the Taft-Hartley Act, "The 1935 act was necessary in view of the way in which labor had been exploited. But that act . . . tipped the scales in favor of labor against management. They gave labor dominance."[17] According to a "Connecticut Housewife," as a letter to *Life* magazine was signed, "Thirteen years ago, the New Deal swept into power on the premise of abolishing special privilege, but in 13 years it has succeeded only in transferring that special privilege from Wall Street trusts to Organized Labor."[18]

Even though the Taft-Hartley Act had supposedly addressed this issue, the Right continued to paint U.S. labor laws as unbalanced in favor of unions, "in avalanche proportions," as Barry Goldwater claimed in 1960.[19] The *Saturday Evening Post,* for instance, editorialized in 1959 that, "It's Time to Stop Coddling Unions; They're on Top Now!"[20] Even as late as 1978 the Right continued to claim that labor laws unfairly favored unions. According to the *National Review,* the drive to amend the Labor-Management Relations Act during the Carter administration would, if successful, further "tilt the labor management equation even more decisively in favor of the unions than is now the case."[21] As a poll taken that same year showed, such arguments resonated with a wide section of the population. According to Cambridge Reports Inc., a plurality felt that "the present labor laws . . . tend to favor labor unions [rather than business] in a dispute."[22]

The notion that the power of organized labor was equal, or even superior, to that of business had been a staple of antiunion rhetoric since the early part of the century. During the Depression, however, this image lost whatever credibility it had ever had and was replaced by the image of unions as the underdog. After World War II, labor's enemies revived the old image of powerful unions as a central component of their effort to undermine labor's legitimization myth.

Evidence to back this claim was not hard to find. In discussing the changed status of unions since the 1930s, popular magazines invariably pointed to the many signs that unions had "won acceptance and security."[23] Their "millions of dollars in assets" were mentioned frequently.[24] Special attention was also given to the "lordly desks in the glass and marble headquarters of giant labor unions."[25] The following description is from a 1962 article in the *Saturday Evening Post*: "marble palaces stand as monuments to the financial and numerical strength of the great international brotherhoods of teamsters, carpenters, hod carriers and electricians and to the AFL-CIO itself. . . . Huge murals grace the walls, and in the lobbies goldfish swim in marbled pools where artificial lilies float. Deep carpets spread from wall to wall in the paneled offices where the high paid presidents sit, and in the corridors soft music plays."[26] The Teamsters' headquarters was specially noted. Its "marble structure cost a fat $5 million which will not seriously dent the Teamsters' reserves of $35 million. . . . [It has] a 478 seat movie theater, and for the union's President Dave Beck, a suite which any big business or government executive might envy."[27]

The phrase "monopoly unionism," in particular, became one the organizing themes of antiunion rhetoric from the 1940s through the '70s. As with the image of powerful unions, talk about the "labor trust" dated back to the turn of the century. Herbert Croly, for instance, although not an antiunion ideologue, claimed in 1909 that labor unions "have been very successful in accomplishing their object. . . . Whenever [they have] had the power, [they have] suppressed competition as ruthlessly as have [their] employers."[28] The Supreme Court itself seemed to endorse this view in its Danbury Hatters and Buck Stove decisions.[29] After the hiatus of the Depression, attacks on unions' efforts to "take the wage out of competition" were revived.

Despite the great deal of ink spilled over this issue, however, it seems doubtful whether it ever became part of the image most Americans held of unions. It is significant that in none of the many articles that discussed the issue did the author explain how the "labor monopoly" worked. At most, a critic might complain about wages that were set "irrespective of local conditions and irrespective of the circumstances of individual firms."[30] No doubt this lack of explanation resulted from a desire to avoid the disagreeable fact that competition in the labor market came from pitting workers against each other in a dog-eat-dog fight over jobs and wages.

Polling data indicate that although a plurality of Americans believed that unions should be covered by the antitrust laws, this still represented less than half the populace. Further, this attitude may have reflected a belief that the antitrust laws could correct certain abuses by unions without necessarily affecting their ability to achieve a standard wage in their industry.[31] For instance, Thurman Arnold, Franklin Delano Roosevelt's leading "trust buster," and no enemy of labor unions, frequently argued that the antitrust laws should be changed to cover unions to correct such abuses as "featherbedding" and collusion between unions and employers to keep competitors out of a market. According to Arnold, such a change need not affect "legitimate labor objectives," including, presumably, standardizing wages.[32] Even the more conservative critics of unions framed their calls for including unions within the scope of the antitrust laws as a way to curb union abuses and not as a way to spur wage competition. In any event, the equivalence between "price fixing" and "wage fixing" seems not to have been generally accepted. Instead, the declaration that "the labor of a human being is not a commodity or article of commerce," as found in the Clayton Anti-Trust Act, seems to have reflected the feelings of many, if not most, Americans.[33]

Although Americans may not have embraced the image of unions as monopolies, the outcry against the "labor trust" does appear to have resonated with a concern that many people harbored with respect to the size and power unions had attained in the postwar period. As the *New Republic* put it, "Such phrases as 'labor monopoly' and 'union bosses' call to mind an image of power-hungry opportunists who, from the lavish central offices of their national headquarters, can by snapping their fingers order the shut-down of one industry or the unionization of another."[34] As early as 1939, an article in the *Saturday Evening Post* was claiming that "the bargaining power of a great corporation was inferior to that of either the AFL or the CIO."[35] According to one analyst, this impression resulted from a "tendency . . . to generalize from cases like the Teamsters or the building trades, where large unions confront typically small and weak employers in competitive industry."[36] As an example, one article entitled "Should Unions Have Monopoly Powers?" related the following anecdote about a company threatened by a strike by the Teamsters: "When the storage company reminded the union delegate that his union had signed a no-strike contract, the delegate laughed. 'We've been sued by better people than you,' he said."[37] Although cases like this may partially explain the phenomenon, widely publicized strikes against the auto and steel companies dramatically demonstrated how some unions could shut down even the strongest corporations. The steel strike of 1959, for instance, prompted *Life* to comment that labor's "strike weapon is more powerful than anything in management's arsenal."[38] The public, apparently, agreed with this sentiment. For instance, a 1977 survey of employed persons found that over two-thirds agreed with the statement "unions are more powerful than employers."[39]

Apart from the effects of unions' size on their character and relations to employers, the public also worried that "big labor" was overly influential in politics. For instance, a 1955 editorial in the *Baltimore Sun* asserted that "of all the organized groups in the country, the labor unions through their bosses, now exert the greatest political and economic power."[40] In 1960, Barry Goldwater railed against "the enormous economic and political power now concentrated in the hands of union leaders," while in 1962, Senator John McClellan asserted "their power over the country [is] almost supreme."[41] And a 1971 article in *Readers' Digest* claimed that "American labor unions . . . constitute the nation's most powerful political force. No other organized group can match labor's bloc of voters, its armies of election workers and lobbyists, its campaign treasury or its immense influence in Washington and state capitals."[42] This refrain about labor's political power found an increasingly receptive audience among the general public. A 1959 poll by the Gallup organization found that 43 percent of those queried believed business had the most influence in what legislation was passed, whereas 34 percent believed that organized labor was most influential.[43] By 1978, 50 percent felt that unions had "more power," as opposed to 33 percent who felt that businesses had more power. And when asked in 1976 whether "labor unions have too much influence on American life and politics," 64 percent said this was true, while 25 percent felt union influence was "the right amount," and only 5 percent felt it was "too little."[44] As early as 1950, Samuel Lubell found that Ohio voters, including many union members, voted to reelect Senator Robert Taft, co-author of the "slave labor" Taft-Hartley law, because "we didn't want labor running the country," "it isn't good for labor to have too much power," and "if labor had beaten a man like Taft with somebody like Ferguson, it would have been the end of our democracy and freedom."[45]

The increased size of unions was responsible for other problems as well. For instance, union democracy was frustrated by the large size and remoteness of international unions where "individual members have become submerged in huge organizations."[46] The following assertion by Cyrus Ching, onetime head of the U.S. Mediation and Conciliation Service, indicates that many people also appeared to believe, though he did not agree, that labor unions' more unsavory aspects were simply a reflection of their size: "I don't believe the unhealthy operations revealed by the McClellan Committee were due to any union's size . . . The important thing is not how big or powerful a union is, but how it uses its power."[47] The impression that a union's size was one factor explaining its tendency towards corruption was no doubt related to the fact that the huge Teamsters union was at the center of the McClellan Committee hearings. Indeed, as David Witwer has written, several members of that committee hoped to use the hearings to show the link between union size and corruption. For instance, he quotes Senator Carl Curtis as saying, "I believe that unions pose a serious economic threat because they are large and wealthy organizations."[48]

Despite this concern about the effects a union's size had in shaping its character and behavior, Americans, somewhat contradictorily, disagreed with the sentiment that unions had grown too large. In 1947 only 22 percent of those polled felt that unions were too big, and by 1954 this proportion had dropped to just 10 percent, where it remained at least until 1966. Over this same period, the number who felt that unions had "grown large enough" held steady at about 50 percent, while those who felt unions should grow larger hovered around 25 percent.[49] The public, apparently, was willing to accept the status quo ante despite its misgivings about unions' apparent power. What it did *not* want, however, was any *increase* in union size. Unfortunately, 1966 was the last time the Gallup organization asked this question.

Antiunion rhetoric went further than simply trying to show that unions were no longer the underdog, that their power now equaled or even exceeded that of businesses. Many critics of organized labor claimed that unions were no different than corporations. Indeed, as one article after another asserted, "Labor Is Big Business." Unions had "become the most powerful selling organizations in the nation. Their job is to peddle to American industry, on the most favorable terms possible, the services of some 15,000,000 wage earners," according to the *Saturday Evening Post*.[50] *Reader's Digest* described unions as "a cooperative society banded together to market a common product, it's labor."[51] Even Mills claimed that, "More than the businessman of comparable power, the national labor leader has built up a business; his commodity is labor, and he bargains for its price."[52] Likewise, union leaders might be labeled labor "entrepreneurs."[53] Far from denying this, some union officials were more than ready to admit such was the case. "'I run the union just like a business. We deal in one commodity—labor,' once explained Dave Beck, president of the Teamsters union," reported the *New Republic* in a 1955 article.[54] Thirteen years later, an article in *Life* magazine quoted Roy Siemiller, the president of the International Association of Machinists (IAM), as saying, "It's just like any business. You can only pay out what you're taking in." The article went on to note that "the only way to take it in is to have the members to get it from. That is why Roy has gone on such a concerted membership drive."[55]

As with Siemiller's membership drive, many union organizing campaigns were portrayed as nothing more than a search for customers to whom they could peddle their product, or, more darkly, who they could coerce into buying it.[56] One writer arguing for a "right to work" law made clear this parallel between unions and business: "We are naive enough to think that one American is pretty much like another, and that selling a union membership in the long run isn't so different from selling a vacuum cleaner."[57] Union "make work" rules were viewed in a similar manner. "Featherbedding has become an established business procedure; it makes more jobs for more members who pay dues," argued one article.[58] And jurisdictional disputes among unions were portrayed as "nothing but private wars among union leaders in search of dues paying members," who could finance their palatial offices and pay their large salaries.[59]

This supposed transformation of unions into mere labor marketing enterprises was offensive to the principles on which organized labor had been founded. As one liberal critic remarked, "unionism needs to be a social movement with some idealism, not just the 'union business' of which [James] Hoffa speaks."[60] Unlike "business [which] is organized for an economic end, without moral pretense,"[61] "a union is not a business run for personal profit. It is a public-service institution, and union leaders are, in a sense, public servants," argued the more conservative Lester Velie.[62] Nicholas von Hoffman, writing in 1978, summed up these higher standards to which unions were held: "Corporate heads who enlarge profits are hailed as masters of the bottom line; union officials who do the equivalent for their stockholders—the dues-paying members—run the risk of being castigated for fueling inflation. . . . Capital can be autocratic; labor must be democratic. . . . Businessmen who break the law commit white-collar crime; union officials who do the same are racketeers."[63] Some historians of the labor movement, writing in the 1980s from a New Left perspective, went so far as to blame the decline of organized labor as a whole on the transformation of CIO unions into mere "business unions."[64]

Overpaid and Arrogant Union Leaders

Organized labor's "generosity to its leaders" was another manifestation of its changed status following World War II.[65] Now that criticism of rank-and-file union members had become less tenable, both because of their increased numbers and because of the changed image of the working class wrought during the 1930s, criticism of "union bosses" became more intense. The issue of high salaries for union leaders, in particular, became a focus of unfavorable comment. This was because, as the *New Republic* argued in 1955, "The thousands who were attracted to the CIO in the 1930s came looking not for an easy way to make a fast buck, but for a life vocation of service to their fellow men. For them, unions were the underdogs, whose officials were jailed regularly, tarred and feathered, blacklisted and even murdered."[66] By 1965, however, "dedicated youngsters, who in the thirties would have been on labor's picket line, [were now] marching to a different drummer. They [were] fighting elsewhere, for civil rights, peace, or better garbage collection in a slum."[67] One suggestion for correcting this problem, was that "[i]t would be good if something were done to curb the high salaries, the unlimited expense accounts, and the general plush living of so many of the top union leaders, whose moral position as champions of the erstwhile underdogs is seriously compromised by their own self indulgence."[68]

High salaries for union leaders flew in the face of this long-standing objective of achieving social and economic equality for the working class. They also isolated leaders from their rank and file, and disqualified them from speaking for workers. To truly represent their members union leaders were expected to live no differently than those they led. For instance, in 1948 Mills found that a common way for a union official to condemn a union leader was to claim that he had gotten "too far above" the rank and file.[69] Thirty years later, von Hoffman noted this same phenomenon: "A union official who makes more than the boys in the shop is considered hypocritical."[70] Indeed, one critic of organized labor, writing at the same time as Mills, continually referenced "professional union leaders," betraying what may have been a widespread feeling that leadership positions in organized labor ought to be conducted on a voluntary and temporary basis. The use of the adjective "professional" to describe union leaders with its pejorative connotations indicates a belief that people should not make a career out of unionism, much like the term "professional politician" is used by those who believe that people who make a career out of politics are less than honorable.[71] At a minimum, according to popular sentiment, labor leaders should "live unpretentious lives."[72]

Instead, as one article after the other asserted from the 1940s through the '60s, union leaders had "grow[n] fat on baronial salaries."[73] They were referred to as "labor tycoons with wide business interests, ostentatious wealth and the ethics of a medieval robber baron," and "$30,000–a-year labor magnates who ride about in armored cars."[74] Particular attention was given to their ability to vacation on sunny beaches. "Following the example of the nouveau riche," commented one article, they "joined the best country clubs and got reserved seats on winter excursions to Florida beaches."[75] Another article claimed that "many [labor leaders] regard working people as raw material out of which smart entrepreneurs can fabricate Florida haciendas, racing stables and vast political power."[76] The 1959 meeting of the AFL-CIO executive committee in Puerto Rico was even criticized by President Eisenhower. When "asked what he thought of a Reuther suggestion that the nation's unemployed stage a protest march on Washington[,] the President answered . . . 'Their people must be on the sunny beaches; I don't know whether they are going to march from there over to this foggy Washington or not.'"[77] The fancy cars they drove were further examples of their moral dissipation, as were their palatial homes.[78]

The common use of the pejorative "fat" in describing unions and their leaders is especially interesting in conjunction with the supposed moral equivalence between business and labor. The rotund figure, dressed in top hat and tails (like the "tycoon" character depicted in the game *Monopoly*), had long been cartoonists' standard caricature for capital. Obesity was commonly associated with great wealth and moral dissipation.[79] By the late 1950s, this caricature was being used to describe unions; the same imagery now portrayed both "Big Business" and "Big Labor." William Puette, for instance, found in a survey of editorial cartoons depicting unions, "Artists are fond of representing labor as fat and unproductive."[80] That organized labor's principal spokesman was the overweight, cigar smoking president of the AFL-CIO, George Meany, only reinforced this image. As William Winpisinger, president of the IAM, put it in 1978, "A picture of George Meany on the front page of an American newspaper has the same kind of impact a picture of Jay Gould or J. Pierpont Morgan once had: that of a cigar-smoking, affluent patriarch."[81]

These criticisms (as with most of the postwar offensive) were not new. For instance, Louis Adamic, writing from a Leftist perspective, produced a similar portrayal of the leaders of the AFL in 1934:

> Most of them are prosperous-looking, Babbitt-like, middle-aged or elderly men, well-dressed, carefully barbered, fat-cheeked, double- and triple-chinned, vast-bellied, with gold watch-chains across their paunches and stickpins in their ties. They drive good cars or travel in taxis between their hotels, which are the best in town, and the convention hall. Their hands are soft and pudgy, eager for the shake. They are breezy, genial men, professional good fellows. The bulk of them have "grown up" together in the "movement," which now is

their "movement." They practically own it. . . . They all know one another, these panjandrums of American labor. They are, for the most part, presidents and vice-presidents and chief organizers of the various national and international unions with salaries ranging from $7500 to $20,000 a year "and expenses." Prosperity or depression, their salaries never stop. Under their brilliant leadership some of the unions have so amended their constitutions that now the presidents—"Tsars"—can raise their own salaries almost at will.[82]

The impression that union leaders were only in it for their personal enrichment was reflected in a number of polls taken during the 1970s and '80s. A 1976 survey found that 76 percent agreed with the statement "Many union leaders have used their union positions to benefit themselves financially."[83] In 1977, a poll by the Survey Research Center claimed that "approximately two-thirds of the respondents agreed that . . . [union] leaders are more interested in what benefits themselves than in what benefits union members."[84] When presented with a list of adjectives to describe union leaders, participants in a 1984 Roper poll picked "self-seeking," "ruthless," "not sufficiently competent," and "behind the times" as their top four choices. By contrast, business leaders were described as "self-seeking," "forward looking and progressive," "able and competent," and "very intelligent."[85] And when asked to rate various occupational groups for their ethical standards, Americans responded that out of twenty-five different occupations, only car salesmen ranked worse than labor leaders when it came to "honesty and ethics."[86]

Unions Versus Workers

More than just asserting that unions and their leaders were no longer the underdogs they had been in the 1930s, critics of organized labor also claimed that the labor movement was failing to "speak[] for the underprivileged."[87] Indeed, much of the discussion about organized labor attempted to show that, in the words of a New York jurist, "instead of being one of the most important agencies for the betterment of the laboring man, [unions had] become a most powerful means of his oppression."[88] Rather than the friend of the underdog, unions were portrayed as his enemy, no better than the corporations against which they had fought.

The most fundamental problem with unions, in this regard, was their supposed lack of democracy. As Wellington Roe, who at one time was connected with the railroad brotherhoods but then became a bitter critic of unions, expressed it in 1947, "our trade unions, which should be models of democracy, are often dictatorships in which labor bosses are the autocratic rulers of the dues-paying members."[89] This problem was acknowledged by both the Left and the Right. Indeed, the issue of union democracy became one of the main components of the debate over the Landrum-Griffin Act, passed in 1959, though it had appeared much earlier and would continue to be an issue for years to come.

The impression conveyed by the press was that, in most cases, the membership had little or no say in running the union. Instead, as Donald Richberg, an attorney for the railroad brotherhoods in the 1920s, a member of the Nation Labor Relations Board in the 1930s, and, by the 1940s, a rabid critic of unions, claimed, "workers [had] rid [themselves] of one set of industrial masters, called employers, [only] to substitute a new set of masters, called labor leaders."[90] Rather than creating an "industrial democracy," union leaders had proved no less autocratic than the managers against whom they had fought. "To many unionists," claimed Roe, "it is becoming increasingly clear that the very men who took them out of the dark woods of employer coercion have taken them into the dark forest of organizational autocracy."[91] Union leaders had become, as an editorial in *Life* asserted, "malefactors of great power who today stand in the role once played by malefactors of great wealth."[92] As a result, "The relation of laborer to union leader is much like the earlier relation of serf to feudal lord."[93] "Feudal lord" was just one of the terms used to describe labor leaders. They were also referred to as "dictators," "tyrants," "despots," and "autocrats."[94] The most common term for a labor leader, however, was "boss." As Puette has observed, newspaper "reporters refer respectfully to the president or CEO of a business, but to them labor unions are led by chiefs or bosses, words that obviously suggest a lack of democratic selection."[95] It was not just the media that portrayed labor leaders as dictators, however. Unions themselves engaged in such mudslinging. For instance, Mills, writing in 1948, quotes a 1925 speech by the legendary labor activist Mother Jones, "The rank and file have let their servants become their masters and dictators. The workers have now to fight not alone their exploiters but likewise their own leaders, who often betray them, who sell them out, who put their own advancement ahead of that of the working masses, who make the rank and file political pawns."[96]

The impression the media conveyed, that unions were for the most part undemocratic organizations, was shared by the public. A poll taken in 1976 found that three-fifths of those surveyed agreed with the statement: "Most union leaders have become arrogant and no longer represent the workers in their unions." (Also of note here is the pollster's echoing of the pejorative "arrogant.") Another poll done in 1977 revealed that 65 percent believed that "unions force members to go along with decisions they don't like." And a 1985 survey by Opinion Research Corporation showed 60 percent agreeing with the sentiment that "union leaders express their own views rather than those of their members when taking public stands." In fact, 68 percent of those responding to a 1978 poll felt that "unions that do not fairly represent their members" was a bigger problem than "companies that unfairly deny their workers a chance to join a union," a position held by only 17 percent of the respondents.[97]

How did this state of affairs develop? "In many unions power gravitates naturally to the International," explained Lester Velie, the labor editor for *Reader's Digest* during the 1950s.[98] The result was that "individual members have become submerged in huge organizations" where their voices were less likely to be heard or noticed.[99] The *New Republic* pointed to the 1957 election of David McDonald, president of the United Steel Workers, to show how democracy had been subverted in one major union. In that case, the leadership's control of the union press ensured that no bad news appeared about the president, while no news at all appeared concerning his opponent.[100] As Velie noted, "Even in legitimate unions, where elections are held, member self-rule is frustrated. The union boss controls all of the union's political machinery."[101] In addition, as Roe explained, "Union constitutions and bylaws are largely written to ensure absolute compliance with officers' wishes."[102] "United Mine Workers' conventions sometimes sound like a Nazi congress," claimed Velie in another article. "Members are so well trained they even yell from the floor that they are against self-rule."[103] More serious were those cases where unions held no elections at all. "In Chicago's Hod Carriers' Union, for example, there has been no election for 29 years," wrote Thurman Arnold, head of the Justice Department's Anti-Trust Division under Franklin Roosevelt, in 1941.[104]

When the leadership's control of the press and the workings of the union constitution did not suffice, union "bosses" resorted to intimidation and violence to get their way. According to the *New Republic*, "CIO unions founded in the mine workers' tradition, have eliminated political opposition largely by strong arm methods."[105] And, of course, the association between unions and violence was both ancient and widespread. As a contributor to the *Saturday Evening Post* reminded his readers, "It is stupid to make believe that the labor movement is conducted by sweet persuasion."[106] Thus, "when intimidation fails to get leaders' wishes through rank-and-filers' skulls, the skulls can be cracked."[107]

Perhaps the most important source of union leaders' control over their members, however, was closed- or union-shop agreements. Union-shop agreements required that new employees join the existing union, whereas closed-shop agreements forbade the employer from hiring anyone who was not already a member of the union. They were organized labor's method of dealing with the free rider problem. As Garet Garret, political affairs editor for the *Saturday Evening Post* from the 1920s though the early '40s, argued, "A union which has a government conferred monopoly on the right to work in a given industry has no cause to heed the opinions of its rank-and-file."[108] Indeed, according to Bill Hard, a roving editor for *Reader's Digest* during the '40s, union-shop contracts "provide dictatorial labor leaders with their strongest weapon for perpetuating their dictatorships."[109] This was because the "power of union officers lies in their right to expel a member for an infraction of union rules. Since, in many industries, a worker cannot get or hold a job in his trade unless he belongs to the union, he is understandably anxious not to arouse the ire of union officers. . . . Under such conditions the dues-payer has the lean choice of expressing his opinion and losing his job, or keeping quiet and having the leaders speak and act for him regardless of his own desires."[110] Or as an editorial in *Life* put it in 1957, "If a business agent throws them out they can't even work at their jobs. So they don't dare squawk."[111] Even the liberal publication *New Republic* had to admit this practice was hardly foreign to organized labor. "The leadership of a large union in Chicago," related one article, "eliminates any rank-and-file opposition by persuading the employer to fire the rebels."[112]

A lack of union democracy, according to many critics, helped explain the existence of racketeer- and communist-dominated unions.[113] For instance, the *New Republic* argued, "The only things wrong with trade unions today are the fringes of racketeering in some parts of the labor movement. This could be remedied by an act making periodic elections mandatory in all trade unions and providing for publicity of accounts."[114] Likewise, Leo Huberman, an apologist for the labor movement and editor for the Left-wing *Monthly Review,* argued that racketeering could be eliminated from unions "if true rank and file democracy replaces the autocracy in the racketeer-infested unions."[115] For those on the Right, it was the union-shop contract, in addition to an absence of democracy, that made this situation possible. Typical of this sentiment was the title of one editorial in the *Saturday Evening Post,* which bluntly stated: "A 'Right to Work' Law Might Help Rid Unions of Goons."[116] (Right-to-work laws forbade unions from negotiating closed- or union-shop agreements. The Taft-Hartley Act permits the states to pass such laws but does not itself contain a right-to-work provision.) The congressional investigation of labor racketeering led by Senator John McClellan conducted during the later half of the 1950s supposedly proved this link. "The files of the McClellan committee," asserted one writer, "contain many tragic letters from men who are walking the streets in search of work after incurring the displeasure of a union leader and have lost their job because of union shop agreements."[117] Likewise, during the 1940s when communist domination of some unions was a widespread concern, the *Saturday Evening Post* claimed that communist union leaders "have been able to get rid of dissenters by dismissing them from the union on bogus charges. Then, under closed shop contracts, the dissenter is automatically fired from his job."[118]

Far from making workers "industrial citizens," then, unions had deprived them of their rights as political citizens, including the rights of free speech, a free press, and free and fair elections.[119] As the *New Republic* noted, "There is a general absence from union constitutions of anything approximating a bill of rights, a protection of the basic civil and political rights of members."[120] The need to write into law such a "bill of rights" for union members was a theme that recurred in the press from the 1940s through the '70s.[121] Such a measure was needed not only to ensure internal union democracy, it was necessary to ensure that members' political rights outside the union were preserved.[122] For example, Jack Swigert, a partner in Senator Robert Taft's Cincinnati law firm, writing in defense of the Taft-Hartley Act, claimed that workers had been thrown out of unions for campaigning for politicians whom their leaders opposed.[123] And the editors of the *Saturday Evening Post* claimed that "union leaders use their power to police the private opinions of their members."[124] As Donald Richberg argued in 1947, "no American should be forced to adopt his economic philosophy or his political program at the dictation of a union."[125]

Another violation of workers' political rights was the use of union funds, without the consent of the membership, for political purposes. As one article after another argued, "There are millions of Republicans in organized labor who are being forced to pay the campaign expenses for Democratic office seekers as a condition of employment. . . . if they object to this sort of use of their dues money, they are insulted, baited and labeled antilabor by the very same labor leaders who claim to be defending their individual rights and freedoms."[126] The impression conveyed by the conservative press was that union-shop contracts had given unions enormous leverage over not only their own members, but also the workings of the national political system.

American labor unions . . . constitute the nation's most powerful political force. No other organized group can match labor's bloc of voters, its armies of election workers and lobbyists, its campaign treasury or its immense influence in Washington and state capitals. . . . Almost every year, labor groups lead the list of top spenders for lobbying in Washington. . . . The development of this awesome political muscle became possible after Congress granted unions the power to make contracts forcing workers—if they want to keep their job—to join unions and pay dues.[127]

National Review even claimed in 1974 that the use of union dues for political purposes was a bigger cover-up than the Watergate scandal. "The biggest of all coverups relates to how—year in, year out—organized labor first extracts a billion or so of dues money from its members under compulsory union contracts (of the closed-shop, union-shop, or agency-shop variety) and then diverts a good part of this money into political activity that contravenes the spirit if not the letter of the law."[128]

As this list of union abuses shows, compulsory unionism was portrayed as playing a role in most aspects of organized labor's oppression of the working man. Perhaps the biggest problem with union-shop contracts, however, was not that they were a tool of the leadership for controlling the membership, or that they artificially increased unions' political power, or even that they were the method by which gangsters and communists came to dominate many unions. Rather, union-shop contracts, in and of themselves, were considered undemocratic, even "un-American."[129] Typical of this sentiment is the following statement by Garet Garrett, a frequent contributor to the *Saturday Evening Post* in the late 1930s: "The statutory closed shop principle has no place in a democracy."[130] This was because it gave union leaders power over, not just their own members, but nonmembers as well. Arguments against the closed shop sometimes strangely echoed those unions had made in the nineteenth century against "wage slavery." "The demand for the closed shop, now sugar-coated with the union shop formula, is a raw demand that every worker be compelled to join one of the elite national organizations in order to earn a living."[131] "Should the right to work be confined to members of labor unions?"[132] "In a free society the cost of getting or holding a job ought not to include compulsory tribute to a union."[133] The impression given by these writers, obviously, was that if organized labor had its way, in order to work at all a person would need to join a union. For certain trades this was already the case. Yet, "[t]he American people . . . believe that admission to all trades should be open to every aspiring person without having to pay large sums to labor leaders."[134]

The more conservative writers, as these excerpts indicate, seemed to be under the impression that most workers had joined unions as the result of compulsion.[135] As the *Saturday Evening Post* argued in 1946, "the government [is] party to a system which . . . forces employers to compel the workers to enlist and pay union dues—so they will be able to make war on the public with an imposing but largely conscript army."[136] Thirty years later *National Review* was claiming that "the government has been doing George Meany the favor of compelling millions of people to join labor unions."[137] In the most outrageous instances, workers were not even given the choice of whether they even wanted union representation. Instead, unions would engage in "organizing at the top," organizing the employer instead of the employees.[138] The following was one example of this practice:

> A contractor working on a small defense housing project in the Philadelphia area was approached by representatives of the Philadelphia building trades unions, who demanded that he sign a agreement to employ none but union men on the premises and to impose the same conditions on all subcontractors. The employer was asked to organize his men enmasse, whether they liked it or not. He refused, with the result that his project was picketed, although there was no strike and none of his employees had indicated any desire to join the union. This is typical of hundreds of so called disputes throughout the United States.[139]

Another article purported to quote letters written by workers at Allis-Chalmers who claimed they had been coerced into joining the union.

> "I am a member of Local 248," wrote one man, "just to avoid union wrath, which some extremists demonstrate by throwing bricks and light bulbs filled with paint through the windows of our homes." Another wrote: "Because of strong arm methods, I'm a member." A third signed his letter, "just another one of the forced members." An employee of twenty-two years' standing explained that he had joined the union because organizers inside the plant made the non-unionists' work "eight hours of living hell."[140]

From the 1950s on the impression that most workers joined unions under compulsion no doubt gained credence, even among union members themselves, as those workers involved in the initial organizing drives of the CIO dropped out of the work force and were replaced by workers who had joined the union because of a union-shop contract. As one union steward complained in 1963 in regards to lack of member participation in union affairs, "people are taking unionism for granted . . . when they come here to work and to join the union; they join it because they have to. And that's it. . . . Their dues are taken off and they never lift their head again."[141]

The antipathy towards the closed- or union-shop, of course, was of long standing. The open-shop drive of the 1920s was, after all, called the "American Plan," with its clear implication that closed shops were "un-American."[142] The terms of the debate were of equally long standing. As the *New Republic* said of the 1965 debate over repealing the right-to-work provisions of the Taft-Hartley Act, "The terms are the same as in the Congressional Record of June 1935; the literature on both sides could be reprinted from a generation ago."[143]

Despite this long opposition to closed- and union-shops, however, most Americans held conflicting views of unions when it came to this issue. To the extent that unions violated an individual's freedom of choice by forcing all workers to join, Americans opposed compulsory unionism. But when it came to an individual's responsibility to contribute to an organization that had directly benefited him, they believed that organization could reasonably demand support. Barry Goldwater, a vociferous critic of unions, articulated this dichotomy as follows, "let us not express our contempt for some men [i.e., free riders] by denying freedom of choice to all."[144]

Polling data clearly points to this dichotomous view. During the 1930s and '40s, 75 percent of people answered no when asked if they were in favor of closed-shop contracts.[145] During the '50s, when asked if they would vote for a right-to-work law, two-thirds said yes.[146] One poll from 1957 was particularly interesting. When asked if they agreed with the statement, "no American should be required to join any private organization, like a labor union, against his will," 73 percent said they agreed, the same proportion as had opposed the closed shop. Yet when the question was phrased to represent the union view—"when all workers share the gains won by the labor union all workers should have to join and pay dues"—a small plurality supported the idea of a union shop.[147] And despite their supposed willingness to vote for right-to-work measures, during the great right-to-work drive of 1958, voters decisively rejected such laws.[148] During the 1960s fewer than half of those surveyed, though still a plurality, disagreed with the statement "a person [should] be required to join a union if he works in a unionized factory."[149] By the 1970s, however, the number of those opposed to union-shop contracts increased to between 60 and 70 percent. But as with the 1957 poll, when the question was framed to better reflect organized labor's view, approval for union-shop clauses showed greater support. Thirty-nine percent of those polled in 1978 agreed with the argument "that if a majority of employees of a firm or factory want to have a labor union, then every employee should have to pay dues to the union since the union will be representing them," whereas 46 percent disagreed. The phrasing of this question, however, was less favorable to unions than the similar question in the 1957 poll and may better account for the different results than the passage of time does.[150]

The critical issue in the debate over the right to work, like the more general concern about union democracy, centered on the general impression that unions had imposed themselves on the workers and, thus, had violated their freedom. If workers themselves wanted a union shop, instead of having it forced on them by a leadership hungry for dues money and power, then it was all right. This view, interestingly, was confirmed by the brief history of one provision of the generally antiunion Taft-Hartley Act. In accordance with the belief that most workers had been forced into joining unions, the Taft-Hartley Act required that the National Labor Relations Board (NLRB) hold a secret ballot election of the workers involved to determine their wishes before a union could negotiate for the inclusion of a union-shop provision in a contract. For the brief period this provision was in effect, "union-shop agreements were ratified 97 percent of the time."[151] Because of this overwhelming endorsement of the union-shop, Congress amended the Taft-Hartley Act in 1951 to eliminate such ballots, supposedly because they were unnecessarily increasing the NLRB's caseload. (Another reason may have been, as the *New Republic* suggested, because it "had the practical effect of strengthening a union's bargaining hand when it asked the employer to sign a union-shop contract."[152]) As a result of this provision, the debate over the closed-shop virtually disappeared from the media. From 1948 until 1954, the issue of compulsory unionism was not brought up in any of the articles examined for this study, except to mention that workers had overwhelming voted for such contracts. Likewise, Gallup polls did not ask about union-shop contracts between 1948 and 1957. Only several years after this requirement was repealed did people again begin to speak about compulsory unionism as though it was something imposed from the top instead of coming from the workers themselves.

In addition to denying to members a democratic choice on whether to join the union, and on who would lead the union, another way in which union leaders supposedly oppressed workers was in denying them a say in whether the union would strike. The preamble to a 1939 antilabor ballot initiative in California contained the following justification for the measure: "Workers are arbitrarily ordered to engage in strikes, boycotts and picketing in support of controversies in which they have no interest."[153] William Green, president of the AFL, far from contradicting this sentiment may have actually encouraged it. Here is what he had to say in 1937 in regards to unions affiliated with the CIO: "In a union controlled from the top the members have nothing to say as to policy. They strike when they are told to strike. They go out on a sympathy strike when the order comes—no matter whether they are or are not in sympathy with the strike called by another union."[154] That same year, Westbrook Pegler, a nationally syndicated columnist whose exposés of labor racketeering won him a Pulitzer Prize in 1941, reminded his readers that, "It is well to recognize that strikers often strike against their will."[155] Lester Velie, *Readers' Digest* labor editor during the 1950s, gave the following evidence for such claims: "Last summer [1954] 6,000 automobile workers voted, by a show of hands, to strike the Studebaker Corp. Company officials urged a second poll with voting machines. In the privacy of the voting booth the men voted against striking, eight to one." Moreover, he asserted that "in only one of every four national unions surveyed [by the National Industrial Conference Board] do men have the right to vote secretly on strikes."[156] As Leo Huberman confirmed in 1946, "The man on the street has been led to believe that strikes are called at the whim of a handful of top labor leaders."[157]

As with the debate over compulsory unionism, the widespread assumption that workers only struck because they were forced to by their leaders led to legislative action. "The wartime [1943] Smith Connally law required NLRB secret ballots before a strike would be 'legal.'" As with the Taft-Hartley provision requiring elections for union-shop contracts, "the workers voted so overwhelmingly for strikes that in 1945 Congress refused any more appropriations for conducting the ridiculous ballots." Nevertheless, "the doctrinaire notion that union members wouldn't strike if it weren't for the 'labor bosses,'" continued to influence public policy.[158] For instance, as the *New Republic* noted about one provision of the Taft-Hartley act, "mandatory cool offs [waiting periods required by the act before a strike could be called] presuppose that strikes are called by power hungry union leaders without consulting their rank and file."[159]

Even when the rank and file did have a say in whether to strike or not, the tendency was to portray the losses caused by a strike as outweighing any possible gains. The most prominent hardship endured by strikers, of course, was the loss of pay. In a synopsis of sixty-two television scripts dealing with unions during the 1970s and '80s, William Puette found that five episodes dealt with the issue of lost pay resulting from a strike. In an episode of *What's Happening!!*, for instance, while a majority of workers at a supermarket voted to strike, the lead character, Raj, is confronted with the choice of scabbing or being unable to pay the doctor bills for his sick mother.[160] Likewise, a 1981 article in *Readers' Digest* portrayed the plight of three strike breakers at an

Arkansas factory. The reporter in this case was careful to detail how each of them was forced to scab to pay the medical bills for a sick relative and the consequent violence visited on them by their striking coworkers.[161] In one installment of *All in the Family,* when Archie Bunker's union goes on strike, he is forced to let his wife Edith take a job to help pay the bills. Similarly, in an episode of *Eight Is Enough,* a strike by the pressmen at Tom Bradford's newspaper forces him to concede to his wife's demand that she be allowed to look for work. And in another episode of the same show, Bradford is forced to file for unemployment when the pressmen again go on strike.[162] Strikes, according to these television shows, then, led not only to financial hardship, but humiliation and emasculation for those involved.

In addition, the salary gains achieved from a strike, according to several different sources, were never enough to make up for the pay the workers lost while out of work. As one commentator noted about the GM strike of 1946, "not until early 1948 will GM workers be as well off as they would have been had they not struck and had they worked steadily without any wage increase whatsoever."[163] And in an episode of the 1970s series *Laverne and Shirley,* Shirley Feeney (Cindy Williams) argues against a strike at the brewery where she works by claiming that "Every year we go out on strike and what do we wind up with? A nickel raise that doesn't make up for all the money we lose by striking."[164] When coupled with the tendency to paint unions as "strike happy" these portrayals of the likely results of a strike conveyed the impression that workers who joined a union would, in all probability, lose more than they could possibly gain, either through being forced to strike or by being subjected to reprisals if they decided to scab.

Although all of these issues went into making up the popular image of labor unions, the most dramatic way in which organized labor was seen to oppress working people was its apparent affinity for racketeering. The connection between organized labor and organized crime formed the premise for much of Hollywood's treatment of unions. A list of movies dealing with union corruption includes *Racket Busters* (1937), *On the Waterfront* (1954), *Edge of the City* (1957), *Slaughter on Tenth Avenue* (1957), *The Garment Jungle* (1957), *Never Steal Anything Small* (1959), *Blue Collar* (1978), and *F.I.S.T.* (1978). In Puette's survey of television dramatic and comedy series, he found that of sixty-two episodes dealing with unions, nine of them had union racketeering as their premise. This figure actually understates the racketeering theme since it includes comedy series. When it came to detective shows, for instance, the only time a union (almost always a truckers' or longshore union) was included was when it was run by mobsters.[165] Additionally, of the

450 magazine articles examined for this study, sixty-nine of them, stretching from 1937 to 1978, were either wholly about union corruption or at least mentioned the issue.

The association of racketeering with organized labor was not new to the postwar period. Writing in 1931, Louis Adamic claimed that *labor racketeering* was a term that came into use in the 1920s.[166] In 1938 Harold Seidman published *Labor Czars*, a book length history of union racketeering, and Westbrook Peglar, a syndicated columnist, won a Pulitzer prize in 1941 for his exposé of racketeering in some Hollywood unions.[167] Already by 1941 the *New Republic* was talking about "the ordinary middle-class American [and] his fantastic conviction that all labor leaders are racketeers."[168] Leo Huberman acknowledged in 1946 that "union-haters" had been successful in "mak[ing] it appear as though unionism and racketeering were one and the same."[169] These assertions were backed up by a 1941 Gallup poll that showed 72 percent of respondents agreeing with the statement that "many labor leaders are racketeers," and only 14 percent disagreeing.[170] In addition to the spectacular nature of the charges, the reason this issue drew so much attention was because it starkly contrasted with the way unions were supposed to behave according their legitimization myth. As an article in the *New Republic* commented, "the corrupt union leader is more offensive than corrupt leaders in other walks of life because he betrays a trust given him by underprivileged people."[171] In any event, the association of unions with corruption has formed the core of most peoples' image of organized labor since the 1940s.[172]

The consequences of union racketeering for workers were not only a lack of democracy within the union and the threat of violence associated with mobster rule, but lost pay because of "sweetheart contracts." According to Lester Velie, "the most heartless racket in labor is the sale to crooked employers of 'sweetheart contracts' that depress the wages of captive union members."[173] Likewise, *Life* magazine listed as one of the many crimes that the McClellan Committee brought to light the "betrayal of the union members through substandard contracts with employers." To protect workers, the editors of *Life* urged Congress to pass a law that would prohibit "sweetheart contracts."[174] Somewhat contradictorily, these diatribes against unions that "sold out" their memberships could be found in the very same magazines and journals that blasted organized labor for raising wages too high and causing inflation.

* * *

The postwar offensive against organized labor had a lasting impact in shaping Americans' ideas about unions. Most of the tropes invoked were not new to this period, but they were espoused with enough vehemence and frequency to convince the general public of their veracity. Most important, these critiques helped begin the process of undermining organized labor's legitimization myth that had been established in the 1930s by showing that unions were failing to live up to their ideal as the champion of the underdog. Indeed, much of this offensive centered on showing how unions had become the enemy of the working man, rather than his friend. As much damage as this offensive caused to labor's reputation, however, it would be the changed circumstances of union members themselves that would eventually sour Americans on unions.

3

The Postwar Boom and
Organized Labor's
Lost Legitimacy

Although the postwar offensive against unions by conservative and business interests caused severe damage to labor's reputation, Americans' "approval" for unions (admittedly, a nebulous concept) continued to remain at a high level into the early 1960s. It was only in the late '60s that union approval would begin a significant, enduring decline. It was not the "Free-Enterprise Campaign" that would sour Americans on organized labor. Rather, as with the shift in attitudes during the 1930s, it was a changed perception of union members that led to declining support for organized labor.

Accusations about the ways in which labor unions oppressed the very people they were supposed to be fighting for could be found in the press almost unchanged from the late 1930s into the '80s. They were, however, most prominent during the '40s and '50s. As the '50s turned into the '60s, criticism of union members themselves became more extensive. Less often were unions accused of exploiting the underdog. Instead, they were increasingly charged with completely ignoring him.

Labor's apparent success in raising its members into the ranks of the middle class, combined with the effects of the post-war boom, convinced most Americans that blue-collar workers were no longer the underpaid and exploited victims they had been in the 1930s. Instead, with the rise of the Civil Rights Movement, a new underdog came to the fore—African Americans and other minorities. Issues related to economic class were eclipsed by those related to race. Unions, which were understood to be primarily, or even solely, economic institutions, appeared to have little to offer this new underdog. Indeed, many unions, particularly those in the building trades,

Workers' approval of unions. Data compiled from Gallup polls.

seemed to have interests directly antagonistic to those of minorities. The increasing divergence between the ideal image of unions as the champion of the underprivileged, and the way in which organized labor was perceived to operate in "reality," caused many Americans to become disillusioned with the labor movement by the 1970's.

The postwar boom, and the accompanying rise in income for unionized workers, not only undermined organized labor's image as the champion of the underdog. In combination with the effects of the second red scare, it also seemed to deprive unions of their own preferred image of being a force for reforming society. By the end of the 1950s, issues of class and economic inequality seemed moot. As John Kenneth Galbraith wrote in his *Affluent Society* in 1958, "few things are more evident in modern social history than the decline of interest in inequality as an economic issue."[1] Blue-collar factory workers, organized labor's perceived primary constituency, were an ever smaller segment of the work force. Increasingly, Americans appeared to be on the way to becoming "Organization Men" for whom unions had no role.[2] Even the appearance of Michael Harrington's *The Other America* in 1962, failed to seriously undermine this view.[3] In 1974, for instance, Andrew Levison felt compelled to write a book, *Working-Class Majority*, arguing against the popularly held belief that most Americans had joined the ranks of the white-collar middle class.[4]

At the same time that the bottom of the class structure was disappearing from view, the top was fading from consciousness as well. C. Wright Mills, for instance, published his study, *The Power Elite,* in 1956 to demonstrate that the super-rich were still as powerful and decisive, indeed, more so, than they had ever been. Nevertheless, the rich qua rich no longer received the attention they once had. Instead, the public's attention had shifted from the "Leisure Class" to "Café Society." It was only by making themselves into celebrities that the rich gained notice anymore. (Mills's section on debutantes brings the contemporary example of Paris Hilton instantly to mind.)[5]

This decreasing interest in class issues was reflected in the number of articles and editorials about unions that appeared in popular magazines during the period. Whereas these were plentiful during the 1940s and '50s, the attention given to organized labor during the 1960s and '70s fell off precipitously. Clearly, the labor movement had become irrelevant to the major social and political issues that concerned most Americans.

Not only had America seemingly become a "classless society," but capitalism itself seemed to have been vindicated. It was now delivering the goods, so to speak. In such an environment, talk of reforming the economy seemed not only irrelevant, but even subversive. This latter view was reinforced by the onset of the Second Red Scare in the later half of the 1940s, which seemed to sap organized labor, in particular the Congress of Industrial Organizations (CIO), of its reformist visions. In 1949 eleven communist-led unions were expelled from the CIO, and the organization lost much of its radical tinge. This trend was confirmed when the CIO was absorbed into the larger and more conservative American Federation of Labor (AFL) in 1955, becoming just another department alongside the building trades department.[6]

Whereas organized labor once was associated with an ideology that embraced a more economically just society—an ideology most middle-class Americans had nonetheless rejected as revolutionary and un-American—it now seemed to be entirely devoid of ideas. It came to be seen as a mere special interest, speaking only for its own members, not society as a whole. As Seymour Martin Lipset put it in 1986, "like big business, [unions] are seen as powerful and *essentially self-serving.* But corporations have an advantage in that the public also thinks they inherently contribute to the community in the form of jobs, goods, and services. Unions [on the other hand] are viewed as *giving low priority to the public interest.*"[7]

Unions not only appeared to have forgotten the underdog, they no longer seemed to offer a broader vision of what American society should be like and what their role in achieving that better society would be. These two interrelated changes led many Americans to turn against unions by the 1970s.

Unions Versus the New Underdogs

Perversely, unions' success in "lift[ing] the common man out of poverty to the greatest prosperity enjoyed by any people," opened them to a new form of attack.[8] As an article in the *Saturday Evening Post* claimed, "the widespread public sympathy and support the labor movement enjoyed when it was fighting against starvation wages and subhuman conditions have been replaced by public irritation."[9] A pair of articles on the 1967 strike against Ford are an excellent example of this attitude. On the Right, *National Review* sarcastically noted that, "Mr. Reuther's [president of the United Auto Workers] defenseless peons are earning, after all, something like three times the minimum wage established by the government."[10] On the Left, the *New Republic* expressed exactly the same feelings, "The Ford Motor Company, the nation's second largest corporation, does not run a sweatshop. Its 160,000 wage workers average more than $4.50 an hour; yet they are on strike. Their protest is not against the kind of exploitation out of which the labor movement was born, or the documented anomie of the assembly line. Affluent workers want to be more affluent."[11] And, as both articles concluded, the results of the strike would simply mean more inflation.

Union workers' new "affluence" created the impression that "the AFL-CIO is just another protective association; speaking for the possessors and not the dispossessed. The unions . . . care more about repealing a section of the Taft-Hartley Act than about the poor, are more concerned with security and seniority for themselves than with a better life for all."[12] As a result, an editorial in *Fortune* asserted, organized labor "can no longer plausibly claim . . . that it speaks for the underprivileged."[13] Union leaders themselves probably reinforced this conclusion. The following is from a 1959 article in the *New Republic*: "Union leaders also point out that some of those suffering most from long term inflation are in occupations which 'refuse' to organize. A Steelworker district staff man's remarks are blunt, but typical: 'We want to bring them into the same economic fold as our people. But until they get off their fannies and organize to fight for their economic rights, they are going to take a little of the brunt of our economic expansion.'"[14]

Unions had not only ignored the unorganized underprivileged, then, but their policies had actually contributed to their imisseration. For instance, as the previous quote indicates, high union wages were blamed for inflation. They also meant lower pay for nonunion workers. As the *National Review* argued in 1971,

successful unions must restrict or ration entry into their trade, thereby reducing the supply of that particular sort of labor, while simultaneously increasing
the supply of labor in unrestricted trades. The resulting flood of labor into low
skill job markets causes weak union and non-union wages to be lower than
they would otherwise be. The gains of strong unions, then are at the expense of
other workers, especially at the expense of those who are arbitrarily excluded
from the employment of their choice by the unions' closed-shop policy.[15]

Or as another article put it, "by increasing the share [of income] going to relatively skilled employees (who were the highest paid even before unionization)
unions have contributed substantially to income inequality." Moreover, "by
pursuing apparently suicidal wage demands, a majority of union members,
through seniority protection, are able to vote newcomers out of a job."[16] As a
testament to the widespread acceptance of this critique, economists Richard
Freeman and James Medoff published a book in 1984 that attempted to refute
the idea that unions increased income inequality and reduced the number
of jobs available to lower-skilled and younger workers.[17]

Among the most prominent of the "newcomers" hurt by unions were
African Americans. Criticism of AFL unions for their racially exclusionary
policies had appeared in the Northern media at least as far back as the 1940s.[18]
As the Civil Rights Movement gained momentum, however, this issue became increasingly prominent.[19] Herbert Hill, head of the labor division of
the National Association for the Advancement of Colored People (NAACP)
in the 1950s and '60s, gave added impetus to this critique by accusing not
just the building trades but many industrial unions of racially discriminatory
practices.[20] And when the New York City local of the American Federation of
Teachers went on strike in 1968 to protect the jobs of nineteen white teachers
who had been transferred out of a local school district composed largely of
African Americans, the interests of unions and African Americans appeared
to be diametrically opposed.[21]

The Ocean Hill–Brownsville strike also highlighted another fundamental
conflict between public employee unions and inner-city African Americans.
As an article in the New Republic argued, "militant union pressure has upset
the balance of power existing previously in our cities, and poses an even
greater threat to newly emerging pressure groups like the poor, blacks and
other minorities, whose claim on public resources may be more just than
the unions'. . . . if blacks do inherit control of our central cities they will find
them impoverished by exorbitant settlements made hastily by white mayors
to public employee unions composed mostly of whites."[22] The conclusion to
be drawn from all this, reached by an editorial in Life, was that unions "are

more hindrance than help to equal job opportunity for Negroes, and they have done little to organize the lowest paid wage earners, such as farm labor."[23]

It should be noted, however, that whereas unions were criticized in the North for discriminating against African Americans, in the South in the 1940s and' 50s, the criticism was just the opposite. The CIO was demonized by southern employers and newspapers for its racially egalitarian principles.[24] By the 1970s, however, such appeals appear to have largely faded away, though employers might raise the specter of African American domination of a local union to discourage whites from joining.[25]

When major organizing drives *did* target African Americans and other minorities, they were often portrayed as more a part of the Civil Rights Movement than as part of labor's effort to "organize the unorganized." For instance, it is commonly forgotten that Martin Luther King Jr. was in Memphis to support black sanitation workers in their effort to gain union recognition when he was assassinated. One of the highest profile union drives of the 1960s was the effort by the United Farm Workers and their leader Cesar Chavez to organize Mexican American grape pickers. Unlike many other organizing drives covered by the media, Chavez's movement received mostly positive coverage because it was viewed primarily as a push for racial equality by Mexican Americans.[26] As Nicholas von Hoffman put it, "Chavez is seen principally as a Chicano leader and only very indistinctly as a colleague of George Meany."[27] Likewise, a 1969 drive by the hospital union 1199 to organize mostly African American hospital service workers in Charleston, South Carolina, only attracted attention when major civil rights organizations intervened on behalf of the workers.[28]

Despite the impression conveyed by the media that unions were either irrelevant or even a hindrance to the Civil Rights Movement, African Americans generally supported organized labor. For instance, unions found that the African American community was its strongest supporter when it came to defeating right-to-work laws in the late 1950s and early '60s.[29] Likewise, Timothy Minchin, in his study of African American employment in the postwar textile industry, shows that African Americans were often more supportive of unionization than whites were.[30] A Department of Labor survey done in 1977 also showed much greater support for unions among African Americans than among other workers.[31] As with the first and second generation immigrants who formed the core of the CIO, it would seem that African Americans were more receptive to organized labor in part because of their partial isolation from and rejection of the dominant white, middle-class culture.[32]

Unions as a Special Interest

If one effect of the postwar boom was to make unions appear to be the representatives of the haves, rather than the have-nots, another, related effect would be to rob them of their image as a force for social reform. Instead, the idea that unions were merely another special interest group "like the cash farmers or the Shingle Binders' Association," although not a new idea, came to dominate Americans' thinking about organized labor in the later half of the twentieth century.[33]

Unfortunately for unions, the perception that their primary purpose was to represent the downtrodden worked against their desire to be seen as more than just economic organizations. Though many twentieth-century unionists from the second decade through the 1940s claimed their ultimate objective was to democratize all of industry, this mission was overshadowed by the emphasis given organized labor's struggle against "starvation wages and subhuman conditions."[34] Indeed, the public's most basic conception of unions' role from the 1950s on was that of raising workers' wages and improving working conditions. When unions were credited with increasing purchasing power or, more frequently, blamed for causing inflation, it was in the context of a general understanding that their primary function was to increase workers' pay.

Such an emphasis narrowed labor's appeal rather than broadened it. If unions mainly functioned to correct substandard wages and defend workers against arbitrary treatment, then what was their relevance to workers who did not feel they were mistreated or underpaid? To paraphrase Gerald Johnson, a columnist for the New Republic during the 1950s, if organized labor's only goal was "higher wages and shorter hours . . . it inevitably admits that organization is not a way of life but an expedient to attain certain ends which, once attained, will render organization superfluous." By the end of the '50s, these ends seemed to be "already in sight" and so, presumably, had made unions "superfluous."[35]

As early as 1947 the New Republic was complaining that "even the CIO has been guilty of safeguarding its apparently selfish interests at the expense of the community."[36] And in 1955 the same magazine lamented that the days when "[t]he CIO used to be a kind of special spark to the New Deal, the main labor channel of organized liberalism in race relations, foreign policy, political action, anti-colonialism and many other issues broader than pure bread and butter unionism" were long past.[37] By 1959 labor's reform agenda had been so eclipsed by its image as just another "business," that even Life magazine was editorializing that it needed to recapture something of its earlier idealism. "Thinkers about the labor movement are almost unanimous in feeling that it cannot go farther until it redefines its goals. . . . It lacks, praise be, the swamplight ideologies that have misled so many foreign labor movements. But it also lacks the conscious aim and purpose that will keep a great reform movement from degenerating into a mere bureaucracy of a racket."[38] This criticism was, at best, disingenuous, for it was precisely such "swamplight ideologies" that had been the basis for labor's claim to be a "great reform movement" in the first place. Yet it was only after the power of the labor movement had been safely contained by the late 1950s, and it no longer seemed capable or even desirous of achieving such ends, that more conservative critics started to lament that it had "lost the evangelistic fervor which sustained it through nearly three decades of surging growth."[39]

The idea that unions were "a mere bureaucracy of a racket" was not new. During the first third of the twentieth century, many commentators, not all of them hostile to organized labor in principle, such as Herbert Croly, Thorstein Veblen, and Louis Adamic, had similarly accused the AFL of being nothing more than a special interest intent on profiting at the expense of the public.[40] These accusations, however, had coexisted with the idea that organized labor was a potentially revolutionary movement as well. But in the aftermath of the 1930s, the fear of a working-class revolution had disappeared. In addition, the Second Red Scare of the late 1940s and '50s seemed to drain unions of whatever radical edge they once had. As a result, the image of unions as a special interest came to dominate Americans' thinking about organized labor.

The notion that unions were just another special interest, a notion reinforced by the belief that their primary mission was to champion the underdog, probably did more damage to their long-term interests than any other image people held of unions. Contrast organized labor's failure to portray its goals as being in the public interest with the success of the Civil Rights movement, the other "great reform movement" of the twentieth century. At its height, organized labor directly represented about a third of all workers. African Americans, on the other hand, constituted little more than a tenth of the population. Yet the Civil Rights Movement, by calling on Americans to live up to their stated ideals of equality and justice for all men, successfully identified its goals as being in the general interest. The result was that, even though organized labor claimed to speak for all workers, it was unable to fend off such legislation as the Taft-Hartley and Landrum-Griffin Acts, whereas the Civil Rights Movement achieved such notable victories as the 1964 Civil Rights Act and the 1965 Voting Rights Act.

Even organized labor's most competent spokesman, Walter Reuther, proved incapable of bridging the perceived gap between the interests of labor and those of the public. His most dramatic attempt to show this identity of interests, the 1946 strike against General Motors (GM), proved to be a significant failure. Reuther's stated objective in this strike was to gain a 30 percent wage increase for the workers and a pledge from GM to not raise the price of its cars. This goal, if achieved, would result in not only a noninflationary wage settlement, but also support a mass consumption economy by increasing workers' purchasing power. The strike ended when Reuther settled on a smaller wage increase without an agreement by GM to not raise its prices. Not only did the strike fail to achieve its objectives, Reuther's own comments on the reason for the strike revealed an implicit acceptance of the idea that the "public" and "labor" were two separate and, frequently, antagonistic groups. His oft repeated comment that "We are part of the community. We intend to make progress with the community and not at the expense of the community," is very revealing of this dichotomy.[41] First, it shows that Reuther was conscious of a general impression that labor's gains were at everyone else's expense. Second, instead of claiming that labor's interests were identical with those of the public, it places them in a subordinate position. Rather than asserting that the community would benefit by the progress of labor, Reuther promised that labor would not be a hindrance to the community's progress. As Nelson Lichtenstein has shown, by the late 1940s and early '50s, Reuther's demands for supplemental unemployment benefits, health insurance, and private pension plans, although meant to spur congressional action on these issues, could hardly be distinguished from the business unionism of Dave Beck.[42]

Reuther's justification for wage increases, that they would contribute to national purchasing power, were a repetition of the policy justification for the National Industrial Recovery Act and the subsequent Wagner Act. Much of the New Deal had been based on the premise that the Depression had resulted from not paying workers enough to purchase all the goods they were capable of producing. The idea of underconsumption replaced the more traditional overproduction explanation for the Depression. Based on this analysis, the government chose to strengthen unions so that they could force employers to raise wages. Thus, the assumption that the primary function of unions was to increase workers' pay came to be seen as being in the national interest.[43]

After the war, however, inflation, rather than deflation, became the problem. In an environment of full employment and rising prices, the role of unions in raising wages was seen less as a benefit to the economy and more as a liability. This transition in thinking did not take place at once, of course.

During the great strike wave of 1946, most of the discussion of unions' effects on the economy centered on their limiting production.[44] Far from increasing purchasing power, these strikes "threaten[ed] to push this country into an inexcusable man-made depression."[45] Or as the title of one editorial put it, "Loafing Creates No Purchasing Power."[46] Nevertheless, blaming unions for inflation had already started.[47] By the 1950s, even though an occasional reference to "the great contribution union power has made to our high wage, mass consumption economy"[48] could still be found, most of the discussion centered on unions' responsibility for the "wage-price spiral."[49] Such talk reached a peak during the steel strike of 1959, when the main question was, "Steel: How Inflationary?"[50]

Though unions would continue to be blamed for inflation through the 1980s, the government's fiscal and monetary policies were increasingly seen as the main culprit for this problem.[51] For instance, when Gallup asked about the cause of inflation in 1959, the choices it gave were between higher wages and higher profits—37 percent blamed higher profits and 33 percent blamed higher wages.[52] By 1974 it had expanded the choices to include government policies, along with business and labor policies. In this case, 48 percent blamed the government, 19 percent blamed labor, and 16 percent blamed business.[53] Nevertheless, the link between "high union wages" and inflation continued to be sounded into the 1980s. One writer for the *New Republic*, for instance, editorialized in 1981 that "[t]he labor movement needs the kind of leadership that is willing to tell a labor audience that the country can have full employment and easier money again only if working people take the first step to control inflation by cutting wage demands drastically."[54]

By the 1970s the effect of high union wages included not just inflation, but the loss of American jobs to foreign competitors as well. Here is columnist von Hoffman's lament from 1981 in reaction to this increasingly prevalent idea:

> During the protected summer of the Republican ascendancy from Lincoln to Hoover, one of the party's perennial campaign principles was that the American working man was or should be the highest-paid worker in the world. Coolie labor was an un-American idea. Throughout that long period it would have been unthinkable to criticize American workers because they were making more than foreigners like the Japanese or Germans. The proof that America was great was that Americans made more money, that the American standard of living was the highest in the world. No more. Henry Ford—the greater, not the epigone bearing his name—made himself a national hero by introducing the eight-hour, five-dollar working day. Now, whatever the occupation, unless it is chairman of the board, the person is being paid too much.[55]

In addition to high union wages, union work rules were also blamed for America's loss of competitiveness. The 1959 steel strike, in fact, centered on the insistence by the Steel Workers Union that its previous work rules be maintained in spite of their purported impact on American competitiveness.[56] By the 1980s the conviction that antiquated work rules were the main hindrance to increased productivity had become widespread. For instance, Michael Piore and Charles Sabel published their influential *Second Industrial Divide* in 1984, which argued for a new form of industrial organization that would do away with the "job control" practices of American unions; and in 1992 Lawrence Mishel and Paula Voos felt it necessary to publish a volume of essays, *Unions and Economic Competitiveness*, to refute the idea that union work rules were responsible for America's lost competitiveness.[57] (This issue of union work rules, or "featherbedding," as it was commonly called, will be discussed in more detail later in this chapter.)

Strikes and the Public

Although organized labor's effect on the economy—whether in aggravating inflation or decreasing American competitiveness—may have painted it as a special interest, strikes were what most dramatically differentiated the interests of unions from those of the public. Strike violence disturbed the "domestic tranquility" and turned cities into "jungle[s] of industrial strife."[58] In addition, as an article in *Reader's Digest* put it in 1971, "The strike is a means for any group of workers with a stranglehold on some vital service to bring the community at large to its knees. It is rarely employed to ensure justice to mistreated workers, but is used frequently to make well paid specialists more affluent."[59] Whether through violence or the denial of vital services, strikes pitted the interests of a small set of workers against those of the rest of society.

Strikes and violence were essential components of the public's image of unions. As the *New Republic* put it in 1980, "when the Pullman workers went to the barricades in Chicago in 1894, violence followed. There's been violence in labor disputes ever since."[60] This, of course, actually understated the ancestry of strike violence, ignoring such incidents as the Homestead Strike, the Haymarket Riot, the activities of the Molly McGuires, and the Great Railroad Strike of 1877. In the mythology of the Right, strikers and union "goons" were the source of violence, whereas in the view of the Left, strikers were invariably portrayed as the victims of company "thugs."[61] In either case, the message was that strikes led inevitably to violence. As the *New Republic* reminded its readers, however, this association was largely a creation of

Playing on images of strike violence. *Bloom County,* 1987. Reprinted by permission of the *Washington Post* Writers Group.

the media: "it is well to remember that it is the sensational event, involving conflict and violence, that command the most space in the newspapers, and that these are sporadic and exceptional rather than characteristic."[62] As if to demonstrate the truth of this statement, *Life* magazine, with its emphasis on photojournalism, was especially fond of publishing photo essays about incidents of strike violence, even at the same time it was claiming "strikes and labor violence make news by their infrequency."[63]

More basic than the association of strikes with violence was the belief, at least among many middle-class writers, that strikes were inherently a form of violence. They were labeled "economic warfare," "economics by bludgeon," and a "reversion to force."[64] As such, they were the complete opposite of rationality. "Strikes, as everyone knows, are neither appeals to.reason nor sound methods of arriving at justice," claimed one critic.[65] This was because, "mere strategic power [should] not be the determinant of who gets what."[66] Strikes were no different than "medieval trial by battle in which the strongest was declared the winner of the dispute."[67] Indeed, they were "barbaric," and as "outmoded" as "dueling."[68] The *New Republic* went so far as to editorialize that "[i]t is obvious that we must do away with strikes before we can pretend to call ourselves a civilized society."[69]

This revulsion to strikes seems to have sprung from an instinctual dislike of conflict. (The constant calls for bipartisanship in Washington are no doubt similarly inspired.) The attitude of these writers appears to have been that reasonable people could resolve all disputes without resorting to coercion. As Mills noted in 1948, "the new unionists believe that class struggles and all other forms of bitterness are wholly due to a simple failure of intelligence on one side or both."[70] Strikes represented a "failure of intelligence."

This attitude may have also reflected the class background of these writers, even those who were more sympathetic to unions. Reinhold Neibuhr, for instance, writing in 1932, commented on the hypocrisy of the middle and upper classes in their condemnations of strike violence.

> Every effort [on the part of workers] to disturb the peace, which incorporates [economic] injustice, will therefore seem to them to spring from unjustified malcontent. They will furthermore be only partly conscious of the violence and coercion by which their privileges are preserved and will therefore be particularly censorious of the use of force or the threat of violence by those who oppose them. The force they use is either the covert force of economic power or it is the police power of the state, seemingly sanctified by the supposedly impartial objectives of the government which wields it, but nevertheless amenable to their interests. They are thus able in perfect good faith to express abhorrence of the violence of a strike by workers and to call upon the state in the same breath to use violence in putting down the strike. The unvarying reaction of capitalist newspapers to outbreaks of violence in labor disputes is to express pious abhorrence of the use of violent methods and then to call upon the state to use the militia in suppressing the exasperated workers.[71]

Even worse, strikes were a tangible demonstration of a fundamental division in American society. They revealed the falsity of the oft repeated claim that workers and managers were partners, not rivals. Moreover, during the 1930s and '40s when concerns about union radicalism were more prevalent, strikes pointed to the basic class divisions in America. "Usually discussed in purely economic terms—in increases in pay, in higher costs, and loss of output or of time—strikes far too frequently result also in hatreds and other social damage that is not susceptible to measurement," wrote one critic for the *Ladies Home Journal* in 1947. "They tend, even here in America where individual freedom and personal equality was once looked on with almost religious reverence, to create class feeling and class hatred."[72]

In addition to the association of strikes with violence, the media's tendency to focus on strikes, as opposed to all other union activities, also created the impression that this was the usual means by which unions settled disputes. In a survey of television dramas and comedies, for instance, William Puette found that of sixty-two episodes dealing in some way with unions, forty-two episodes (over two-thirds) depicted a strike or the threat of a strike.[73] According to one writer for *Ladies Home Journal*, "Strikes, which, in principle, should be the very last resort, are, in the hands of certain labor leaders, frequently the first."[74] As Leo Huberman, a Left-wing apologist for unions, noted in 1946, "The man on the street has been led to believe that the prime purpose of unions is to call strikes. . . . The man on the street has been led to believe that unions are quick to call strikes."[75] Indeed, the terms "strike drunk" and "strike-happy" show up fairly frequently in descriptions of organized labor.[76]

This apparent tendency of organized labor to strike at the drop of a hat ran counter to the public's expectations of how "responsible" unions should behave. As the liberal George Soule wrote in 1946, "Believers in organized labor used to say that conflict was caused largely by the fact that true collective bargaining was not practiced. . . . A secure union, it was argued, accepted by employers, will develop concern for the welfare of its industry; it will usually be able to gain justice without stopping production; it will bring to the surface responsible leadership and will be slow to strike except in extremities."[77] Philip Murray, president of the CIO, claimed in defense of the federation, "We do not like to strike. We would rather cooperate with industry for constructive peace than fight in industrial war. Picket lines are the last resort, after all other lines of communication have failed."[78]

When unions did strike, the public expected that it would be for certain limited and "legitimate purpose[s]—better wages, hours, safety conditions, and so on."[79] Jurisdictional strikes, "which are nothing but private wars among union leaders in search of dues paying members," for instance, were condemned even by union leaders.[80] In a 1942 campaign against a group of craft unions affiliated with the AFL to represent the three thousand workers at DuPont's plant in Belle, West Virginia, District 50 organizers pointed out that "much of the criticism of organized labor has been the result of strikes, walkouts, and shut-outs caused by disputes, not between the boss and workers, but between two or more unions that belonged to the same central labor body."[81] Industrial unionism, according to these organizers, had the virtue of eliminating the jurisdictional strike. Likewise, Huberman noted that "[j]urisdictional disputes are a good example of the kind of thing that has helped give labor a black eye."[82]

Although many critics may have been troubled by the tendency of strikes to result in violence, the contribution of strikes to the creation of "class feeling," and the frequently illegitimate goals of strikes, of more immediate concern was the threat strikes made to the delivery of vital goods and services to the public. Nothing so solidified the view that unions were a special interest than when a relatively small group of workers wreaked havoc on an entire community, or even the entire nation. The litany of woes caused by such strikes seemed endless. Here is the *Saturday Evening Post*'s summary of the effects of the strike wave of 1946: "In city after city, people get along without milk, do without buses and streetcars, forgo the morning newspaper, shrug off the prospect of the winter without fuel, speculate on when the trains will be running and on how many days a city can last without bringing in food, wait optimistically for mobs of pickets to release the things they need from struck warehouses."[83] And here is how *National Review* brought together in one hypothetical citizen the effects of a series of strikes that took place in New York City in 1972: "a New York dockworker unemployed by the tugboat strike, sitting in a cold house with his car locked up and out of gas, his dead wife unburied, and his children left without milk."[84] Strikes in transportation, communications, and electric utilities were especially objectionable, as were strikes by public employees, in particular the police and firemen.[85]

Industry-wide shutdowns in basic commodities were also condemned. According to the *New Republic,* coal miners were "always being told that babies will freeze if they strike to support their claims." A strike in one industry might also mean layoffs in companies that depended on that industry's product, resulting in the interests of one set of workers being pitted against those of another. For instance, the same article also claimed that "steel mills have been known to shut down dramatically but needlessly amid a blare of trumpets in order to help the coal operators to drive home their point with the public."[86] Even Philip Murray, president of the Steelworkers and the CIO, conceded that "No nation can prosper when its basic industries and transportation arteries are shut down for long periods because of industry-wide disagreements between managements and unions."[87]

Unions as Anachronism

Unions' seeming success in lifting its members into the ranks of the middle class and their apparent devolution into a mere special interest created the impression among many observers that unions had outlived their purpose. As Gerald Johnson had observed in 1955, "Mr. Reuther continues to harp on higher wages and shorter hours, not as an immediate necessity, but as a long-range program. He ignores the fact that it is a closed program whose end is already in sight."[88] By the 1960s the consensus was that this end had been achieved. Thus, a 1985 poll found that 58 percent of those queried agreed that "most employees today don't need unions to get fair treatment from their employers."[89] On the other hand, in 1981 when asked directly whether they agreed with the assertion that "Unions served a useful purpose once, but they've outgrown their usefulness," only 35 percent agreed.[90] Nevertheless, the idea unions were increasingly a thing of the past seems to have been gaining ground in the late 1970s. The framing of this question, for instance, seems to indicate that the pollster was seeking confirmation that his or her own view of union obsolescence was widespread.

For many people, the labor movement that had come to maturity in a blue-collar, manufacturing economy seemed to have little relevance for the increasingly white-collar, service economy the United States was developing. Daniel Bell's widely read book *The Coming of Post-Industrial Society* helped popularize the notion that the United States had moved beyond industrialism. According to Bell, "If the struggle between capitalist and worker, in the locus of the factory, was the hallmark of industrial society, the clash between the professional and the populace, in the organization and in the community, is the hallmark of conflict in the post-industrial society." Unions, in other words, could not provide a model for worker organization in the future. "The crucial fact," asserted Bell, "is that the 'labor issue' *qua* labor is no longer central, nor does it have the sociological and cultural weight to polarize all other issues along that axis." In fact, Bell went so far as to predict that "by the end of the century the proportion of factory workers in the labor force may be as small as the proportion of farmers today."[91] So, whereas unions may have been essential to the industrial society of the United States during the first two-thirds of the twentieth century, they seemed to be irrelevant to the postindustrial society that had emerged by the 1970s.

The concept of a "postindustrial" society that developed in the 1960s and '70s was not the genesis of the notion that unions were archaic, however, but simply reinforced a conviction held by at least some critics as early as the '40s. Several writers associated unions with medieval guilds, and the terms "archaic," "outmoded," and "medieval" were not uncommon in describing unions and their practices.[92] In fact, one writer presaged the idea of postindustrialism as early as 1941 to support his contention that the United States was witnessing the "Twilight of Communism." According to Stuart Chase:

> We swing from the machine age to the power age. In the machine age, armies of men sweat in huge, smoke blackened factories, amid a roar of belts and steam. In the power age, a few skilled inspectors, dial watchers and repair men, in fluorescent lighted modern plants, direct electrical energy through automatic mechanisms, which turnout goods "untouched by human hand." . . . The hod carrier has been replaced by hoisting engineer. With his electrical motor and tackle, he can lift 100 times as many bricks in a day, and his work is dignified and interesting. He is a director of power, not a generator of power.

He does not consider himself "masses." When the brotherhood of hoisting engineer's throws a banquet, the brothers appear in tuxedos.[93]

Although this argument was advanced specifically to refute the communist doctrine of the inevitability of class conflict, it could also be seen as an argument that unions, as the institutional embodiment of such conflict, were becoming obsolete.

It was the issue of union work rules, or featherbedding, however, that most strongly created the impression that unions were a relic of an early age. As an editorial in *Life* put it, "featherbedding is a throwback to the protectionism of the medieval guilds."[94] It reflected an "archaic attitude" and a "very old superstition that the technical and mechanical means whereby the productivity of labor is increased tend to dispense with labor."[95] As Leo Huberman conceded:

> union rules, which prevent the introduction of modern machinery, create superfluous jobs, and force unnecessary work to be done, have acquired the satirical name of "feather-bedding."
>
> Every one of them is bad. They restrict production. They stand in the way of progress. They hurt the consumer by forcing prices up. And they hurt unions because . . . they help to give labor a black eye.[96]

The issue of featherbedding had been brought up as early as the 1940s and found legislative expression in a provision of the Taft-Hartley Act that forbade unions to negotiate contract provisions that would allow payment for work not done.[97] It was the relationship between union work rules and foreign competition, however, especially that from the Japanese, that did the most to solidify the attitude that unions were obsolete. For instance, in 1984 Michael Piore and Charles Sabel published an influential book that argued for a transformation of the "job control" form of production common in American industry. Even though they did not intend their argument to mean that unions were no longer needed—in fact they believed an earlier form of craft unionism should be the model for the future—even they could not escape the feeling that union work rules were antiquated. According to these authors, "The modern American system of shop-floor control in mass production had produced a parceling of de-facto rights to property in jobs that would bring a smile of recognition to the lips of any historian who had studied the struggle between lords and peasants in medieval Europe."[98]

One other conception about union rules received little to no attention in the media but appears to have been widespread. Many workers viewed union work rules as restricting the flexibility they had in doing their jobs. For instance, Mills quotes one white-collar worker in 1951 as reporting that the union representatives at her friend's place of employment "brow-beat them in her office. They [the union representatives] walk up and down the office and watch what people are doing, and if a file girl types even a label, they threaten to have her fired."[99] Similarly, during my interviews with workers at Frank Ix and Sons half a century later (see chapter 4) one worker described union rules thus: "[There are] certain things you're not supposed to do. You have a job title and you're supposed to do that job, you're not supposed to do anything else. . . . There's other things to be done and they [the union] catch you doing it and a lot of times they get you for it, and write you up for it."[100] As Sanford Jacoby has observed, "Organized labor was most successful where Taylorism was strongest. Confronted with scientific management as a *fait accompli*, the new industrial unions pragmatically constructed their regulatory systems around the division of labor wrought by Taylorists. Hence unionism's contractual restraints recapitulated Taylor's unimaginative approach to work design." Quoting James Worthy, head of personnel research at Sears, Jacoby observes that the result of the Taylorist system is a work place where "there are many layers of supervision [and] employees feel restricted, controlled, and policed." According to Jacoby, this was "a powerful critique not only of scientific management but also of modern unionism."[101]

Unions and White-Collar Workers

Talk about postindustrial society and the irrelevance of unions, of course, assumed that unions were strictly a blue-collar institution. As the *New Republic* noted in 1959, "The image of unionism is so closely linked in the public mind with industry and with the building trades that it is easy to forget how many non blue collar people have already been organized."[102] Despite the number of white-collar workers that had "already been organized," all through the 1960s, unions and students of industrial relations continued to examine how unions could break the "collar barrier."[103] This idea that unions were primarily for manual workers no doubt reinforced the view that organized labor was a special interest, a belief that would only be strengthened in the postwar period as the number of white-collar jobs increased relative to blue-collar jobs.

The association of unions with blue-collar trades also created an impression that unionism was opposed to professionalism. For instance, according to Puette, "a common theme running through some of the most popular television dramatic series . . . is the conflict between professionalism and union loyalties." Typically, a lead character, usually a doctor, police officer, nurse, or teacher, is faced with the choice of standing with his or her colleagues or crossing a picket line to fulfill his or her responsibilities to the public. Invariably, the character chooses to scab. The message is that individualism, not solidarity, is the only appropriate choice for a professional.[104] Further, the assumption that unions were solely concerned with increasing their members' wages went against the "norms of professionalism" which, according to Daniel Bell, did not have "economic self-interest" as their guiding principle.[105] As Mills wrote in the early 1950s, "The businessman, it has been thought, egotistically pursues his self-interest, whereas the professional man altruistically serves the interest of others."[106] The result of this attitude, as one student of labor issues noted in 1959, was that, "To some technical and white-collar groups who see the world in terms of more than shorter hours, higher wages and grievance procedures, unions appear selfish and expedient to the extreme."[107]

Of more direct import for white-collar workers was the feeling that joining a union threatened to deprive a person of his or her middle-class status. For instance, Mills, writing in 1951, claimed that "[t]he status psychology of white-collar employees is part of a 'principled' rejection of unionism." He quotes one worker as saying, "It is not possible that a union would start in my business, but if it did I do not think I would join because . . . people think less of you."[108] Likewise, Leonard Sayles, in researching attitudes of union members during the early 1950s, concluded that "[t]he 'American ideal,' and in particular the middle-class ideal, is one of self-sufficiency and individual initiative." By joining a union, workers "surrender some of their middle-class aspirations. Unconsciously perhaps many feel that some degree of shame is attached to union membership."[109] Perhaps Sayles was simply projecting his own feelings about unions onto the blue-collar workers he was interviewing, but the idea that "some degree of shame is attached to union membership" was unquestionably widespread among white-collar workers.

Besides violating the "American ideal of self-sufficiency and individual initiative," another reason, at least during the 1940s and '50s, for the perception that unions would deprive white-collar workers of their middle-class status was undoubtedly unions' association with immigrants and the children of immigrants. As Mills noted, "In the United States, white-collar people have been able to claim higher prestige than wage-workers because of racial, but to a greater extent and a more direct way, national origin." According to Mills, part of white-collar workers' "'principled' rejection of unionism" resulted from the "prestige based on their not being 'foreign-born, like workers,'" a distinction that would be lessened if they joined a union. Despite Mills's prophesy that the passage of time would probably "erase the prestige cleavages based on descent," it did not, at least by the 1970s, erase the "prestige cleavages" based on occupation.[110] For instance, David Selden, president of the American Federation of Teachers from 1968 to 1974, summarized the attitude of teachers towards organized labor in his memoirs: "Professionals were upper class; nonprofessionals were working class. Professionals received salaries or fees; nonprofessionals worked for wages. Professionals worked with their brains; nonprofessionals used their hands and bodies. Professionals were clean; nonprofessionals were dirty. In short, professionals belonged to professional associations, and nonprofessionals belonged to unions."[111] And in a 1975 study of engineers' attitudes towards unions, a researcher felt it appropriate to ask if they agreed or disagreed that "[m]embership in a union tends to decrease a person's professional status" (79 percent of those queried agreed).[112]

By joining a union, a person became part of "a faceless proletariat, from which no man could hope to rise by dint of superior character and talent," as an editorial in the *Saturday Evening Post* phrased it in 1946.[113] "White-collar workers are especially concerned," noted one scholar, "with the threats unionization might pose to their individual autonomy and independence."[114]

Labor's own self-image could, on occasion, contribute to this impression. Elizabeth Faue, for instance, has reprinted a 1934 cartoon from the union paper the *Organizer,* in Minneapolis, which "portray[s] the masses of workers in the same solid gray mass behind its leader." Although this particular cartoon may not have had a wide circulation, it is the image of organized labor that many white-collar workers harbored and which they found so objectionable.[115] As the president of the Office Employees International Union commented in 1964, "One of the real problems facing us . . . is in our inability to get across the idea that unionization doesn't mean the loss of individuality."[116] Likewise, one researcher who studied the attitudes of engineers towards unions in 1975 found that 64 percent of those queried agreed with the statement: "Union representation results in employees' being treated with less dignity and receiving less consideration as individuals."[117] (As indicated previously, that this researcher asked this question also indicates the widespread nature of this attitude.)

This idea that union membership would result in a loss of dignity is especially ironic considering that union leaders, along with many of the rank and file, believed that organized labor's greatest success was in attaining dignity for its members. As Philip Murray asserted in 1947, "Our unions . . . brought a new sense of personal dignity to employees in our large corporate

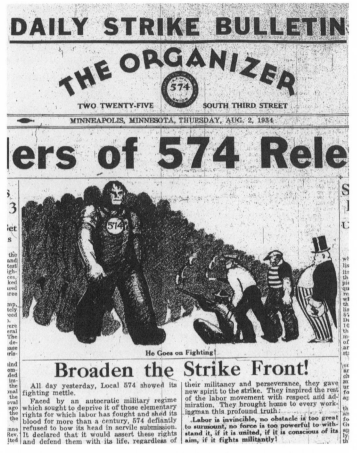

Labor and the loss of individuality: labor's faceless masses. *The Organizer*, Minneapolis, Minn., Aug. 2, 1934.

enterprises."[118] Yet, "to many office employees, signing a union card is proof of lack of success, of defeat—an index of a decline of importance," as one researcher noted in 1964.[119] For the middle class, joining a union represented a personal failure to live up to the ideals of individualism; it was an admission of their lack of power to control their own lives. This is no doubt what lay behind the conviction that union membership lowered a professional's status. By joining a union, by not "getting ahead on their own," professionals would be forced to admit that they were not superior to the working class, which relied on solidarity and mutual support for advancement.

This ideal of individualism, of getting ahead on one's own, may have made union membership appear to some white-collar workers as a sign of effeminacy. Donald Richberg and Maurice Franks, both associated with the railroad brotherhoods at one time, but, by the 1950's, both bitter critics of organized labor, extolled the virtues of "real men" who dared to cross picket lines to provide for their families. Real men did not need unions; they could brave the forces of the market on their own. Franks was especially incensed about labor leaders, such as Walter Reuther, who preached an ideology of collective advancement. In his view, such leaders were "pantywaists."[120]

Just how widespread this image of union membership was is hard to say. For most Americans, unions were seen as masculine. As Alice Kessler-Harris argues, the term "worker" itself was assumed to be a masculine term through much of the twentieth century. (Indeed, more than just masculine, "workers" were also understood to be *white* men.[121]) As both she and Elizabeth Faue have shown, unions themselves did much to reinforce the image of unions as a masculine institution.[122] Not only were they dominated by men and composed of male members, the very idea of unionism—its association with strikes, conflict, and economic warfare—embodied a masculine ideology, as Wayne Urban argues.[123] Thus, the idea that unions were masculine was no doubt dominant. In partial contradiction to this view, and yet in some way coexisting with it, was the idea that union membership would lead to emasculation.

UNIONS AND THE MORAL ECONOMY

The relegation of organized labor to the status of a special interest was reflected in it's inability to reshape the dominant culture's ideas about economic justice and the way American society should be organized. For instance, rather than successfully challenging Americans' implicit (sometimes explicit) acceptance of a hierarchical economic order, unions were seen to violate Americans' ideas about how workers should be compensated and why. Unions were seen as protecting inefficient and lazy workers, discouraging hard work, and being against progress. Most fatefully, perhaps, was the idea that unions stood in the way of creating a harmonious work environment: that they embodied conflict rather than cooperation. Considering labor's goal of "democratizing industry," this last impression is most ironic and emblematic of organized labor's failure to present it's goals as being in the public interest. Overall, unions were unable to challenge any of Americans' most cherished ideas about what constituted a moral economy.

Union work rules, for example, helped create the impression that unions were opposed to the American devotion to progress. Many critics blamed unions for "slow[ing] down the technological progress that is making a better life for all of us."[124] They were "shackles which hold enterprise in bondage."[125] If unions had their way, according to one writer, "the wagon-and-buggy industry [w]ould have been featherbedded against development of the automotive industry."[126] Union spokesmen felt compelled to address this widespread feeling. For instance, Sydney Hillman, president of the Amalgamated Clothing Workers (ACW), asserted in a 1939 article that "[l]abor will continue to reject the short sighted policy of attempting to stem the utilization of more efficient equipment and improved methods of work."[127] Hillman's assurances, however, had little effect on the popular impression that unions stood in the way of technological progress.

The issue of featherbedding also reinforced the impression that unions were "organized to protect inefficient workers."[128] According to Thurman Arnold, "the rules of some of the building trades spread a great deal of labor over a very little work; it is demanded that musicians be hired as standbys even when there is nothing for them to do; itinerant trucks are required to pay for the services of local drivers—even if they are not used—when passing through certain cities."[129] In addition, as Donald Richberg asserted in 1942, unions allowed "a few slackers, grouchers and saboteurs, by demanding union discipline and the enforcement of union rules, [to] prevent great numbers of loyal workers from giving all out service to their country in time of war."[130] In fact, according to another critic, "fast workers are threatened with fines or loss of membership card's (and their jobs) unless they slow down."[131] Forty years later, Robert Bellah, in his widely read *Habits of the Heart,* related an incident from 1981 that showed the continued vitality of this image. A Chrysler dealer in Suffolk county, Massachusetts, while defending the federal government's bail-out of the car maker to his local Rotary Club, neverthe-

Parodying union work rules. *Wizard of Id,* 1987. Reprinted by permission of the John L. Hart FLP and Creators Syndicate, Inc.

less blamed the UAW for Chrysler's plight. "Now I'm not against unions," he stated, "but those workers there weren't putting in a full day's work. They wanted to get paid for not working. . . . The unions have funds so that you'll not only get paid when you work, but you get paid when you don't work."[132] High union wage scales were especially galling in light of this impression that unions went out of their way to protect lazy workers. Not only did they contribute to inflation and make American industry noncompetitive, many people believed unions were simply just a racket to extort more pay for less work instead of ensuring that workers were not mistreated.

Combined with the impression that union members were paid too much for too little work was resentment at the fact that a few blue-collar unionists made more than higher status white-collar workers. For instance, one reporter noted in 1961 that "[a]t Vandenberg [Air Force Base] electricians have averaged $510 a week—$145 more that the combined pay and allowances of the base's missile commander, Maj. Gen. Davis Wade, a 25 year veteran. Elevator operators have collected as much as $363 a week, truck drivers $324, warehouse clerks $262—all in excess of the pay of the major I had talked to, who must ready million dollar missiles to be fired on 15 minute notice."[133] In the same vein, Senator McClellan fumed that "[s]ome mechanics [at Cape Canaveral] earned more in a week than does Secretary of Defense McNamara, or Dr. Werner von Braun, or any of the astronauts."[134]

Union policies for determining who got what and how fast a person could advance were also seen as violating the ethic of meritocracy. As Albert Blum observed in a 1964 study of labor's prospects for organizing white-collar workers, "labor has the disadvantage of bearing the reputation of favoring mainly seniority as a basis for promotion while white-collar employees tend to favor merit."[135] And with respect to pay, a 1964 study of engineering unions found that "the conflict between the principles of individualism and equality in salary administration has bedeviled every engineering union. . . . Almost every engineering union avowedly supports the principle of allowing people to rise on the basis of individual merit. Yet the traditional union objective is to get more money for its members on a collective basis."[136] In addition, by compressing wage differentials between not just individuals, but also occupations, unions discouraged workers from acquiring more education and skills. According to an editorial in the Saturday Evening Post, "It is plain that a lot of young fellows think there isn't much incentive to acquire a skill, when a man with a mop can earn only a little less than a man who is driving a train."[137]

Finally, the public had certain expectations about the way in which unions should achieve their objectives and what those objectives should be. Ideally, unions would cooperate with management for the benefit of both parties and the public at large. Over the years many articles were written extolling some union or union leader for the way they worked with management to increase a company's productivity and sales. Titles such as "This Union Prospers by Producing," and "This Union Found the Best Way to Raise Wages" give some indication of how people expected unions to go about realizing their goal of increasing their members' wages.[138] In holding up the Typographic union as a model, William Hard, an editor for *Reader's Digest* during the 1940s, praised it for teaching its members "that 'labor should not be unfriendly to capital'; that 'capital and labor both are essential to efficient and economical production'; that the union should insure high class workmanship; that it should 'strive to reduce unit costs'; that the employers of the Typographical Union have virtually never broken a contract with the union, and that no local should ever break a contract with any employer; that every local should regard itself as a 'partner' with the employer in the production process."[139] In other words, an ideal union should resemble a professional association.

Union leaders themselves often subscribed to this cooperative ideal. Sidney Hillman, president of the Amalgamated Clothing Workers, was famous for implementing Taylorite methods in ACW shops and working with employers to increase worker productivity.[140] According to Hillman, labor should "give its full cooperation to further industrial efficiency, recognizing that the improvement in the living standards of the workers must, in the main, come from increased productivity."[141] Or as Walter Cenerazzo, president of an independent New England watchmakers' union, explained, unions needed to "become the active partners of management for more and more productivity and prosperity."[142]

Unfortunately for organized labor, as with many aspects of the union image, most Americans did not believe that unions lived up to this ideal. Indeed, the emphasis on strikes and union-employer conflict in the press created the impression that unions were solely organized to engender discord and antagonism. In essence, this impression was correct. Unions were an institutional outgrowth of the irrepressible conflict between workers and employers in the capitalist system. What was unfortunate for organized labor was its failure to make (or even attempt to make) Americans understand that such conflicts of interest were unavoidable, that these clashes were woven into the very fabric of capitalism. Instead, by largely subscribing to the cooperative ideal, unions set themselves up for failure when such efforts at cooperation eventually and inevitably failed.

* * *

Part I has gone into great detail about how Americans had come to view organized labor by the late twentieth century. It would be a mistake to think that all of these different images would come to mind if you asked your typical American to think about unions; nonetheless, there can be little doubt that a powerful antiunion culture existed in the United States, coloring the way most people viewed organized labor.

Although Americans believed that unions had helped society by raising wages and by promoting such measures as the eight-hour day, the five-day work week, social security, and the minimum wage, those days were gone. Rather than helping the underdog, unions had become his enemy. In most peoples' views, unions were run by leaders who were motivated by greed and who cared little for their membership. They forced workers to join so they could collect more dues money to pay their own salaries. They deprived members of basic democratic freedoms. Leaders regularly forced members to strike, which often resulted in violence and always meant lost pay. Often these strikes would directly impact the general public by denying it basic and essential services. Moreover, union work rules straight-jacketed workers into narrow job classifications that destroyed flexibility and creativity, reproducing the worst aspects of Taylorism. Most alarmingly, Americans assumed that many, if not most, unions were run by organized criminals, an obvious threat to the safety and welfare of the membership.

Organized labor's impact on society was seen as even more deleterious than its treatment of its own members. Organized labor was viewed as a greedy special interest whose goals were most often at variance with the good of the nation. By protecting lazy, inefficient workers, by securing for them wages beyond what they deserved, and by slowing down the introduction of new machinery and work processes, unions contributed to inflation and reduced productivity. Union work rules and high union wages also hurt American competitiveness, leading to the loss of numerous industries to foreign competitors.

The postwar boom further reinforced the idea that unions were just another special interest. Blue-collar workers were no longer seen as the underpaid victims they had been in the 1930s. Instead, they seemed to have joined the ranks of the middleclass. The "labor question" seemed to have become moot. Issues of class were eclipsed by those of race. Rather than representing the interests of the underdog, then, unions seemed organized solely to make "affluent workers more affluent." The steady decline in blue-collar jobs relative to white-collar ones further amplified the impression that unions were a special interest. Because they were so deeply associated with blue-collar work, they were seen as increasingly irrelevant to the postindustrial economy of late twentieth-century America and representative of an ever smaller portion of the workforce.

PART II

Antiunion Culture
at Work

In this culturally centered account of union decline, there were two important changes in the postwar era that intersected in the 1960s and '70s and that had a decisive impact on Americans' ideas about organized labor and, more to the point, on its ability to gain new members. The first change involved the generally negative shift in Americans' perception of unions, which was detailed in the preceding section. The second important change involved a transformation of the composition of the workforce. This change was both structural and social in nature. On the one hand, white-collar occupations greatly expanded in comparison to blue-collar trades during the postwar period. On the other, the ethnic, blue-collar working class was largely assimilated into the dominant, Anglo culture during this period. These changes in the composition of the work force were what made the attitudinal change so important.

By 1950 unions had organized the bulk of the blue-collar working class. A large portion of these workers, of course, were ethnic Americans and African Americans; in other words, they were those workers who were least assimilated into the dominant, Anglo culture and therefore least likely to have been influenced by the pervasive, generally negative image of unions in that culture. To grow, unions needed to crack the so-called collar barrier and organize white-collar workers. Yet these were precisely the workers who were most likely to have absorbed the antiunion bias of the dominant culture.

These white-collar workers not only could be expected to have a more negative view of unions than blue-collar ethnic and African Americans, but they were also affected by the fact that one of the major components of the union image was that they were meant for blue-, not white-collar workers. This perception both reflected the reality of the composition of union membership (what Nelson Lichtenstein has referred to as the "unionized blue-collar ghetto"[1]) and was implied in the idea that unions represented the underdog, that is, the lower-income worker. As the relative number of blue-collar jobs declined in the postwar period, then, unions found it increasingly difficult to keep pace with the growth of the labor market.

A second trend at work during the 1950s and '60s would extend the reach and influence of America's antiunion culture. As noted in the introduction to part one, this period saw an increased homogenization of American culture. The rise of national networks in radio and television, and mass consumption of standardized consumer goods tended to wash out regional, ethnic, and class-based cultural differences. Second- and third-generation immigrants, the backbone of America's working class, became increasingly assimilated into the hegemonic, Anglo culture, with its individualistic and antiunion biases. Thus, unions not only had problems dealing with occupational shifts taking place in the postwar period, they also were confronted with a workforce that harbored an increasingly negative view of organized labor.

Part I revealed the cultural image of organized labor; part II examines just how deeply that image affected labor's efforts to reach out to unorganized workers in the later half of the twentieth century, just as union membership was about to experience a precipitous decline. Not all aspects of this cultural image of unions were operative when unions sought to enroll new members. For instance, consider the widespread belief that unions were more powerful than employers. Although this impression may have been useful when antiunion legislators attempted to pass new laws further limiting organized labor's ability to grow, there is no evidence that it had any impact on organizing drives. In just one example, when employees at Frank Ix & Sons, a Charlottesville, Virginia, textile mill, were confronted by an organizing drive in 1980, the employer was unquestionably more powerful than the union (see chapter 4). Indeed, it is hard to imagine that any union would want to be seen as weak and powerless when appealing for worker support. On the other hand, images of unions as undemocratic, prone to strikes, only interested in extorting more dues money to pay the large salaries of their leaders, and ridden with corruption would surface in practically every organizing drive. Indeed, many unions studied workers' attitudes towards organized labor and prepared literature in advance to help dispel these very images. Considering the power and scope of America's antiunion culture, however, in many cases these efforts were not enough to overcome workers' doubts.

With respect to this culture's negative influence on workers' attitudes in the 1970s and '80s, two issues were particularly important. One issue was organized labor's seeming devolution into a mere special interest. With the loss of a broader vision for reshaping society, unions increasingly appeared to be little more than economic institutions. As unions seemed more and more solely concerned with issues of pay, employers found it much easier to defeat organizing drives by matching the pay scales at unionized companies. With all the costs associated with joining a union, both financial and nonfinancial, it made little sense to many employees to support unionization if they felt they were already receiving most of the benefits the union could offer (i.e., a union pay scale). For instance, at Frank Ix & Sons, the textile union found that the issue of wages generally did not work in its favor. Instead, it tried to emphasize the issue of arbitrary and differential treatment of the mill workers. Most employees, however, did not feel they were treated unfairly and doubted that the union had anything else positive to offer. In the cases examined here, only the Leftist District 65 articulated a broader vision of society in its pitch to workers, issuing leaflets about its positions on women's rights, civil rights, and opposition to the Vietnam War. Yet, by 1971 it had dropped these appeals for purely instrumental concerns, no doubt in reaction to seeing unionized hard hats beating up antiwar protestors in the summer of 1970. Unlike workers in the 1930s, who were told "the President wants you to join a union" and believed that their joining a union contributed to a broader reformation of American society, workers in the 1970s viewed unionization almost purely in instrumental terms. Consider, for instance, the Little Steel Strike of 1937, during which workers went on strike for union recognition despite the fact that their employers had granted them a ten-cent wage increase and had matched almost all of the provisions of the contract between U.S. Steel and the Steel Workers Organizing Committee (SWOC).[2]

The other major issue negatively influencing workers' attitudes toward unions in the 1970s and '80s was the image of unions as being dedicated to confrontation and conflict. Most workers wanted a work environment that was friendly and cooperative, both among their fellow workers and between employees and employers. They harbored a Mayoist vision of the workplace.[3] In addition, many of them saw—particularly in the face of increased foreign competition during the 1970s and '80s—a mutuality of interests between themselves and their employers. Creating or maintaining a friendly, cooperative work environment, therefore, was a vital component in their considerations about how a union would affect their working conditions. The popular idea that the raison d'être for unions was to foster conflict, then, worked against organized labor as it sought to win over workers.

The following chapters provide case studies of several organizing drives from the 1970s, covering a variety of occupational groups: blue, pink, and white collar. The goal is not to show why unions won or lost certain representation elections, but to provide a deeper insight into the concerns these workers had about joining a union. In the first two cases, the union lost the election, but even if it had won, these cases would still provide a window into workers' concerns. The kinds of appeals both employers and unions made to workers during these campaigns reveals just how deeply America's antiunion culture biased workers against joining a union. These workers didn't vote against the unions because of the fear of being fired, threat of disciplinary action, or worries about seeing their place of employment go out of business. (Indeed, these fears would have been applicable only in the first case studied.) Rather, many of these workers were simply convinced that a union was unnecessary or would make their work environment worse.

4

Union Outsiders
versus the Ix Family

Blue-Collar Workers and Unions in the Late Twentieth Century

The year 1980 was one of the most hopeful years for textile unionism since the 1940s. As cloth production in America continued the shift from the North to the South, a shift that had begun in the early 1900s, the Textile Workers Union of America (TWUA), which had never made any substantial inroads into the South, had dwindled in numbers and health in parallel with the decay of its Northern base. By 1976 the union was in such poor shape that it was forced to merge with the Amalgamated Clothing Workers (ACW). The resulting organization, the Amalgamated Clothing and Textile Workers Union (ACTWU), though much weakened from years of membership losses in clothing manufacturing as well as in textiles, was reinvigorated when, after years of effort, it finally negotiated its first contract with one of the South's largest textile manufacturers, J. P. Stevens.[1]

Though this breakthrough proved fruitless when only a small number of Stevens plants voted for the union, at the time the union's leaders hoped it would form a beachhead from which the ACTWU could finally expand and organize a majority of the South's textile workers. To build on this success, therefore, the union launched a wide-ranging organizing drive across the South in 1980. To generate interest in the union, it printed up flyers heralding its triumph at J. P. Stevens and distributed them to workers at textile mills across the South.[2]

One of the companies targeted by the union during this drive was Frank Ix & Sons. Ix was a relatively small company that produced synthetic yarn and was still owned and operated by members of the founder's family. Ix owned three mills: one in Pennsylvania; one in North Carolina, which it had just purchased the year before; and one in Charlottesville, Virginia, which was its largest and oldest facility. It was the Charlottesville mill that the ACTWU attempted to organize.[3]

This drive began in August 1980. By November the organizer, Lou Agre, had reached an impasse. Out of approximately 480 workers, only 160 had signed cards indicating they wanted to be represented by a union. Although this was enough to allow the union to petition for an election with the National Labor Relations Board (NLRB), it was nowhere near the number needed to ensure a victory. Despite this shortfall, the ACTWU decided to press ahead and file for an election. In part, this decision may have been motivated by a desire to keep faith with the Ix employees who had worked to form the union. Agre also expressed the hope that once a petition was filed and an election date set, those employees who were undecided and therefore reluctant, or scared, to sign a union card would feel freer to come out in support of the union.[4] The election was held on February 5, 1981, and resulted in a decisive defeat for the union: only 105 workers voted for the union, whereas 318 voted against it.[5]

A window into the issues that concerned these employees can be gained through a close examination of the literature distributed to the Ix employees by both the union and the company, as well as interviews with some of the workers involved. This examination reveals the extent to which their acceptance or rejection of organized labor was conditioned by the generally anti-union culture in which they lived.

Although these two contestants for worker loyalty, the company and union, never engaged in a face-to-face debate (the union did ask for such an opportunity[6]), they did spar with each other via speeches, letters, leaflets, brochures, posters, and so forth. To convince workers to cast their votes either for or against unionization, both Ix and the ACTWU played on the various pre-existing ideas workers had about unions. In waging this contest, both sides drew on their long experience in conducting campaigns of this sort. The ACTWU had been involved in numerous representation elections and had an organizing department at its New York headquarters that researched the best ways to approach workers and the messages most likely to win them over to the cause of the union. The ACTWU had also learned about the misgivings workers had about unions and prepared material to convince workers that these fears were unfounded. Though Ix itself did not have this same level of experience, it drew on the expertise of its Richmond law firm, Hunton and Williams, whose labor law department handled not only Ix's affairs when confronted with such labor issues as unemployment claims and complaints to the Equal Employment Opportunity Commission (EEOC), but also provided companies with advice and guidance on how to defeat organizing drives.[7] Ix also communicated with other companies that had been targets of organizing drives to learn how they had dealt with unions. In addition, members of the management team attended conferences and seminars on how to avoid unions.[8] Thus armed, both sides waged a battle calculated to heighten or mute the worries workers harbored about organized labor, worries inherited from America's antiunion culture.

A study of textile workers can help illustrate how deeply some blue-collar manufacturing workers, organized labor's traditional constituency since the 1930s, were affected by America's antiunion culture. Because these are Southern workers, however, an added complication arises. Volumes of scholarly material have been written concerning Southern mill hands; much of this material posits that these workers were different from other manufacturing workers in one way or another.[9] Certainly, the rate of unionization in the South was much lower than that in the North. By 1980, however, unionization rates were falling even in the heart of America's Rust Belt. Indeed, Clete Daniel argues that it was not Southern mill hands that were unique, but Southern employers, who fought unionization tooth and nail even as their Northern counterparts gave into government pressure and agreed to recognize unionization as inevitable in the 1930s and '40s.[10] In any case, much of the literature on Southern mill hands covers the period before World War II. Only a few historians have focused on the postwar period.[11]

By 1980 it would be hard to argue that Southern textile workers were significantly different from manufacturing workers elsewhere in the nation. Whereas textile mills had once been all white, African Americans now made up a significant portion of the workforce. (At Ix, for instance, 87 out of 460 workers were African Americans, or about 19 percent of the workforce.) Mill villages, once owned by the employer, had disappeared as employees purchased the homes or bought cars and commuted to work. The isolation of the prewar period was broken down through the widespread introduction of television. The educational level of Southern mill hands climbed in the postwar period as well.[12] In many ways, Southern mill hands underwent the same assimilation into the dominant, national culture that ethnic workers in the North experienced.

At any rate, very little about the campaign at Ix indicated that these workers were significantly different from workers in the North. In only one regard could the situation facing the ACTWU be considered especially Southern: the very low union density in the South. This low rate of unionization hurt the ACTWU, because the workers at Ix had little firsthand experience with unions, making the impact of America's pervasive antiunion culture that much greater. But as will be shown in chapter 5, even workers in New York City, one of the most heavily unionized locales in the United States, were so steeped in this culture that unions found it difficult to expand there as well. Rather than demonstrating the uniqueness of Southern mill hands, then, this study shows that the workers at Ix provide a representative example of late twentieth-century blue-collar workers, their attitudes towards organized labor, and how these attitudes affected the ability of unions to gain new members. In fact, most of the major problems unions faced elsewhere appeared during the ACTWU's attempt to organize Ix.

At its core, workers' decision to support or oppose the union rested on their understanding of what it, and organized labor in general, had to offer workers. In line with the general culture, most workers, particularly those who opposed the union, saw organized labor as simply and solely concerned with economic advancement. Although this appealed to some workers, the majority believed that if that was all the union had to offer, there was no reason to join because they were already making as much as the union could hope to get for them. Indeed, many of them felt the union might actually threaten their livelihood rather than enhance it.

The ACTWU itself recognized that an economic appeal was insufficient. Thus, its main pitch to workers centered on the issue of favoritism and arbitrary, differential treatment, which it proposed to cure by the introduction of formal work rules. African American workers found this pitch particularly appealing. Yet, for the majority of workers, it was precisely the prospect of a rigid, Taylorized work environment—which was how they pictured union work rules—that caused them to oppose the union. Their fear, which was in line with the general culture's portrayal of unions as being dedicated to opposition and confrontation, was that the union would ruin the family atmosphere at Ix and replace it with a bureaucratic and impersonal system that made no allowance for individual circumstances.

The Economic Perils of Unionism

WAGES

When asked about their memories of the campaign, former Ix employees invariably mentioned pay as being an important issue. Sam Crawford, a member of the plant organizing committee, recounted that he supported the union because he thought it would be able to increase his wages.[13] Similarly, Tammy

H. voted for the union because she thought her pay was so low, "it couldn't get any worse."[14] Even Charlotte Dudley, who voted against the union, felt the main issue of the campaign had to do with pay. She believed that workers in the weave room were the main supporters of the union because "they thought they wasn't getting a fair share. . . . they thought they wasn't getting enough money for the job they were doing." In sharp contrast to Tammy H., however, Dudley opposed the union because she felt her pay was already as good as it could be. "We [workers in the spinning department] thought we were getting a fair share. We'd already had somebody check Comdial [another Charlottesville factory] and different places. They made, maybe, a few cents more than we were making, but still we were making the same thing they were making."[15]

In evaluating the economic benefits of unionization, this question of comparability was key. Some people may have measured their pay in relation to the cost of living. Others may have considered how much their employer profited from their labor versus what portion of that profit was returned to them. How their wages stacked up against other *similarly situated* workers, however, seems to have been the most important factor in determining their position on this issue. Henry Peregoy, for instance, opposed the union because "I checked around and Ix was paying union wages anyway."[16]

When considering their pay, Ix employees pictured themselves as belonging to a particular regional and industrial job market. They had a geoeconomic map of the world that marked the boundaries of where they could reasonably expect to obtain employment, and they wanted to know that they were doing as well as other workers within those boundaries. They did not take into account the wages of auto workers in Michigan when evaluating their pay. (In fact, Crawford, who supported the union at the time, twenty years later had turned against unions because he felt they were hurting consumers. He was especially dismayed by the "outrageous" salaries of auto workers, which, he felt, made cars unaffordable.[17]) Although they may not have compared their pay to Northern industrial workers, they did consider the pay of textile workers in other parts of the world as directly relevant to their own situation. According to Peregoy, the union "couldn't raise the pay down here much higher than we got. . . . There was a limit on how much you could pay a textile worker."[18] This limit was set by what textile workers in India and Korea were making. In part, this way of thinking about wages and working conditions was the result of the limited mobility of these workers, both geographic and economic. In addition, both the company and the union encouraged these workers to think in such limited terms.

A major aspect of the company's campaign to defeat the union was to convince its employees they were already doing as well or better than other textile workers, especially those represented by the ACTWU. In a letter sent to Ix employees, plant manager John Todd pointed out that the union "cannot expect to obtain for you any more wages and benefits than they have obtained at other companies like ours."[19] Just before the election was held, the company put up a large poster comparing Ix's pay scales for twenty-seven different job classifications to the pay scales of "employees represented by the ACTWU at a nearby company." Although later proven to be untrue, this comparison purported to show that in most cases Ix employees were already paid more than those at the unionized competitor. The poster also compared the benefits at Ix with those of the "nearby company," as well as with those at J. P. Stevens (which had recently signed a contract with the union). It concluded that Ix employees were already doing as well as workers at unionized companies without incurring the costs of union membership.[20] As plant manager Todd expressed in his final talk to the employees, "you do not need a Union to get what you already have."[21]

For its part, the ACTWU also encouraged employees to think about their wages and benefits in terms of other textile workers. One union leaflet, referring to the recent victory at J. P. Stevens, exhorted workers not to be left behind in the drive to organize the textile industry.[22] Another union handout referred specifically to Ix's wage comparison and rhetorically asked the company if it would be willing to give the same contract to its own workers.[23] The union also criticized the Ix retirement plan, claiming that its own members had a better plan.[24] Only one leaflet mentioned what unionized workers in another industry earned. This leaflet stated that "an automobile worker makes more per hour than both a man and his wife receive at Frank Ix." For obvious reasons, however, it did not claim that the union would be able to bring wages at Ix into line with those of the auto industry.[25]

In spite of all this talk about wages, the question of pay was hardly decisive in determining how Ix employees evaluated what the union had to offer. An analysis of Ix's records on how employees planned to vote in the representation election, including such factors as age, length of service, pay, race, and gender, shows that pay was not a significant factor in these workers' decisions.[26] This is not to say that *expectations* about how the union would affect their wages were not significant, just that what employees made at the time—whether above average or below average—had no statistically relevant correlation to how they planned to vote. This was also reflected in the lack of emphasis the union gave to this issue in its appeals to the workers. One union handout listing seventeen benefits of unionization placed better pay and benefits far down on the list, in places thirteen through sixteen.[27] Likewise, according to a report by the company, one of the initial union meetings included "very little about wages."[28]

If anything, the union was on the defensive when it came to the question of wages. A great deal of the company's campaign against the ACTWU involved threats of *lower* pay and benefits, or even the loss of work altogether if the union won. As a result, in one leaflet after another the union was forced to rebut the charge that if it won Ix employees would "lose breaks, get less money, get more work and lose benefits."[29]

Although such open threats by the company would have been a violation of the National Labor Relations Act (NLRA), management was very careful about the way it discussed this issue. Rather than directly saying that a union win would result in lower pay and lost benefits, it claimed that in negotiations with the union it could bargain from any starting point.[30] As a result, "it's all up for grabs," as the antiunion film shown to employees explained.[31] Or as Todd put it, "everything's negotiable."[32] This, of course, was assuming that the company even bothered to negotiate. As was pointed out in one company posting, according to the NLRA management was not required to *agree* to anything. It was only required to negotiate in good faith.[33] Referring to the ACTWU's recent breakthrough at J. P. Stevens, Todd explained that negotiations "have been known to take anywhere from a few months up to a few years or longer. As you know, this Union recently spent several years negotiating one contract."[34] Even were the company to agree to a contract, "you can be sure it will be one we can live with. The company can't lose one way or the other."[35] As Ix tried to convey in all of its messages, only the workers themselves had anything to lose if the union won; its campaign against the union was based on its concern for the workers and not selfish motives. The union's reply was that "if the Union made workers work harder for less wages, Frank Ix would make us join the Union."[36]

Some workers also believed that a union could threaten their pay through time spent on strike. Fred Carey, for instance, although he thought the union was needed and felt that workers at unionized companies "were getting a better pay scale," also qualified this benefit by noting that "those people would be on strike at times and we never did. . . . They [Ix employees] had their jobs year round."[37] To counter this concern, the union took pains to discount the possibility of any strike occurring. "Ninety Seven percent of all Union contracts are settled without a strike," one leaflet maintained. "There is more work time lost in this Country due to the common cold than to strikes."[38]

Another handout tried to reassure employees by pointing out that "no committee, officer, representative or official of the Union can call a strike at your plant. The only people that can call a strike at your plant are the workers at the plant by majority vote."[39] Lost pay due to strikes, according to the union, was a remote possibility.

JOB SECURITY

More serious than the possibility of lower pay and lost benefits, however, were threats by the company that workers, by voting for the union, were endangering their very jobs. Though the company denied the charge, and the NLRB found it innocent, some supervisors apparently told their employees that if the plant were unionized it would be shut down or have its operations moved to the North Carolina plant.[40] Over and over, the union tried to assure the workers that the plant would not be closed if it won the election. The union invoked the aura of the federal government in refuting this charge: "The Government of the United States says that Frank Ix cannot close the plant, lay you off, or move production to another plant because you form or join a Union. If anyone tells you different, then they are saying that the Government won't protect you."[41] It also quoted Jerome Ix, the administrative manager, as saying the plant would not close were the union to win.[42] And it appealed to the workers' common sense, pointing out that since the plant was making money it would be foolish to close it.[43] For some workers, at least, this last argument was convincing.[44]

According to the company, however, a vote for the union would threaten this profitability. Even if supervisors did not claim that the plant would be closed as a *direct* result of a union victory, they were instructed by the law firm in charge of the company's antiunion efforts to tell the employees that this could be the *indirect* consequence of a vote for the union. Because the union might take them out on strike at any time, the company warned, it might lose customers who were worried about Ix's ability to deliver its product without interruption.[45] Or the company might be forced to shutdown as the direct result of a strike. Such was the message of one posting that consisted of a mosaic of newspaper headlines. Most of the headlines were about strikes at different Virginia companies; others blared the message that some of these same companies had gone out of business.[46] Union boycotts were also pointed to as another potential threat to the continued existence of the company. In a letter to employees, plant manager Todd raised the specter of Farah Manufacturing Corp. in Texas where two thousand employees lost their jobs when the company was forced to cut back following an ACTWU sponsored boycott.[47]

More vaguely, the antiunion film shown to employees warned that, "There have been instances when union pressure has caused a business to become unprofitable and it had to close."[48] The 1970s, of course, had been a time of increasing foreign competition, especially from Japan. The U.S. government, by insisting on concessions from the United Auto Workers (UAW) as one of its conditions for bailing out Chrysler Corp. in 1979, had reinforced the message that overpaid, work-rule bound, unionized workers were one reason for America's growing noncompetitiveness. Todd pointed to the example of Chrysler to show just how "union pressure" could cause a company to go out of business.[49]

Whether because of lost profitability, or simply because they believed the company was determined to run union free, many workers thought a union victory could lead to the plant being shut down. Although some workers may have accepted the union's argument that a profitable company would not shut down, many other workers were less sanguine. As one employee recalled, the company's argument, "if you go for the union the plant is going to close," was an abiding fear among many of the employees.[50] Likewise, Crawford related that many of the older workers had "seen what unions do. . . . Company shutting down because they don't want unions in the facility."[51] Though he did not say so, this may have been a reference to the Miliken plant in South Carolina that had shut down in the 1950s after the union had won an election there.[52]

Even if the company itself were not put out of business by the union, individual workers might still lose their jobs if the union won. In conjunction with its threat to not bargain with the union, the company warned that workers who went on strike to win a contract would be permanently replaced.[53] To drive home the point, the anti-union film the company had its workers watch pointed out that they had almost no chance of winning such a strike. "If we had 80 percent of our employees walk out, we could probably still do business." And unlike the auto companies with their thousands of employees, Ix was small enough that it could easily find enough replacement workers from the surrounding community.[54]

In response, the union pointed to the provisions of the NLRA that protected striking workers. The union especially referred to the sections of the law that provided that workers striking over unfair labor practices could not be replaced, and emphasized that failure to bargain in good faith constituted one of those unfair labor practices. "You are being told that if you strike, you can lose your job. . . . If you, at Frank Ix, vote to strike because of unfair labor practices that your Company could commit, you would be protected against other workers taking your jobs. . . . Unfair labor violations are re-

fusing to bargain with a Union in good faith . . ."[55] The union also pointed
to the company's hypocrisy in claiming to be opposed to the union because
of its concern for its workers' welfare, and at the same time threatening to
fire them out of hand should they strike. In a letter addressed to John Todd,
Robert Freeman, the union organizer, wrote, "How could you tell the workers that they have protection with the Company then tell the workers that
if they dared to exercise their rights as guaranteed by Law to strike, that the
Company could replace them with new employees? That's about the most
un-American statement I have ever heard. How can you love a worker, then
give his job to another worker and let the worker who has been with you for
years starve just because he exercises his rights to be an American?"[56]

As in much of the debate between the union and the company, both sides
tried to interpret the provisions of the NLRA to the workers. The union
pointed to those portions of the law that protected workers to assure Ix employees that they wouldn't suffer from supporting the union; the company
emphasized those sections of the law that made the union appear either powerless or malignant. Moreover, the company demonstrated through its actions
that federal labor law was a thin reed to rely on if the company decided to
retaliate against individual workers. The union tried to assure workers that the
company would not know whether they had signed a union card, nor would
it know how they voted during the representation election. "The company
does not see the card you sign. The United States Government guarantees
this secrecy. The Company can't ask you if you have signed a card or try to
keep you from signing."[57] "No one but you, and God Almighty, will ever
know how you vote in the election."[58] Nevertheless, one worker I interviewed
believed that some people may have voted against the union simply because
they could not be sure that the company would not know how they voted.
Such worries were not unfounded. As this worker recounted, Ix supervisors
regularly sat in their cars outside the motel where the union held its meetings to see who attended. They also held numerous one-on-one interviews
with employees to determine how they were going to vote in the upcoming
election.[59] Records left by Todd attest to the effectiveness of this surveillance.
The company knew who was attending union meetings and what was discussed at those meetings. In addition, it had a complete breakdown on how
each worker was expected to vote in the upcoming election; workers were
coded red if they were going to vote for the union, green if they were going
to vote for the company, and blue if they were undecided.[60]

More serious than company surveillance of union meetings or one-on-
one interviews with employees, however, were cases where individual union

activists appeared to be the victims of company retaliation. In the middle of the campaign, two employees were fired and a third union activist, Nellie Toler, was transferred to a lower paying job. In the case of the fired workers, the NLRB later exonerated the company of charges of unfair labor practices.[61] Nevertheless, the message to employees was clear. According to Crawford, "they were pushing to set an example. . . . Just to let you know 'Maybe we can do a little bit of trouble.'"[62] And though the company lost in the case of Toler, the resolution of this case could hardly have been encouraging for potential union supporters. In a letter to Ix employees excoriating the company, Freeman, the union organizer, charged that "your Company signed an agreement with the Federal Government stating the Company would stop intimidating, coercing, and discriminating against Nellie Toler. The Company has paid absolutely no attention to this agreement. Your Company's word and signed agreement with the Federal Government meant nothing."[63] Though no doubt meant to provoke a hostile reaction among Ix workers against the company, such a charge only reinforced the belief that the union was powerless to help them.

Even if the company did not retaliate immediately because of someone's support for the union, workers still had to consider the long-term consequences of pro-union activism for their career at Ix. Such was the implication of one union leaflet claiming that, "Lately some people, mostly bosses' relatives and friends and *people who expect to be boss*, have been wearing shirts that say 'Support Frank Ix.'"[64] At the time, Crawford, who was a member of the plant organizing committee, was young and single and didn't care if the company fired him. Looking back twenty years later, however, he was surprised that the company eventually promoted him to facilities manager because "I always just kind of figured that deep down somewhere they were holding it against me."[65] For older, married workers with two or three children, worries about job security and career prospects were much more acute. "I was fearful," recounted Fred Carey, "that if I had done anything against the company they would have hurt me as far as my children were concerned." Mr. Carey's children, besides relying on his income for shelter and food, had directly benefitted from Ix's educational loan fund to attend college.[66]

Union Outsiders versus the Ix Family

If the economic consequences of unionization were uncertain, at best, the noneconomic implications in many ways loomed as a larger issue both for those who supported the union and those who opposed it. As we have seen, the union did not make the issue of wages the primary focus of its campaign, even if many employees, both pro and con, did believe this was the central issue. Rather, its main focus was the issue of favoritism and the creation of fair and evenhanded treatment for all the workers at Ix. Where the union promised equal treatment for all Ix's workers, however, the company and many employees saw a threat to the personal, friendly, family atmosphere at the mill.

According to management, unionization would mean the imposition of regimented and rigid working conditions and "deteriorate[] your friendship with each other and your relationship with your supervisor."[67] Ix's personnel relations were premised on the idea of personalism. As the company expressed it, when there were problems at Ix, "we've been able to solve them on a face-to-face basis."[68] A union would change this. It would "come between you and your company."[69] No longer would an employee "be able to talk to [his or her] boss about problems."[70] Instead, "if a union represents you, the company is bound to deal with them, not you. Problems then would be resolved the way the union, or those few of our employees who are in this thing for their own personal gain, wants them resolved."[71]

In place of personalism, the union would substitute bureaucratic and rigid working conditions. Union work rules would eliminate the company's ability to exercise discretion in cases where workers violated company policy. Even the mere appearance of a union organizer, according to Crawford, caused the company to begin tightening up on its "flexibility." "They did start documenting more stuff when the union came in. 'We know you've been late fifty times in the last ten years. We don't have it documented. But, we found you've been late three times in the last two weeks and we've got all this documented.'"[72] Minor transgressions that had formerly been passed over were now cause for a reprimand. The way Crawford remembered it, the essence of one company flyer could be summarized as:

> Rules are going to be rules and they're going to be followed. You may have gotten by with doing this and that in the past, but if there's a union in here, then you won't get by with that anymore because you're going to have to follow the union rules. You can't lay out two days [one] week any more and not get fired because you're one of our better employees when you *are* here. Once a union's here, that won't happen anymore. We're not going to be the Ix family anymore. We're going to be the union.[73]

The poster to which Crawford was apparently referring was entitled "Job Security?" and listed sixteen work rules the ACTWU had included in its contract with J. P. Stevens. According to this poster, employees at J. P. Stevens were "subject to *immediate discharge*" for violating such rules as stealing, being drunk on the job, fighting, refusing to "perform assigned duties or to obey instructions," possessing firearms on company premises, failing to report to work for three days without notifying a supervisor, and so on.[74] Though the union promised to enhance workers' job security through such measures as a fair seniority policy, stopping unfair discipline, and by providing "a grievance procedure that fights for you," the company pointed to these work rules and asked, "Are these the union's idea of job security?"[75]

This poster is remarkable for several reasons. Although it is obvious that these work rules (no doubt boilerplate), were included in the contract at the insistence of J. P. Stevens, Ix made it appear as if the union were responsible for their inclusion. In this regard, Crawford's remark "you're going to have to follow the union rules" is very revealing. It shows how the company was able to portray the union as just another disciplinarian the workers would have to put up with. As supervisors were instructed to tell their employees, "Remind employees they could wind up with 'two bosses' instead of one if they join the union."[76] Instead of placing the blame for stricter work discipline on their actual "bosses," employees were encouraged to believe that it would be the union that was responsible for Ix's loss of flexibility.

Perhaps more remarkable, however, is what this poster says about just how "flexible" Ix was in its treatment of employees. All of these work rules would seem to be standard policies at any company. Yet Ix portrayed them as new and rigid regulations that would be forced on employees if the union won the election. To a certain degree, this may have been the case. As John M. recalled, "they were slack on things . . . They never really had any written rules that they had presented to us."[77] Crawford related just how this flexibility worked in practice, "There were employees there that, maybe they were out of work once and a while and they wouldn't get fired for it because they were good employees. They were reliable employees, except for maybe once in a while. . . . It was a flexible thing because they were good employees. If they had a guy that, he just wasn't really working good, then if he lays out on Monday two or three times . . . then they've got an excuse [to fire him]."[78] With a union, however, Ix would be forced to treat "reliable" and "unreliable" workers the same.

Although Ix may have prided itself on its flexibility, such differential treatment of its workers was perhaps the major source of the union's appeal. As a company memo listing items discussed at one union meeting reported, "employees with discipline problems are complaining about supervisory treatment—favoritism and partiality."[79] Leaflets passed out by the organizer consistently listed ending favoritism ahead of increased pay and benefits as one of the reasons to vote for the union.[80] At one of the very first union meetings, favoritism headed the list of issues discussed, according to a company memo, while they discussed "very little about wages."[81] And in one of its activity reports, the company noted that one union activist was wearing a shirt that said "Vote Union, Stop Favoritism."[82] John M. also recalled that "there was a lot of family there; at times there was some favoritism there."[83]

The desire to end favoritism may partially explain why African American employees tended to side with the union.[84] Tammy H., for instance, remembered that all the blacks she knew were for the union.[85] A statistical analysis of the company's records confirms that memory: there was a significant correlation between race and the way an employee was expected to cast his or her ballot in the representation election.[86] Although race relations at Ix seem to have been relatively congenial, between January, 1980, and October, 1981 (i.e., contemporaneously with the organizing drive) the company was accused of racial discrimination by two different employees.[87] In one case, James Morton complained to the EEOC that his wages had been reduced when he transferred from Beamer Tender to Beamer Helper, while this had not been the case for a white employee.[88] In the other, Gregory Brown was fired for sleeping at work on two separate occasions. Yet, according to Brown, white workers who fell asleep were only given reprimands.[89] Although Ix was exonerated in both cases, that they were brought in the first place indicates that black employees had a perception of disparate treatment.

In this regard, it is also useful to recall the union leaflet indicating that "some people, mostly bosses' relatives and friends and people who expect to be boss, have been wearing shirts that say 'Support Frank Ix.'"[90] At the time, Ix had only one African American manager in the small warehouse department. So blacks' expectations of becoming a "boss" would have been much less. As John M. put it, "although they had a couple of black supervisors . . . if you wanted to advance it wasn't the place for a black person to be."[91] More important, most African Americans would not have had any relatives in management. One accusation that the union made against the company was that relatives of management received more favorable treatment.[92] Though the company denied this charge, it may help explain why employees with the same last name as a supervisor were significantly less likely to support the union.[93] John M., for instance, claimed that supervisors, "for family and friends, they would ease them past" more senior employees, and pointed to an instance where a supervisor's wife was able to obtain a job on first shift even though more senior workers had been seeking to move to that shift. In any case, on top of their perceived disparate treatment based on race, none of Ix's black employees could expect to benefit from more favorable treatment based on family connections to management. Even Fred Carey, the sole African American supervisor working at Ix at the time, "felt it [the union] was necessary because the blacks were getting less money than anyone else."[94] The union tried to exploit these sentiments by claiming that "blacks have [a] better chance with [the] Union" at one of its meetings.[95]

In addition to creating a more rigid work environment and changing how workers related to management, the union would also, according to the company, negatively affect how workers related to each other. Todd asked the workers to "think about the atmosphere around here for the past few months. The arguing, bickering, the tension, etc."[96] As already indicated, much of this increased tension could be blamed on the company itself. One-on-one interviews, surveillance of union meetings, firing union activists, and instituting a tighter work discipline were all bound to contribute to a deteriorating work environment. In addition, one union activist charged that "management had tried to discourage workers from conversing among themselves since union talk began."[97]

Management, however, was not solely responsible for the heightened tension at Ix. Workers themselves lined up into warring camps over the issue of the union. Whereas some workers wore T-shirts saying "Support Frank Ix," others donned shirts urging support for the ACTWU.[98] Crawford recalled that a woman he had known for ten years slammed the door in his face when he went to visit her about supporting the union.[99] Another worker, who wrote a letter urging his fellow employees to vote against the union, complained that some people had called him "crazy" and had accused him of acting at management's behest, which he denied.[100] In another instance, "Anna Davis told her supervisor that Nellie Toler made some nasty remarks to her in [the] ladies rest room because she would not sign [a] union card," according to a company activity report. Likewise, "Barry Lawson made threats to Donald Davis [about?] not signing card." From the other side, it was alleged at one union meeting that "Eddie Jones made threats to Jenny Woody against [the] union."[101] Workers also defaced both company and union leaflets. The company posted several copies of a newspaper article detailing a case of union corruption and asked "Is this the leadership *you* want to pay dues for?" On one copy someone wrote "This is not our union." On another someone responded that, "Nixon blew it! Carter blew it! Does that make Jefferson, Washington and Lincoln bad too? There [sic] someone bad everywhere. *Like Here.*"[102] Likewise, a manager found an ACTWU leaflet that had been defaced by an opponent of the union. Next to the portion describing "Rights on the Job," this person had written "Lie like a dog." In the section requesting contact information, he or she had filled in the name of a member of the organizing committee and listed her address as being "whorehouse avenue," and her shift as being the fourth (i.e., nonexistent).[103] Another employee wrote letters to her congressman and senators complaining that the NLRB was biased in favor of the union and got sixty-two of her coworkers to sign these letters.[104]

For most workers, of course, one's stance on the union was not decisive in how they related to each other. Familial and social connections outside of work and the desire to maintain a livable work environment were more important in this regard. For instance, both Crawford, the union activist, and the company reported that people who had no intention of voting for the union would sign a union card when approached by a fellow worker. They did so both to mollify their fellow employee and to "be left alone."[105] According to Charlotte Dudley, "most people kept it to themselves," while Fred Carey recalled that "nobody talked about it."[106] Nevertheless, it would seem, as Todd claimed, that "some of our employees are not as friendly with others as they might have been in the past."[107] And should the union win the election, Todd warned, "the tension, distrust and arguing [would] continue."[108] (In addition to the general image of unions as masculine institutions dedicated to conflict, this increased tension at Ix may partially explain why women tended to be against the union.[109])

In sum, then, by imposing a new and regimented work discipline, and by altering workers' relationships with their supervisors and each other, the union would end the "harmonious family atmosphere" at Ix.[110] Or as Sam Crawford recalled the company's message, "We're not going to be the Ix family anymore. We're going to be the union."[111]

This symbol of the family was key to Ix's campaign against the union. By defining this family to include both management and workers, Ix converted the "us versus them" message of the union from that of workers versus management to one of the Ix "family" versus union "outsiders." Ix attempted at every turn to bring home the message that management was part of "us," whereas the union was one of "them." It was implicit in the company's claim that it opposed the union, not for selfish reasons, but out of concern for its employees. And it could be seen in Todd's lumping managers and workers together when he claimed that the union "deteriorates your friendship with each other and your relationship with your supervisor."[112] But most explicitly, the company told its employees in one letter: "The other reason we oppose the ACTWU is because it is the beginning of an attempt to breed distrust of the Company by our employees; to disrupt our relationship with each other."[113] In the context of this letter, and others, "each other" could easily be misread by the employees to mean both management *and* workers.

Distrust of one's employer, of course, is a central reason workers unionize in the first place. Unions represent workers' means to counter the economic power of their employer to set wages, determine the conditions under which they will work, and whether they will even have work at all. Unions are the "us" meant to limit the power of the management "them." It was this logic of organized labor that Ix aimed to subvert.

The company did not simply claim that the "Ix family" was composed of both workers and management and leave it at that, however. To make this claim persuasive, it tried to elicit worker empathy for management and to heighten the worker's sense of the union as foreign. Todd asked Ix employees to "think about some of the things that the Union has said about us and about you" again trying to lump management and workers together. "In some of their handbills, they have called the Frank Ix management team some very dirty names. . . . They have even referred to some of our management members as lying S.O.B.'s. This is certainly not the way we like to deal with our people as we have always tried to treat our people in a manner that was morally correct."[114] Such an appeal to workers' sympathy and sense of propriety seems likely to have resonated with at least some employees. One person opposed to the union wrote a letter to his fellow workers that echoed management's appeal. "I know you have heard talk about the UNION AND FRANK IX, but we do know what FRANK IX is, but not the Union. Most of us know the so call[ed] TOP DOG'S, really they are not all that bad, they want to be our friends if we let them and not just BOSSES."[115] Even had this worker been asked by management to write this letter, which he denied, it shows that there was at least the expectation that workers could more closely identify with the local management than they could with a bunch of outsiders who "run the ACTWU from New York," as one company poster reminded them.[116]

The company also tried to show how its interest in its workers made it one of "us," whereas the union's interest made it one of "them." As the antiunion film shown to the workers explained, "You are being placed in a position where you have to decide who is going to look out for you, who really has an interest in your feeling good about where you work, the company or some union outsiders. . . . without the people we've [the company] got nothing."[117] The union's interest, on the other hand, was merely to obtain dues "to pay big salaries to the union bosses!!" who shared little in common with the workers.[118] For instance, should the workers go out on strike, "the union organizers still get paid, the union negotiators still get paid, the company management still gets paid . . . but the only employees who get paid are the ones who come to work."[119] And unlike the company which spent thousands of dollars on such items as bowling teams, educational loan funds for employees' children, Christmas parties, and so forth, to keep its workers happy, "last year the union did *not* pay one dime to its members!!"[120] As the antiunion film summarized it:

> You see a union is a business and for a business to survive, it has to have customers. . . . you represent another potential dues paying member and dues are the biggest source of income for the unions. That's why unions often spend thousands of dollars even hundreds of thousands to organize individual facilities just like this one. And, where do they get the money for these expensive organizing efforts? Mostly from dues, dues paid every month by hard working honest employees in other companies like this one. . . . the company not the union provides the jobs and the job security the people want and the company not the union has the greatest interest in making sure that employees feel good about their jobs and their future here. Its easy to make promises about higher wages and more benefits, but only the company has the ability to deliver on those promises.[121]

The flaw in the logic of this argument is transparent. After all, the company's interest in its workers was to make money to pay high salaries to "bosses" and shareholders, the same as the union's supposed interest. And, it would seem, the union's stake in keeping the workers happy would have been as large as that of the company's.

What made this argument persuasive was the size and location of the union versus that of Ix. Although Ix's corporate operations were located in New York, the Charlottesville plant was the oldest and largest in the company's relatively small empire of three textile plants, one of which had only been purchased the year before.[122] Members of the Ix family still worked at the Charlottesville facility. For all practical purposes, Ix continued to be a family-run operation that could easily be seen as local to the Charlottesville area. The ACTWU, on the other hand, was based in that favorite whipping boy of small-town populism and moralism, New York City. This reference to New York may have also been a hangover from Southern antiunion campaigns of the 1940s and '50s which, as Robert Zieger shows, extensively employed anti-

Semitic slurs. By linking the union to New York, which was in turn linked to Jews, Ix may have been trying to draw on the stereotype, widespread in the immediate postwar period, that unions were, by and large, run by Jews and Communists, another equivalence popular during the '40s. It is possible, then, that Ix was subtly attempting to play on whatever latent anti-Semitism existed among its workers.[123] In addition, the size of the union far surpassed the size of the Ix workforce. Thus, the ACTWU represented a large, distant, and suspect bureaucracy that was unlikely to take much notice of the needs of a small group of workers located in far away Virginia. The company, of course, was careful to point out these facts using sections of the ACTWU's constitution against it:

> The International Union is run by a General Executive Board. No Ix employee can now be a member of the Executive Board. The union can also combine various local unions into a joint board which could then include people from other companies besides Ix. The joint board would then have the power to make the Local decisions which would also affect you.
>
> 1. Local Unions of ACTWU do not have the power to make a collective bargaining agreement unless authorized by the International Union President or the General executive Board.
>
> . . .
>
> 5. 50 percent of all dues collected goes to the New York headquarters.
>
> . . .
>
> 7. All money, records and property are owned by the International Union and not the Local Union.[124]

The union's own pamphlets may have also hurt it when it came to convincing Ix employees that it cared about their particular needs. They are generally boilerplate in nature and of rather poor quality. They are also inappropriately strident and many of them seem to pay little attention to the specific issues at Ix. Crawford, who was on the organizing committee, recalled that they were put together by the union organizer—the committee had nothing to do with them. He ridiculed them as being "ridiculous."[125]

The Union Police State

Besides the economic danger and the threat of creating an impersonal, rigid, and acrimonious work environment, the third major menace the union posed for Ix employees, according to management, was the loss of control over their own destiny. For, as the company portrayed it, the union represented an alien, malignant dictatorship. The ACTWU was like an inescapable black hole into which Ix's workers would be pulled, and once beyond its event horizon the union would gain control over every aspect of their lives. The union would force workers to act as it saw fit and thrust them into situations they had no desire to be part of. And this would be true whether the worker was actually a member of the union or not.[126]

For instance, the union could decide to "impose" a boycott on Ix and destroy the livelihood of Ix's workers.[127] Also, whenever the company talked about strikes, management was sure to say it was the "union [that would] take you out on strike," or "unions cause strikes," not upset workers or intransigent management.[128] And, naturally, the company circulated newspaper clippings detailing instances of strike violence, while its antiunion consultants advised supervisors to mention strike violence to all their employees, making it seem as if such violence was some impersonal force that accompanied all strikes, not something that either workers or management precipitated.[129] In addition, once out on strike the union's constitution prohibited members from quitting.[130]

The ACTWU, according to the company, was a form of government that imposed all kinds of rules on its members and strictly enforced them through its own judicial system. Moreover, these rules, and the procedures used to adjudicate violations of them, went against the norms expected of a democratic government. "Members who fail to pay an assessment for two months are subject to discipline by the Union. . . . Discipline includes the right of the Union to fine its members, and a civil court can enforce collection of these fines. . . . If a member becomes dissatisfied with the ACTWU and says he or she wants to form or help another Labor organization, the ACTWU can fine that member. . . . Members must go through the union's trial and appeal procedures before any civil court suit can be started. . . . The Union can hold a trial against an accused member even if the member is not present at his or her own trial."[131] Management pointed to one section of the ACTWU constitution that provided for fines for conduct detrimental to the union, and observed that "it looks like they can fine you for whatever they want!!"[132] And in losing the right "to talk to the boss," or to seek the help of another union, Ix employee's risked "Losing the Right to Speak for Yourself."[133] The union, then, violated some of the most sacred concepts of the Bill of Rights.

What's more, this police state would not affect just those who planned to join the union. For, according to the company, the union would force *everyone* at Ix to join. Despite Virginia being a right-to-work state, the company cited cases where the ACTWU had pressured people into joining or had people discharged for resigning their membership. For instance, the company circulated a newspaper article detailing an incident at a Virginia company where the ACTWU had failed to sign a form that would have allowed an employee who had been absent without notice to reclaim her job. According to the newspaper, the union's failure to back up this employee was motivated by a desire to take revenge on her after she quit the union following an increase in monthly dues.[134]

Finally, once installed, this police state would be impossible to topple. As Todd put it:

> We have heard some people say they would just like to vote for the Union and try it for a short period to see if the Union could get them higher wages, better benefits, etc. Please remember you don't try a Union on as you would a new pair [of] shoes to see if you like them despite what the Union would like you to believe. Once it is in, it's virtually impossible to get rid of it. For one year it is impossible. If a contract is negotiated, you can't [get] rid of it for the term of the contract and many contracts have three year terms. Even if there is no contract, the law makes it very difficult for employees to get rid of the Union.[135]

In the face of this onslaught, the union, which had begun the campaign with an offensive against the company, was forced to devote all of its efforts to defending itself against these charges. Initially the union had tried to assure workers that federal law protected them from the *company*. It now had to tell them how federal and state law protected them from the *union*. One letter circulated to employees by the union, but addressed to Todd, stated, "You [Todd] are well aware of the fact that no workers can be made to strike. You are well aware of the fact that any person who tried to make another person strike against his will would be placed in prison."[136] Another union leaflet pointed to Virginia's right-to-work law to assure employees that they would not be forced to join the union.[137] And in case that was not sufficient, the union told employees that anyone forced to join the union could collect $100,000, an obligation, the union said, that could be enforced through the courts.[138]

To charges that it represented an undemocratic bunch of outsiders, the union tried to assure workers that they would be the people who ran the local. The following is from one union leaflet:

> Question: Who is the Union
> Answer: You are the Union
> That's right, Y-O-U, the people that work at Frank Ix are the Union. You will run the Union, you will elect officers, some of you will be officers, shop stewards, and convention delegates of the Union. It is the people at Frank Ix

who will join, form, and run the Union. If the Company says that you don't
need outsiders, then they must be crazy because there are no outsiders. Y-
O-U are the Union.[139]

If a strike occurred, it would not be because "the union took the workers
out on strike" but because the workers themselves voted to strike. "No committee, officer, representative or official of the Union can call a strike at your
plant. The only people that can call a strike at your plant are the workers at
the plant by majority vote."[140]

The union went further than just assuring workers of its own democratic
nature, though. It devoted considerable effort to showing Ix employees how
organized labor, in general, was not only compatible with democracy, but
essential to its survival. Indeed, the union did everything it could to wrap
itself in the flag. As one union leaflet asserted, "Every law that protects you
and your family was brought about through the efforts of organized labor. If it
were not for Unions, there would be no democracy in this Nation."[141] Unions
did not just support freedom in America, according to the ACTWU, they
were also at the forefront of the worldwide struggle for freedom. Referring
to the Solidarity movement in Poland, the union claimed, "[t]he Russians
have accused the Unions of this Country of sending money and support for
workers in Poland. When you join the Union you join in the fight for freedom around the world."[142] Far from being an aberration from the ideals of
democracy and "Americanism," the union claimed to "have shown you that
everybody who stands for Americanism stands for a free labor movement
for working people."[143]

According to the ACTWU, it was Ix that threatened freedom and Americanism. When the company objected to including the maintenance department in the proposed bargaining unit, the union was quick to respond that
it would "protect the maintenance mens [sic] right to vote as guaranteed by
the Laws of this Nation. A person who would deny an American the right
to vote is no different than the Communists."[144] Where the company portrayed the union as a dictatorial taskmaster, the union claimed that it was
the company that was the true dictator. "The reason workers belong to the
Union is to be free to place a price on their labor and to be free to exercise
their rights as free Americans. Workers who do not have a Union to protect
them are no better off than slaves."[145] Nor was it the union that would control
workers' lives as the company claimed. Rather, it was Ix that already exercised
such control. "The only people who fight Unions are people who want to rob
workers of their wages, and who want to control their lives."[146]

The company did not just let such charges pass unnoticed. Instead, it vied with the union to show how it, not the union, was the true champion of democracy. When the union wrote a letter to the company with a pro forma request for recognition based on its having obtained a substantial number of signed union cards, the company responded with the following letter, which it posted on the bulletin board alongside the union's letter:

> We cannot and will not sign away their rights on the basis of some cards signed under pressure in many instances. Instead our employees have a right to make an informed choice in a secret ballot election conducted by the National Labor Relation Board. We will not agree with your proposal to deny the employees this right. Thus, we believe that, if our employees are to make a choice as important to themselves and their families as is this one, they be given the right to do so in a democratic way. We, therefore, refuse your request to recognize your union which would deny our employees their rights guaranteed by law.[147]

As to why it had objected to including the maintenance men in the bargaining unit, the company explained that it was merely trying to be a good citizen by informing the NLRB about a possible violation of the law should they be allowed to join the union. As Todd explained in a talk to the employees, "At the NLRB hearing we brought out the fact that some of our maintenance people worked as watchmen on weekends and shutdown periods. We did this because the NLRB law says that people who do act as guards and watchmen cannot vote with the production people. . . . We simply presented the facts and left the decision as to whether or not they should vote up to the NLRB."[148]

Unions and the Ix Workers' View of the Moral Economy

The representation election also forced workers to consider how the union comported with their sense of the moral economy. Did unionism strengthen or weaken those precepts workers valued in regards to work discipline, individualism, and even the workings of the capitalist system itself?

One theme running through all the interviews with former Ix employees is their pride in how hard they worked. "They were a hard working bunch of people down there. I'll give them credit for that," was how Henry Peregoy put it.[149] They valued their jobs because of the friends they made at work and because it was one of the best opportunities for unskilled workers in the area, not because of the rigorous work discipline required. Nevertheless, one of their bases for judging their fellow workers was whether they measured up to this discipline. Partially, this was simple self-protection: they did not want their own work loads increased to make up for the "slackers." And those workers who were caught up with their work were available to help their fellows either catch up or look after their jobs while they took a short break.[150] For the most part, however, this was a moral judgement. These workers felt an ethical obligation to work hard and expected the same from others. "Like I told them," recalled Charlotte Dudley, "If I'm coming in here to goof off I'll just stay home." This was in contrast to some workers, whom she looked down on, who "didn't care about the job, they were just in there for the pay check."[151] Similarly, Peregoy disparaged lazy workers who were "deadbeats that didn't want to work."[152]

Both the union and the company were aware of this attitude and tried to convince workers that their opponent threatened this work ethic. The issue of favoritism was the union's entrée for convincing workers that the current system favored slackers. As one union leaflet put it, "[b]rown nosers are against the Union because they don't have the ability to run their job unless they brown nose the boss."[153] The company, on the other hand, claimed that it was the workers who could not carry their own weight or workers who had discipline problems who sought the protection of the union. According to management, these workers hoped that the union would allow them to keep their jobs in spite of their lower productivity and poor work habits. One cartoon posted by the company, for instance, contrasted "Jack Hardworker," who had doubts about the union, with "Joe Freeloader," who supported the union.[154] The company's effort to convince its employees that the union threatened their work ethic was no doubt helped by the widespread belief that unions were designed to protect lazy workers.

Along with their belief in the obligation of hard work, these employees also expected that workers who met this obligation should be recognized for upholding this standard. How organized labor fit in with this expectation, then, became another issue of contention. According to the company, such recognition should be on an individual basis. As the antiunion film shown to employees put it, "Fortunately, in this country, the individual still has the right and the ability to work a little harder and be rewarded for it. . . . [Don't] give up your rights as an individual to speak for yourself and make your own decisions about your future with this company."[155] The union also promised that it could obtain the respect that workers deserved. In this case, however, respect was to be gained through collective rather than individual action. "Remember, any worker can work for nothing," one leaflet claimed. "It takes a real worker to demand decent wages, fringe benefits, dignity, and respect from a Company. I believe you possess the courage, the intelligence, and the integrity to demand to be treated with the respect God intended you to be treated with."[156] The true test of individual integrity, then, was not in fulfilling one's obligations to the company as the company defined them, but in standing up to the boss and demanding recognition for the work that they were already doing. As another union leaflet put it, "The reason workers belong to the Union is to be free to place a price on their labor," and not just take what the company decided to give them.[157]

"Placing a price on their labor" was, to some extent, a critique of the workings of the labor market. According to the union, the only way workers could effectively place a price on their labor was through combined action in the face of the employer's greater economic power. Rather than letting the market set the price of labor without any constraints, the union sought to obtain for employees a wage that the employer could pay, not just what the market would bear. Unions commonly referred to this as "taking the wage out of competition."

This critique, it would seem, did not sit well with some employees. Peregoy's comment that "there was a limit on how much you could pay a textile worker," Dudley's reference to "getting a fair share" in her decision to oppose the union, and Crawford's current dismay about the "outrageous" salaries paid to auto workers, all point to an acceptance of a meritocratic ethic that limited these workers' expectations about what they could reasonably demand of the company. Carey, for instance, felt good about working at Ix because of his progress from janitor to supervisor. "I didn't go too far in school. [Yet] I was working up the ladder, doing something good." He obviously felt that pay and responsibility ought to be tied to education and was pleased that he had managed to advance despite his own limited qualifications in this regard.[158] Ix employees' constant comparisons of their own wages with those of other textile workers, and workers in local factories, also show an implicit acceptance of (some might say resignation to) the idea that the market was what set wages. There was, however, a limit to this acceptance. Both Crawford and Peregoy, for instance, felt that unions had been necessary at one time when people worked sixteen hours a day, six days a week, for very little pay. Those days, however, were gone, and unions were no longer needed.[159]

Some workers also questioned the union's right to interfere with how Ix ran its operations. They held that the owners of a property should be allowed to control that property without someone else telling them what they could and could not do. As one employee put it in a letter to his fellow workers: "Why should FRANK IX let a UNION come in this plant without a fight?

Would you let some outsider come in your home and tell you how to run your house? HELL NO! So why should they?"[160] In this case, the ownership of a factory and the ownership of a home were portrayed as essentially the same. And since many employees owned their own homes, they could be expected to respect the principle of the rights of ownership. As Edward Gibson recalled, he opposed the union because "the people owned the business and I thought they ought to be able to run it the way they saw fit."[161] The question of unionization, then, touched on employees' most basic feelings about the value of private property and the proper workings of the capitalist system.

Union work rules, or at least workers' perceptions of them, were especially threatening to this belief that the owner had a right to organize and run his facility as he saw fit. Edward Gibson, for instance, characterized union rules in the following manner: "[There are] certain things you're not supposed to do. You have a job title and you're supposed to do that job, you're not supposed to do anything else." According to Gibson, "That would hinder a lot of work. There's other things to be done and they [the union] catch you doing it and a lot of times they get you for it, and write you up for it."[162] Workers like Gibson saw their job in broader terms than just their particular job title. "Work" meant producing cloth for sale, and not just setting up throwing machines, which was Gibson's particular assignment. This is also the implication of Dudley's remark that some workers "didn't care about the *job*, they were just in there for the *pay check*."[163] A worker who cared about the "job" was not concerned about job titles and jurisdictional boundaries, but in making sure the company was producing its product. Another, unstated, though implicit, concern about union work rules was how they would affect the ability of workers to assist each other. There was, apparently, some trepidation that the union would impose strict job descriptions that would not allow more than a certain number of workers or only certain types of workers to do a job, thus destroying the flexibility workers wanted so they could help each other.

Who Do You Trust?

Amid all these claims and counterclaims, threats and promises, and competition for the mantle of "the good guy," employees turned to those they were closest to for help in deciding how they should vote. Trust, based on how well they knew their friends, family, company, locality, and organized labor, was vital to the success of the company and the failure of the union. Because they knew almost no one that was actually in a union, employees had to rely on each other, the company, and what they had read in newspapers or seen on television to form an opinion about the ACTWU and organized labor in general. Ix was able to exploit this factor with consummate expertise.

Support for the union tended to follow ties of family, race, and department or shift. At union meetings, husbands and wives (assuming both worked in the plant) would attend as a couple. Some company reports on union meetings, for instance, note "Family ties" or "Kinfolk" next to a list of attendees.[164] There is also a tendency (though not statistically significant) in the company's "polling data" to report people with the same last name as being in agreement when it came to how they were going to vote on the union. And as noted previously, employees with the same last name as someone in management were significantly less likely to be in favor of the union. Race was also a statistically significant factor in predicting how a person would vote during the election.[165] Finally, support for the union tended to cluster in a few departments and shifts. The weave room third shift was one such hot bed of union support; the maintenance department, which only worked first shift, was another site of strong union activism. (Hence the company's attempt to exclude them from the bargaining unit!)

How workers responded to the union, then, was not simply a matter of weighing the claims of the union against the claims of the company. Workers also took into account what their peers thought about the union. For instance, one company activity report noted that "Linwood Jordan . . . told Bill Mowell, his supervisor, he was not trying to organize the plant, but if it came to a vote he would vote for the union and others have ask[ed] his advice."[166] Although there was no doubt an element of peer pressure involved in this—the desire of the average person to have his own opinions accord with those of his fellows—the issue of trust was also an important factor in explaining why workers lined up on the union the way they did. The closer the tie between workers—whether that tie was due to race, family, or simply working adjacent to one another—the more likely they were to respect each other's opinions and rely on them for guidance. For instance, Tammy H. related that she would only talk to fellow black employees about the union because she felt she could trust them more than white employees.[167] Even in a generally antiunion environment, then, the scales could be tipped in the union's favor, at least in a few departments, when a few trusted workers decided to throw in their lot with organized labor. Once this happened, the negative image of unions predominant in the popular culture and reinforced by the company would no longer be as effective in influencing their decisions.

The ACTWU was well aware of this phenomenon. The union's Organizing Department compiled lists of factors, both favorable and unfavorable, for selecting potential organizing targets. Among the favorable factors were plants where the workers had spouses who worked for a unionized company, and where several plants in a multiplant company were already organized.[168] In such cases the union would not have to work as hard to gain the workers' trust because many of them would have already been exposed to organized labor and would find it less of a foreign concept. In trying to organize Ix, however, the union would benefit from none of these advantages.

To deal with this problem, the union devoted considerable effort to showing that organized labor was worthy of workers' trust. Hence its constant attempts to link unionism with patriotism, freedom, and democracy. By wrapping itself in the flag, the union hoped to demonstrate that it was as American as apple pie and was not some foreign entity. In the face of such low union density, which was common in the South, it endeavored to show that people worthy of trust had endorsed organized labor and that millions of workers just like those at Ix were members of unions. The following is from one union leaflet:

> Every President of the United States for the past 50 years has advocated and endorsed Unions for working people.
>
> The churches of this Nation endorse and advocate Unions for the workers of this Nation.
>
> The Judges and the courts of this Nation, including the Supreme Court of the United States, protect workers in their rights to have Unions.
>
> Twenty million American workers, just like you, are Union members. They go to the same churches that you go to. They belong to the same civic organizations that you belong to. They are city councilmen. They are mayors. They are pastors of churches. Just as you, they are decent, upright, religious American citizens.
>
> [A list of different kinds of workers in unions] They [the union members] are the backbone of this nation.[169]

Another twelve-page pamphlet cited endorsements of organized labor by "Famous Americans," including FDR, "Scoop" Jackson, Abraham Lincoln, Harry Truman, Martin Luther King Jr., Dwight D. Eisenhower, Lyndon B. Johnson, John F. Kennedy, Hubert Humphrey, and Billy Graham. The center two pages of this same pamphlet also had quotations from leading religious denominations endorsing unions.[170]

When it came to familiarity and trust, however, the company had a distinct advantage. A majority of the workforce had been at Ix for all of their lives.

Some of them had been there since the 1930s. These workers would have been those that had thrived under Ix's system of "personalism." They would have been the ones that Crawford referred to as "reliable employees," who "maybe they were out of work once and a while and they wouldn't get fired for it because they were good employees." Indeed, the age of a worker was the most statistically significant factor in predicting how he or she would vote in the election. According to Crawford, these workers responded to the union campaign with incredulity. "We've worked here all these years, we don't need these outsiders coming in trying to change our lives."[171] Or as Dudley, who opposed the union, put it, "I thought we were better off like we were . . . we left good enough alone, we let it ride."[172]

The company also benefitted from the low union density of the Charlottesville area. There was little chance that Ix employees knew anyone who belonged to a union. Thus, they would have had few firsthand accounts of what they could expect from working in an organized plant. Ix management was well aware of this fact and expressed concern when a factory twenty miles away voted to unionize.[173] Any increase in union membership in the area would threaten its ability to continue sowing doubt about the consequences of unionization. And this was the main thrust of the company's campaign against the union.

Despite management's reprisals against some union activists and its threats to him personally, Crawford characterized the company's campaign as basically "clean." It was not the threats and intimidation that were most prominent in Crawford's memory. Rather, he felt that Ix's primary message to its employees was that they should ask questions of the union. "Go and ask these people this, go ask these people how they're going to get you more money, what are they going to do to make your benefits better."[174] In speech after speech, in its letters, and in its bulletin board postings, the company repeatedly asked the employees "Do you know the ACTWU?" and urged them not to "take the risk" of joining.[175] One such posting simply listed a series of questions employees should ask the union.[176] In another instance, management warned employees that signing a union card was like signing a contract to buy a house.

> [I]f any one of us were signing a contract to purchase a new home, we would probably be doing this with a local banker that we knew very well. We would be very careful to read all of the fine print, we would know exactly where the home was located, the condition of the plumbing, the electrical services, the physical structure of the home, the size of the home, etc., before we signed

anything committing ourselves to a long term contract. Even after we did that and even though we were dealing with a local banker that we had probably known for many, many years, we would still take the contract to an attorney and ask him to be sure that everything was in order. Signing a union card is also a long term contract committing you to certain things in the way of dues, etc., and affecting your legal rights for the future.[177]

The company also claimed that, unlike the union with its unsubstantiated promises, "distorted facts," and its insulting references to management, "we have tried to be sure you had the truth on all issues. . . . We have tried to back up everything we have said with the law, with their Constitution, with their Tax Forms, and with several contracts they have negotiated. In other words we have tried to tell you the facts without making any accusations or promises."[178]

That this message struck home is attested to by the memories of some of the employees that worked at Ix. Not only Sam Crawford, but John M., another union activist, felt the company did not really have negative things to say about the union, per se. Rather, as he recalled, their basic message was "we didn't need it."[179] Thus, even people who supported the union found the company's message to be measured and even tempered, even if not universally persuasive. For those less committed to the union this would have been a powerful way to sow doubt.

* * *

Over and over, Ix drew on the negative images of organized labor that existed in the popular culture to dissuade its employees from voting for the union. It portrayed the ACTWU as a distant, bureaucratic organization that had little concern for the workers at Ix beyond what it could extort from them in the form of union dues to pay for the large salaries of its leaders. According to Ix, the union would likely cost its employees more than they could possibly hope to gain. It would involve them in strikes, during which they would lose their pay, if not their very jobs, and which would almost certainly result in violence at some point. And should the union somehow manage to raise the workers' wages—a very remote possibility, according to the company—then it would most likely mean that Ix would go bankrupt, either because other mills would underbid it, or because of foreign competition. Moreover, the ACTWU, according to Ix, was little better than a police state, with its undemocratic governance and its multitude of rules regulating its members' lives.

The most serious problem, however, was the way in which the union would affect the work environment at Ix. The ACTWU would impose all sorts of new work rules that would interfere with the employees' abilities to do their jobs. The union, according to the company, would represent a new set of bosses to which the employees would have to answer. Moreover, these new bosses, because they were not responsive to workers' needs, would enforce a strict new work regime that would prevent Ix from exercising the flexibility that its employees were used to. Not only would this new work regime affect how workers did their jobs, it would also change how they related to each other as well as their managers. The friendly, family atmosphere at Ix would disappear. It would be replaced by an impersonal environment where strict new rules would regulate everything from how a worker operated a machine to when, and under what circumstances, he could talk to his supervisor. Familial cooperation would be replaced by union-inspired confrontation.

Although some employees were not persuaded by Ix's propaganda—African American's, for instance, did not think that Ix's current "flexibility" worked in their favor—many, if not most employees, were prepared to believe the company's message. During interviews they would mention many things unions did that they did not like, some of them not even mentioned in the company's campaign. Talk about rigid job descriptions, the obsolescence of unions, organized labor's contribution to inflation, and the way in which unions caused companies to go out of business could be heard from even those employees who had supported the union at the time.

In only one respect was there a significant difference between these workers' views and those found in the popular culture: the relative power of the union versus Ix. Whereas most Americans during the 1970s seemed to believe that unions were very powerful organizations that could often bring industrial giants, such as GM and U.S. Steel, to their knees, the employees at Ix could see from firsthand experience that this was not the case, at least at Ix. In fact, the ACTWU recognized that the employees would have preferred a *more powerful* counterweight to Ix's power to hire and fire. To this end it tried to draw on the power of the federal government to reinforce its own weak position. Thus, for instance, it claimed that the government would prevent Ix from closing the mill should the employees vote for a union. It also assured them that the government would force Ix to negotiate with the union, and that it would protect workers from the company's retaliation.

Ix's campaign against the ACTWU was successful because its message to employees was geared to reenforcing an image of organized labor that most of them already held. This was reflected in the union's own literature which, instead of focusing on how the union would benefit Ix's employees, was devoted to refuting the company's charges and assuring workers that the negative things they had heard about unions were not true. Indeed, by the end of the campaign the union was no longer telling workers how the government would protect them from the company, but how it would protect them from the union! In the end, the workers at Ix voted against the union because the culture in which they lived disposed them to distrust organized labor.

5

Antiunionism in the Citadel of Organized Labor

Organizing Clerical Workers at New York University

From the rolling hills of the southern Piedmont, we turn to the concrete canyons of New York City. From an examination of blue-collar workers in one of America's first, and now declining industries, our focus shifts to pink-collar workers in one of the great growth industries of the later twentieth century: college education. Though these two venues, and the workers involved, are so very different, it will quickly become apparent that the same concerns and issues that played such a prominent role in the campaign at Frank Ix & Sons were active in the attempt by District 65, Retail, Wholesale, Distributive and Processing Workers Union (RWDWU) to organize the clerical workers at New York University (NYU) in 1970.

What is interesting about District 65's failure to win over the NYU workers is not only that the same issues evident in the Ix campaign resurfaced here but that this failure took place in New York City. As Joshua Freeman argues in his book *Working Class New York,* New York City had the most favorable climate for unions of any city in the United States.[1] As will be shown, District 65 tried to draw on this asset to woo NYU's employees. Despite this prounion climate, however, workers at NYU proved as skeptical of unions as those at Ix. Even in the citadel of organized labor, the antiunion bias of American culture proved to be a powerful impediment to labor's effort to organize.

* * *

District 65's organizing drive at NYU began in December, 1969, at the invitation of the university's library workers (not the librarians, but the clerical staff). Initially, these workers had turned to Local 153 of the Office and Professional Employees International Union (OPEIU) to help them organize. This effort had come to naught, however, when the State Labor Relations Board (SLRB) ruled in the fall of 1969 that a bargaining unit composed of only library workers was too small. Following this defeat, these workers, who were apparently disillusioned with Local 153, turned to District 65 to help them achieve union recognition. Rather than confining its unionization effort to the library and running into the same obstacle Local 153 had faced, District 65 set out to organize all of the clerical workers at NYU, a bargaining unit with about two thousand members.[2]

This initial effort to create a more broadly based union was apparently not very successful. Three months after the campus-wide organizing drive had begun, District 65 submitted a letter to NYU asking that the university recognize and begin negotiating with the union as the representative for the library staff.[3] It probably came as no surprise when the university turned down District 65's request, citing the SLRB's decision of the previous fall. Instead of returning with a demand that the university recognize the union as the representative for all of NYU's clerical workers, however, the union continued to press for a bargaining unit composed of only the library staff. By the middle of April, workers' mounting frustration at the continued lack of progress prompted the union to call a strike to force the issue.[4]

Although the strike's initial goal was to achieve union recognition for only the library workers, this relatively limited ambition quickly grew to encompass all of the clerical workers at the university. It appears that the union was greatly encouraged by the response to the strike. According to one union leaflet, over three hundred workers signed union cards on the day the first picket lines went up. Other departments around the university voted to follow the library workers out on strike as well.[5] In addition, support from the students and faculty encouraged the union to believe that it was well on the way to enrolling a majority of the workers on campus.[6]

Ironically, by broadening the objectives of the strike, the union placed itself in a somewhat awkward position. All along the university had maintained that the only appropriate bargaining unit was one that encompassed all of the clerical workers and not only those in the library.[7] Now the union was striking, by all appearances, to force the university to grant something it had long ago conceded. Indeed, the day after the union declared its new goal, James Hester, the president of the university, released a statement saying that since the union now agreed with the university's position on the appropriate bargaining unit it should call off the strike. He also announced that, based on the union's call for a campus-wide unit, the university had petitioned the

SLRB for election as soon as possible to determine if the workers wanted a union—an action, he pointed out, the union itself should have taken instead of resorting to a strike.[8] As a result, many workers began to question the purpose for the union's strike.[9] After striking for two weeks, the union decided the best course of action was to simply declare victory and prepare for the campus-wide election that would be held on May 15.[10]

May 1970, of course, was a tumultuous time in the United States, particularly on college campuses. President Nixon's decision to invade Cambodia touched off a wave of protests across the country. The uproar only escalated after four students were killed at Kent State University on May 4. New York University was hardly immune to such unrest. For instance, one group of students calling themselves the Kimball Hall Commune occupied the university's personnel offices.[11] Coming hard on the heels of a strike that had greatly disrupted the university's operations, these distractions may partially explain why the university did not mount a campaign against the union. In any case, the administration sent only one letter to its employees prior to the election. That letter simply pointed out that if the union won the election and negotiated a contract that included a "union security" clause, all employees would be forced to join. Therefore it was important that everyone vote, whether they wanted a union or not. The university made no recommendation on whether they should vote for or against being represented by a union.[12]

The results of the election were quite ambiguous. District 65 received 479 votes, Local 153 (which had reentered the picture after the SLRB scheduled the election) tallied 73 votes, and 320 workers voted against union representation. However, 518 ballots were challenged and not counted. During a representation election, either the union or the employer can challenge ballots if they believe someone wanting to vote is ineligible. For instance, the union may claim that someone is a manager and should not be allowed to vote. Conversely, the employer may claim that someone is not part of the bargaining unit and, consequently, should not be included in the vote. In addition, the election authority, in this case the SLRB, will challenge a ballot when the voter's name does not appear on the list of employees provided by the employer. In any event, when a ballot is challenged, it is sealed and not counted until the authority conducting the election determines if the voter in question is eligible to vote. If it is determined that the voter would be part of the bargaining unit, then the ballot is unsealed and counted. In this case, according to a university memo, the large number of challenges were caused by the inability of the university to provide the SLRB a complete list of employees prior to the election because its personnel office had been occupied by student protesters.[13] Until the SLRB decided which, if any, of these votes should be counted, the outcome would remain in doubt.[14]

Hearings to resolve this issue were held during the summer of 1970. Before the SLRB was able to complete these hearings, however, the National Labor Relations Board (NLRB) intervened by claiming jurisdiction over large private universities. Over the strenuous objections of District 65, which was convinced that it had won the election, the entire process of determining an appropriate bargaining unit and scheduling an election was restarted from the beginning.[15]

It was not until June 11, 1971, that this new election was held. During the course of the year between these two elections, the situation at NYU had changed in several ways that would adversely affect the union. Unrest on American campuses had considerably eased. A state of exhaustion seemed to have set in, sapping the militance of both workers and students. Their eagerness to demonstrate their power by going on strike, for instance, appeared to be much diminished. In addition, the clerical workers at NYU witnessed a seemingly unsuccessful three-month strike by a union of university maintenance workers. After twelve weeks of being out of work, the maintenance workers finally voted to end the strike and accept the university's offer, which they had rejected prior to the strike. This strike ended only a few short weeks before the clerical workers at NYU were scheduled to vote on whether they wanted to be represented by a union.[16] Several acts of vandalism also occurred during the maintenance strike, which no doubt reinforced the association between strikes and violence.[17] On June 7, just a few days before the election, utility workers at Madison Square Garden went on strike, forcing NYU to shift its commencement exercises to Radio City Music Hall.[18] The frequency with which strikes were happening all around them, then, may have reinforced the popular image of unions as "strike happy." In addition to an easing of the general unrest and the prevalence of strikes, a general pay raise at the university helped defuse one of the union's main campaign issues.[19] Employee turnover also was very likely to have had a negative impact on the union. Right from the start of District 65's organizing drive, the union had pressed for a quick election because it was worried about the high rate of turnover in many jobs at the university.[20] As the union argued in April 1970, a long delay would mean that "the staff will go through its annual partial change and some of those workers who know from experience that the union is a necessity for worker bargaining will leave, taking their experience and union support with them."[21]

The most important change, however, was the university's decision to mount a concerted antiunion campaign instead of simply standing on the sidelines. It is possible that this decision to actively oppose the union was motivated by the increasingly dire fiscal situation NYU was experiencing at the time. For instance, the 1970 fiscal year ended with a $4.5 million deficit, up from $1.4 million the previous year.[22] For whatever reason, by the time of the election in June of 1971, NYU was prepared to oppose the union with an intense campaign composed of letters to employees, bulletins, and one-on-one meetings with supervisors.[23] In addition, some of those workers opposed to unionization organized themselves into a committee to lobby their fellow employees to vote against union representation. Before the first election, David Livingston, president of District 65, told a group of NYU workers, "I have no doubt . . . we will win the election, because I don't believe the University will campaign against the union, and there is no clear-cut organized worker opposition. You're working in a climate and atmosphere which is generally pro-union."[24] Clearly, by the time of the second election this was no longer the case.

Because of the large number of votes that were never counted after the first election, it is hard to say just how much support District 65 lost between the two elections. What is clear is that District 65 suffered a devastating defeat. The union's vote total declined to 387 from the 479 it received in the previous election. If, as the union claimed, 275 union members who voted in the first election were among those that had their ballots challenged, then its loss of support was even more dramatic.[25] (Such a claim, however, should be viewed with a good deal of skepticism. Unions, like most political organizations, have a tendency to overstate the amount of support they have.[26]) Local 153, which had never had much of a base at the university, garnered only 118 votes. All together, 926 workers voted against having any union.[27] Clearly, District 65 had failed to convince the employees at NYU that they needed a collective voice.

Although it is impossible to say exactly why the workers at NYU finally voted against unionization, an examination of the campaign literature of the various organizations involved with the election in June 1971 shows that the same concerns that animated workers at Frank Ix & Sons were present here as well, though with varying degrees of emphasis. Although strikes and strike violence were mentioned frequently in the Ix campaign, this concern was even more relevant to the workers at NYU. As at Ix, wages were also an important issue. In this case, however, we can see the actual evolution of a union's strategy away from articulating a broader vision of society and towards a much more narrow focus on workplace issues. Another similarity to Ix was the question of how the union would affect the work environment at NYU: would the union create a regimented, confrontational work environment or was unionism compatible with friendly, personal relations with supervisors? In an echo of the ACTWU's assurances that workers at Ix would not be unique in choosing to vote for a union, the question of whether unionization was appropriate for NYU employees also came up. In this case, though, the concern was not the result of an unfamiliarity with unions—New York, after all, had a higher union density than just about any other place in the United States, and NYU itself had relations with a number of unions—but with whether unions were appropriate for white-collar workers. Despite the very different set of workers involved, then, the same set of concerns about organized labor influenced the thinking of workers at NYU as they had at Ix.

Assessing the Prospects for and Consequences of Strikes

Talk of strikes was very prevalent. All together, three of NYU's nine letters to its employees prior to the election mentioned the possibility of a strike if they voted for a union. At the same time, District 65, in five of it's thirteen leaflets and letters distributed before the June election, tried to downplay the likelihood of a strike, claiming that talk about strikes was simply fearmongering by NYU. Local 153 also mentioned strikes in two of its five leaflets. Like District 65, they claimed that their union achieved good contracts without striking. They also claimed that District 65 was over-anxious to hit the picket lines.[28] In addition, one of the No-Union Committee's four leaflets was devoted entirely to the issue of strikes.

The amount of attention given to this issue was not simply part of the normal campaign literature seen in most organizing drives. Rather, it was especially relevant to the June 1971 election because of the recent strike by NYU maintenance workers. Both NYU and the No-Union Committee made much of the pay these men lost and would not be able to make up. For example, one letter from NYU to its employees claimed that "many employees have recently been asking 'if a union wins at NYU, is there much possibility that it will order me out on strike so that I may end up without pay for weeks on end?'" It's answer, as might be expected, was that "that possibility is extremely real."[29] The No-Union Committee was even more explicit, claiming that the typical maintenance man lost $2,000 in pay because of the strike. To the question: "How could we make up lost pay [due to a strike]," the committee flatly replied, "You can't!"[30] And if the example of the maintenance workers' strike was not enough to convince employees about the dangers unionization posed for their pay, the administration also pointed out that "District 65 has raised the possibility of ordering you to undertake 'joint walkouts' and other actions in sympathy with other University employees represented by other unions involved in labor disputes. That means you might be forced to give up even more pay."[31]

In their own defense, both District 65 and Local 153 claimed that they hardly ever called strikes. In fact, both unions claimed that 99 percent of their contracts were settled without resorting to a strike. As was typical in most organizing drives, the unions pointed out that a strike could happen only if a majority of the membership voted for one.[32] District 65 went even further, claiming that it would support binding arbitration to settle outstanding issues if contract negotiations reached an impasse. One letter, for example, tried to cast the onus of strikes squarely onto the shoulders of the university. It claimed that "the Administration has repeatedly brought up the question of strikes. Why are they so strike happy? We aren't. We believe most NYU employees would prefer arbitration in the event that contract negotiations stall at some point. Why doesn't the Administration ever discuss arbitration?"[33]

This disavowal of strikes by District 65 was quite a turnaround from its position just six months prior to the June election. In January 1971, for instance, a special membership meeting was called to decide whether the union should walk out in sympathy with the maintenance workers. (In this case, the union decided not to go on strike.)[34] And, of course, District 65 was responsible for the two-week strike in April 1970, which resulted in the first election held under the auspices of the SLRB.

That strike, as has already been mentioned, grew out of the frustration of the library workers who had been seeking union recognition for at least a year. As it spread to other departments, however, the union was able to capitalize on the sense of collective strength experienced by the workers who participated in it. Several leaflets and newsletters mentioned the sense of "power" these workers felt.[35] The union's message—"when people band together to secure basic rights, they cannot lose"[36]—seemed to carry special weight in the wake of the April strike.

With the passage of time, however, this sense of empowerment seemed to wane. In part this was due to the general state of exhaustion that set in following the turbulent decade of the 1960s. During the April strike, protests against the war in Vietnam mixed freely with protests against working conditions at NYU.[37] As American involvement in the fighting wound down, this general atmosphere of protest, especially on university campuses, seemed to fade. Likewise, the militance associated with the Civil Rights Movement waned as that struggle moved from the streets to the courtroom.[38] This transition could be seen in District 65's own leaflets and handouts. Whereas in 1970 the union made many references to its positions on women's rights, minority rights, and the war in Vietnam, by 1971 its appeals to workers were almost wholly couched in terms of wages and working conditions.

More important for the union, though, was the effect that employee turnover had in reducing the number of workers familiar with the sense of empowerment gained through the April strike. Already by December 1970, a union leaflet was addressed to new employees who were unfamiliar with the history of the NYU local.[39] By the time of the June election, of course, the failed strike by the maintenance men tempered any sense of what workers could accomplish through collective action, even among those who had participated in District 65's earlier walkout.

Thus, the union was left in a rather awkward position when it came to defending itself against the charge that it was all too eager to engage in strikes. Whereas its earlier willingness to confront the administration had been an asset, by the time of the election in June 1971, this history had become a liability. Indeed, not only NYU, but Local 153 as well, pointed to District 65's earlier strike in order to discredit it. Local 153, for obvious reasons, could not completely disavow the use of strikes. Yet even during the election in May 1970, when the university was largely silent, Local 153 labeled District 65's strike as irresponsible. As one leaflet put it, "If their idea of responsibility and militancy is to call a strike at the wrong time, in the wrong department, for the wrong reasons—who needs them?"[40] It repeated this charge during the June 1971 election, labeling District 65's strike as "needless" and "irresponsible."[41] NYU went further, in essence claiming that the strike had been illegal and amounted to little more than a thinly veiled display of thuggery:

> Only last spring, right here at NYU, District 65 called a strike that resulted in many clerical employees losing up to two weeks' pay despite the fact that it did not legally represent our employees. It might interest you to know that the "compelling" reason District 65 called the strike was to force the University to ignore the Labor Boards and agree to recognize District 65 as the representative of what it regarded as the "appropriate bargaining unit." The University did not accede to that type of coercion and District 65's position was subsequently rejected both by the New York State Labor Relations Board and by the National Labor Relations Board.[42]

In addition to the issue of lost pay, workers were also likely concerned by the specter of strike-related violence. Several acts of vandalism were associated with the strike by the maintenance men and accorded front-page treatment by the student newspaper.[43] NYU itself briefly referred to this violence in one of its letters to its employees.[44] During District 65's own strike, there had been a few acts of vandalism as well. Yet, at that time the university was careful to note that these were carried out by some radical students who were not connected to the union and that District 65 had disavowed these actions.[45] Even its mention of the vandalism during the maintenance worker strike was more of an aside than something that was prominently highlighted. This issue may have received so little attention in NYU campaign literature because the unions distanced themselves from the popular association of strikes and violence. As a District 65 organizer noted at one meeting, "Violence is going to make people anti-union and we cannot have that."[46] Nevertheless, because of the recent example of the maintenance workers strike, it is likely that at least some of this antiunion sentiment was created among NYU's employees.

From Social-Unionism to Business-Unionism

As in almost every union campaign, wages were a prominent issue in the NYU campaign. Starting with District 65's very first leaflet, nearly all of its letters and handouts discussed how the union would improve wages.[47] In fact, it appears that the very low pay for nonfaculty staff at NYU was the main reason the local was formed. Despite this focus on wages, however, when District 65's campaign began, the union presented itself as more than simply an economic institution. Instead, it portrayed itself as part of a broader social movement helping to reform American society. This emphasis on the more encompassing aspects of unionism, however, disappeared as the campaign progressed to the point where District 65 eventually appeared little different from the stereotypical business union.

In December 1969, when the campaign began, the minimum starting salary at NYU was only $80 a week.[48] According to District 65, this was $20 a week less than salaries for comparable jobs in private industry.[49] The university apparently agreed that these wages were too low, because by the time of the June 1971 election, the minimum starting salary had been raised to $100 a week, a 25 percent increase in the space of one year.[50] In addition to better wages, the union also agitated for a better health care package and for unemployment insurance (from which the university was exempt).

The university claimed that its wages were comparable to those paid at unionized colleges and universities, as well as those in private industry.[51] NYU also claimed that its benefits were generally superior to those in industry.[52]

The No-Union Committee repeated this claim. "Aren't the established wages, sick leave, vacations, holidays, etc., of NYU (at no union cost to us) equal to or better than the above unionized corporations [represented by District 65]," asked one of their flyers.[53]

Because the university was already paying union scale, then, it was unlikely that a union could improve salaries. In fact, District 65's talk about wage and benefit increases, according to both the university and the No-Union Committee, were just empty promises designed to win votes. "In every campaign, union organizers make a lot of statements and promises designed to win your vote," intoned one letter from NYU. "[O]nce the election is over, no one can require them to make good on their campaign promises."[54] Or as one of the No-Union Committees handouts summed it up, "Promises . . . Promises. That's all a union can offer you!"[55] Even Local 153 accused District 65 of making a bunch of "empty," "wild," and "radical" promises.[56]

NYU's assertion that its pay scale was at least as good as that at unionized colleges could only be made after it implemented a substantial salary increase in 1970. District 65 repeatedly pointed to this history and tried to take credit for that increase. For instance, one leaflet asked, "When did we ever get such big raises before? Not before there was a union on campus."[57] Another handout claimed that, "It is a matter of record that no increase was announced until the union organization was well underway, and there can be no doubt that the administration is using this device to convince people that their interests are being looked after."[58] Considering its lack of opposition to the initial organizing drive, it is unclear whether the university originally intended this salary increase to be an antiunion measure. By the time of the June 1971 election, however, it did use this raise as evidence that a union was not needed, just as District 65 had predicted it would.[59]

According to the university, because NYU was already matching a union pay scale, NYU employees were unlikely to improve their wages by voting for a union. On the other hand, due to the added cost of union dues, there was no question that they would lose money by voting for a union. Indeed, both the university and the No-Union Committee argued that the union's only real interest in the workers was as a potential source of income. "After all," one of NYU's letters to its employees claimed, "only by getting your vote can they also get your union dues money which is needed to pay their salaries."[60] It is ironic that the founders of the local District 65 unit had leveled this same charge against Local 153 when justifying their affiliation switch in 1969. "They're [Local 153] not really after the best interest of workers," one of the members of the District 65 local told a reporter for the student newspaper, "and would make any deal with the administration selling out the workers just to get more workers in their union."[61]

The costs of union membership versus the potential benefits thus became an issue of contention. In an attempt to reverse the usual argument about the cost of union representation, however, District 65 pointed out that while "[t]he Administration . . . talks about dues[, t]hey never mention what no union costs us." This letter explained how a nominal salary increase would far outweigh the cost of union dues.[62] Another handout reassured employees that they would not have to pay any dues until a contract was signed, "and you obviously would not sign a contract that didn't at least cover the cost of the dues."[63] And if this were not enough, another District 65 leaflet, "Dues We or Duesn't We," listed the nonsalary benefits union members received, such as a discount pharmacy, a credit union, training programs, an employment office for out-of-work members, and a newspaper.[64]

Not only did District 65 need to defend its dues structure from attacks by the university, it had to respond when Local 153 tried to place it on the defensive in this regard as well. For instance, several of Local 153's handouts pointed out that they, unlike District 65, did not have any "organizational fees, assessments, [or] fines."[65] Local 153 also contrasted its monthly dues, which were a flat $6, with those of District 65 which, "go up every time your earnings go up."[66] In its defense, District 65 claimed that it "does not have a flat dues rate as do most other unions because that type of arrangement discriminates against employees who earn less. Our dues are proportional to our earnings because our members have traditionally felt that this is the most democratic method of dues payment."[67] (It should be noted that most unions today base their dues on their members' earnings, typically assessing two hours pay per month. This method seems to have been implemented to keep up with inflation without having to go back to the membership for a dues increase every few years—a measure that was never popular—rather than because it was more "democratic.")

Although the issue of wages had been an important aspect of District 65's campaign from the start, in the spring and summer of 1970, the union had also given a great deal of attention to some of the broader social issues of the day, such as the war in Vietnam and the rights of minorities and women. By the time of the June 1971 election, however, the union had dropped all of its references to its stance on such issues as the war, race, and gender, and came to focus on issues related to the workplace. This may reflect the shock following the incident of May 8, 1970, when about two hundred unionized construction workers marched through the city's financial district, waving

American flags and beating up antiwar protestors. In light of this incident, the union may have decided that its support for radical politics might not appeal to NYU employees the way it had once thought it would.[68] Whatever the reason, by 1971 the union's leaflets and letters were confined to issues of wages and working conditions.

District 65 had long been associated with the left wing. It had been one of several unions that had withdrawn, or been expelled from, the CIO in the late 1940s over the issue of Communist domination. Although it is not clear, it appears that its president David Livingston was a party member. Though it later broke with the Communist party, the union continued to champion left-wing policies through the 1960s. It was particularly active in the area of civil rights, and its antiwar position prompted it to withdraw from the AFL-CIO in 1969.[69]

This history of left-wing activism was reflected in the union's initial pitch to NYU employees. For instance, in May of 1970 the union put out one leaflet devoted exclusively to a condemnation of Nixon's invasion of Cambodia; not once did this particular leaflet mention anything about the working conditions at NYU.[70] It also co-sponsored an antiwar rally in Washington Square in April 1970, along with such organizations as Chelsea-Village SANE, the City-Wide Coordinating Committee on Welfare Rights, the Freedom & Peace Party, the Greenwich Village Peace Center, the NYU Student Mobilization Committee, and Veterans for Peace in Vietnam.[71] And it demanded that the university administration give time off to its workers so that they could participate in antiwar protests.[72]

District 65 made much of its progressive stand on racial issues as well. When the clerical workers went on strike in April 1970, the cafeteria workers, perhaps inspired by District 65's action, staged a wildcat strike of their own. Though they belonged to a different union, District 65 weighed in on the side of these workers, condemning "N.Y.U's racist policy of paying the largely Black and Spanish speaking workers in the cafeterias below poverty wages."[73] In another instance, the union put out a leaflet that asserted that "District 65 will also fight to protect us from job discrimination. . . . We will fight for the end of racist hiring policies and for jobs and pay for our Black and Spanish-speaking brothers and sisters comparable to those of white workers."[74] And one of its contract demands was for the inclusion of Martin Luther King's birthday as a paid holiday.[75]

Reflecting the fact that it represented many female clerical workers, District 65 was also sensitive to women's issues. For instance, it provided free breast examinations and PAP tests for its members.[76] In 1970 it opposed the Equal

Rights Amendment (ERA), because it would eliminate many special protections for women workers. As one union flyer noted, "many jobs, mostly held by black and brown women, but also by other third world and white working class women, provide no protection even now."[77] (Although this position seems contrary to the Left's current position on the ERA, at that time, and dating back at least to the 1930s, conservatives supported the ERA precisely because it would eliminate protective labor legislation for women.[78]) In another example of the union's support for women's rights, one of its contract demands was for a day-care center at NYU.[79] In general, then, the union was supportive of feminist politics.

Not only was District 65 quick to point to its support of left-wing positions as a reason workers should support the union, it also went to some pains to disassociate itself from the AFL-CIO. One leaflet, designed to introduce new workers to the union, "What It's All About," was careful to point out that, "[b]ecause of its commitment to full multi-racialism in the labor movement; its vigorous campaign to organize all unorganized workers; and its firm stand for peace, District 65 has voted to disaffiliate from the AFL-CIO."[80]

Despite District 65's decision to drop any mention of these issues by the time of the June 1971 campaign, they resurfaced in Local 153's brochures. In this case, however, 153 pointed to District 65's politics as a reason workers should vote against District 65, not for it. The Office and Professional Employees International Union, Local 153's parent organization, had been formally chartered in 1945 as the AFL's alternative to the Communist-dominated Office and Professional Workers of America, which was affiliated with the CIO until it was expelled in 1950. From it beginnings, then, OPEIU had been offering itself as the noncommunist, nonradical alternative to left-wing rivals. In its contest with District 65 at NYU, it continued this tradition of appealing to workers based on its more conservative politics.[81] Thus, Local 153 spent a good deal of time castigating District 65's politics. As one leaflet put it, workers "want a union that will not only protect us in dealings with the University, but will protect us against the ravings and rantings of extremist groups, either right or left wing. The union that will not exploit us for political purposes, but is interested in our safety and well being is Local 153."[82] In fact, Local 153's main appeal to NYU employees was based on its claim to being "a responsible trade union, [not] a band, irresponsible, malicious, interested in violence and not our welfare."[83]

This embrace of "responsible unionism"—a phrase that was repeated in almost every one of Local 153's handouts—was not only a reflection of its more conservative politics, it was also part of an effort to assure NYU employees that unionism, and in particular Local 153's brand of unionism, was appropriate for them.[84] Thus, not only did Local 153 point to its extensive experience in representing white-collar workers (discussed in the following section), it also tried to create an image of itself that it felt such workers would be comfortable with. It then contrasted this image of a "responsible" union, with that of District 65, which it portrayed as "irresponsible, malicious, interested in violence" and more concerned with staging "radical demonstrations and needless strikes" than "help[ing] employees to gain better working conditions."[85]

What is most interesting about this aspect of District 65's initial campaign was the manner in which it diverged from the widespread and enervating impression that unions had lost their social-reformist vision and had become mere economic institutions. Yet, it is questionable whether the particular approach District 65 adopted was something that attracted many workers. First, although Local 153 garnered only one-third of the support District 65 did, its attacks on District 65's radicalism reflected its perception that the kind of reformist vision espoused by District 65 was not universally attractive. The OPEIU's long and persistent history of selling itself as a nonradical alternative to left-wing unions indicates that its vision of unionism was more in tune with at least some workers' views than District 65's portrayal of unionism. Second, it is also significant that District 65 itself decided to drop these types of appeals by the time of the June 1971 election.

Finally, we should consider the content of District 65's social-reform message. In the early part of the twentieth century, the issues that animated most reformers were concerned with the economic structure of society. The connection between organized labor and these concerns was clear and direct. By the 1970s thinking about a fundamental restructuring of America's economy had become marginalized. Even the left-wing District 65 failed to articulate such a vision in its communications with NYU employees. Instead, "social" issues dominated both the general discourse as well as District 65's own brand of social unionism. The connections between organized labor and questions of race, gender, and war, however, were much less direct. How, for instance, could an institution centered on workplace organization deal directly with issues of racial discrimination in housing and school funding other than by educating and exhorting its members and the public, something that many other types of organizations could engage in? What special provenance did organized labor have for addressing these issues? At the same time, as the rise of the Reagan Democrats in the 1970s also makes clear, the left-wing position on these issues ran counter to the views of many workers. A version of social unionism that strayed too far from issues of economic justice and an ethical structuring of the relations of production, in many ways seemed as unproductive as pure bread and butter unionism.

District 65's decision to drop these types of appeals in favor of a focus on wages did not mean, however, that it, or the workers involved with the union, saw this issue as simply a matter of economics. Rather, in some ways, the demand for higher wages and union recognition was part of a larger demand for greater respect from the university administration. The leaders of the NYU local, who were themselves university employees, felt the university treated its workers with "disdain and contempt" or, at best, in a "paternalistic" manner.[86] On several occasions the union charged the administration with treating workers as "boys and girls."[87] One thing these workers hoped to gain through collective bargaining was "[r]ecognition that we are responsible adults, competent to have a voice in our own affairs and in the university community."[88] Spokesmen for District 65 continually claimed that the union was needed to make "the University . . . treat their employees with the respect that is due them."[89] They resented their perceived status as second-class citizens when compared to students and professors. According to one handout, "students and faculty have 'privileges' which are denied to the rest of the staff."[90] "It is clear we are not considered part of the 'university community,'" was how another leaflet sarcastically phrased it.[91] The local went so far as to claim that the university "considers us to be its own property."[92] The only cure for this perceived disrespect was for workers to band together and confront the university as a united body. "The only time NYU showed any respect for the workers and listened to their grievances," according to one handout, "was when the workers in a collective action clearly displayed the power they have—during the April strike."[93]

In the end, it appears that the question of wages, even to the extent that this issue encompassed a broader meaning than simple economics, ended up working against the union rather than for it. The university's substantial salary increase in 1970 did much to reduce the salience of this issue. Not only that, it made it appear as if further salary increases could be expected without the cost of a union. And although District 65 tried to take credit for the increase, this claim probably did not carry as much weight as it might have if employee turnover had not been so high. Just as it had when it came to strikes, turnover worked against the union when it brought up the issue of wages. New employees, after all, would have no memory of NYU's pay scale before the organizing drive began. Moreover, the university's claim that it regularly granted wage increases every September would not only be credible to newer employees, but made it seem as if the last increase had been simply a result of standard policy.[94] And although some employees, in particular the leaders of the NYU local, may have felt disrespected by the university, as we shall see, many other workers, particularly those with the No-Union Committee had no problems with their treatment by the administration.

Strength (and Weakness) in Numbers

Another issue that all the parties concerned with the June election debated, though much less than wages or strikes, was how much support they had, both within the university as well as in other universities, and even in the broader white-collar field. As in many other organizing drives, the employer tried to portray the unions as marginal, and the unions tried to convince employees that they would be joining many other workers similar to themselves who had already made the choice to enroll in a union. At issue in this debate was not only the competence with which the unions could represent NYU's workers, but also whether union representation was appropriate for workers like themselves and the level of acceptance an NYU employee could expect by expressing either pro- or antiunion views.

Both Local 153 and District 65 tried to assure NYU employees that they would not be unique in choosing to join a union, and that their own union was especially well qualified to represent workers like themselves. "We know that you will decide to select a union that has experience in representing office and administrative employees," began one leaflet put out by Local 153. "You will select the union that has experience in representing non-profit and educational institutions. That union is Local 153."[95] District 65, in the handout "We are not Alone," went to even greater lengths to reassure employees that joining a union was common for white-collar workers:

All over the country white-collar workers are organizing and joining unions. . . . Just last Friday clerical and professional workers at the Museum of Modern Art voted 3 to 1 for union certification in our national union . . . Legal secretaries and clerks in such places as the New York Civil Liberties Union and Mobilization for Youth and private law firms; non-faculty staff at Fisk University and Hampton Institute [have joined District 65]. Elections are now pending at Yale University, the University of Chicago, and Temple University. Employees at Boston University and Brooklyn Polytechnic Institute have also sought union representation . . . A number of universities across the country have been organized by various unions. Parts of Columbia University have recently joined Local 1199. It is important to note that recent lay-offs there have occurred only in non-union offices. Clerical and secretarial workers at other schools including City College, New School, Stanford, and Berkeley have also unionized.[96]

These assertions, however, and especially those by District 65, did not go unchallenged. For instance, NYU, in a letter to its employees entitled "College and University office staffs have rejected unions," pointed out that the office workers at Boston University and Brooklyn Polytechnic, both of which District 65 had mentioned in its handout, had overwhelmingly voted against the union. "In fact," the letter went on, "aside from one small unit at an institution in Tennessee, District 65 does not represent the clerical, technical or administrative employees of any of the thousands of colleges and universities in this country." This repudiation of unionism went beyond just District 65, however. According to NYU,

> Not only have college and university clerical staffs rejected District 65, however; they have rejected other unions as well. For example, in July, 1970 the staff at Cornell University similarly rejected union representation and voted by an overwhelming margin (2335 to 634) in favor of "No Union." Local 153 also has been unsuccessful in several attempts to gain representation among office and clerical employees at colleges and universities. Like District 65, it also fails to represent office and clerical employees at more than one college or university.

The conclusion to be drawn from this history, as the university put it, was that "unions, especially District 65 and Local 153, do not have a viable, constructive program to offer employees and that employees realize this."[97]

Although Local 153 did not respond to this jab, it did repeat the university's charge that District 65 was unsuited to represent NYU employees. In one leaflet it claimed that District 65 has "no experience in representing large groups of administrative and office employees in educational and non-profit institutions. [It] Overwhelmingly lost elections within the last month at Brooklyn Polytech and Boston University."[98] In the leaflet "They Lie Again," Local 153 went even further in trying to discredit District 65:

> District 65, in recent leaflets, has purported to represent employees at Hampton Institute and Fisk University.
> At Hampton Institute they represent the grounds keepers. And so far have been unable to secure a contract.
> At Fisk University they have no contract. Because of their weakness they have been forced to go to arbitration.

Are you a groundskeeper?
Are you a teamster?
Are you an auto worker?
(Alliance for Labor Action, with which District 65 is affiliated represents these types of employees.)
Vote for experience[99]

Like the unions, the No-Union Committee also tried to reassure fellow workers that their own position was representative. For instance, one of their handouts listed the names and departments of thirty-five people who were members of the committee. The number of departments listed shows a clear attempt on the part of these workers to demonstrate their widespread support. The same flyer also claimed that "More than 200 employees have volunteered time, money and service to support us. It is unfortunate we cannot print everyone's name."[100] Clearly, the committee understood that it was important for employees who had their doubts about union representation to know that they were not alone. District 65 itself recognized the importance of keeping antiunion workers silent to help generate an atmosphere that was favorable to the union. David Livingston, president of District 65, told a group of NYU workers before the first election in May 1970, "I have no doubt . . . we will win the election, because I don't believe the University will campaign against the union, and there is no clear-cut organized worker opposition. You're working in a climate and atmosphere which is generally pro-union."[101] Thus, the appearance of a No-Union Committee, when combined with the active opposition of the university, was a tremendous blow to District 65's efforts to maintain a pro-union climate. No longer would workers who opposed the union feel isolated and demoralized. Instead, they would be free to voice their antiunion opinions in the expectation that others would agree with them, making it possible for a decidedly antiunion climate to be created in which union supporters would be the ones who were ostracized.

"Direct Negotiations" versus "Having a Say"

One of the reasons the university claimed a union was not appropriate for NYU employees was the effect unionism would have for workers' relationship to each other and their supervisors. According to the administration, by bringing in an "outsider" NYU employees would no longer be able to deal directly with their supervisors. Instead, "close personal contact often gives way to the requirements of a formal union relationship," was how one letter portrayed the consequences of having union representation.[102] Another letter warned employees that by voting for a union, "You lose: Your right to confidential, individual consideration of your grievances and problems. Often under union contracts, you are not permitted to discuss your grievances individually and confidentially with your supervisor. Rather you are generally required to discuss your problems only through the union representative or in his presence."[103]

This picture of a union as an outsider that would break up the special relations workers had with their supervisors also featured prominently in the organizing drive at Frank Ix & Sons. In the case of NYU, it was not nearly as central to the employer's antiunion message. Yet it is interesting to see that such very different employers could appeal to the same apprehension that workers might have about how a union would substitute rules and bureaucracy for flexibility and friendship. That this was a real fear on the part of employees, and not just something invented by NYU, was reflected in a District 65 leaflet that directly addressed the question: "How will collective bargaining affect office relationships at NYU?" The union's answer was that "[t]here is no reason why personal relationships should change in any office at the university because of collective bargaining."[104] The fact that this handout was prepared and distributed in late 1970, long before the university had begun its antiunion campaign, indicates that even without the prompting of the employer, employees were already worried about how a union would affect their relationships at work.

District 65 not only tried to allay workers' fears about how the union would affect their work environment, it also tried to make the case that NYU employees currently suffered from the ills of bureaucracy and impersonal treatment. As one handout claimed, "We need the N.Y.U. Local because we work for a large bureaucratic organization which has proven insensitive to the individual or group needs of its workers."[105] According to the union, to overcome this insensitivity, NYU employees needed a collective voice loud enough to overcome the university's deafness. "We know, from the experience of other groups in the academic community, that the Administration is ready to deal with those who speak with a united voice."[106] In one leaflet after the other the union claimed that its primary purpose was to provide employees with a voice, which, according to the District 65, they did not have when dealing with the administration one on one.[107] "Having a union means having a voice," was how one of these handouts summarized the meaning of unionism.[108] In addition, the union claimed that only through unionization would workers gain the respect they deserved: "The only time NYU showed any respect for the workers and listened to their grievances," according to one handout, "was when the workers in a collective action clearly displayed the power they have—during the April strike."[109]

While the union hurled charges of disrespect at the university, NYU fought back by accusing the union of being an outside force, a third party, in which employees would have little role "apart from paying dues, manning picket lines and following the dictates of the union leadership."[110] "Before you cast your vote, look around you," urged one letter. "Who is actively pushing the union? Are they the individuals whom you consider to be capable of handling your problems and into whose hands you are now ready to entrust your future and your affairs?"[111] Did employees really want to be forced to "discuss their problems through, or at least in the presence of, an outsider from the union" instead of dealing directly with their supervisor? "Don't trade a relationship that you understand and that has been steadily improving for a costly deception."[112] To cap off these messages, the university warned its employees that this leap into the unknown was irrevocable: "Once a union wins an election and enters into a contract, it is almost impossible to get rid of the union no matter how dissatisfied you may have become."[113]

District 65 responded to these attacks by denying that it was an outside institution and emphasizing its local origins. "The N.Y.U. local was organized and has been controlled from the beginning by clerical and technical employees of N.Y.U. . . . The N.Y.U. local of District 65 is not a third party seeking to interfere in university affairs, but is the organized voice of N.Y.U. workers," one leaflet reassured employees. The reason the local unit affiliated with District 65 was "to gain experience and strength."[114] Another letter pointed out that, "Those of us who are active in District 65 are your co-workers as you know from seeing us on campus."[115] "The NYU Local of District 65 was created by NYU employees, is composed of NYU employees, and is run by NYU employees," claimed yet another letter. "We have been here for two years and are a well-known part of the University community."[116] And if this were not enough to establish the union's bona fides, it also pointed to an endorsement by the late Dr. Martin Luther King Jr. In a handout entitled "Can you trust *this* union?" District 65 proudly claimed that Dr. King had labeled the union "the conscience of the labor movement" and had contrasted it favorably with the big international unions of the AFL-CIO.[117]

A major part of the university's campaign, then, centered on portraying the union as an alien institution—a busybody sticking its nose into other peoples' affairs and, in the process, breaking up well-established relationships and replacing them with rules, rigidity, and impersonal treatment. NYU sought to capitalize on its white-collar workers' unfamiliarity with—or stereotypes of—unionism by making District 65 seem like a risky proposition. Most of all it asked workers if they could trust the union—was it really interested in their welfare, or just their dues money? For its part, the union tried to reassure the workers that it was not an outsider but composed of, and run by, NYU employees. Moreover, it belittled the idea that workers could accomplish anything on an individual basis. It claimed that the university ignored its workers' needs and even treated them with contempt. The only cure for this state of affairs, according to the union, was for workers to band together to gain a voice loud enough that the university would pay attention to their demands.

Unions and Democracy

Another issue that received some attention was that of union democracy. For instance, the university warned

> What role will you have in their union apart from paying dues, manning picket lines and following the dictates of the union leadership? You can't become an officer of the union for at least a year, according to the latest constitution District 65 has filed with the New York office of the U.S. Department of labor (Article F-2). The union has broad authority over your affairs. While you can vote in the local, the entire local's vote can be overridden by the Union's General Council (Article C). And if the union decides that you've violated the laws of the Union or otherwise acted in a way "detrimental to the welfare of the Union," District 65 can impose on you "such penalties as the best interest of the union may warrant (Part VI. Section 5)."[118]

Likewise, Local 153 could draw on the stereotype of undemocratic unions to warn workers against voting for District 65, "a union which equates dictation with representation."[119]

The most forceful warning about the lack of union democracy came not from the university, Local 153, or even the No-Union Committee, however. Rather, a worker who identified himself only as "JR, an NYU clerical employee" addressed a letter entitled "What Unions do TO You" to his fellow workers which, apparently, was meant to be posted on bulletin boards around the campus. JR opened his letter by warning that "Unions, by virtue of government legislation, *strip the individual worker of practically all volition regarding his or her job.*" He then went on to invoke many of the popular accusations about the evils of closed-shop contracts and the consequences of union monopoly:

Once a union gets 51 percent of the workers to vote for it, all workers within this individual union's jurisdiction MUST join it. The worker cannot decide for himself if union membership is worth the dues; he must belong, he must pay dues, and he must strike if the union says, "We go out!" He must join the union or he is out. . . . Not only must the worker join a union, he must join one particular union. No matter how irrational the union leadership is, no matter how much a bunch of bully-boys they might be, no matter how high the dues, you must join one particular union. You might conceivably, of course, be joining a most rational, benign, and beneficent union, but how many unions have you heard of which are so disposed?

According to JR, the most serious problem with a closed-shop contract would come when the union decided to call a strike. Referring to the failed maintenance worker strike, he warned that, "the worker must servilely accept his union's decisions when he can only either belong to one particular union or lose his job (or scab); do you think that ALL the maintenance workers wanted to stay out on strike for four months, losing four months pay?" He then closed his letter with an appeal to vote for "no union": "A vote to unionize is IRREVOCABLE. Let all clerical workers reflect on their work conditions, wages, and fringe benefits. Are they that bad that they warrant a final decision to vote away freedom of choice regarding their jobs?"[120]

NYU Antiunionism

The one truly unique feature of the organizing drive at NYU was District 65's oft-repeated accusation that the university was antiunion. Talk about strikes, relative wages, union dues, the union as an outsider, and so on, were common in almost any union campaign. To find a union harping on an employer's alleged antiunionism, on the other hand, at least from the 1970s on, was almost unheard of. Employer opposition to unionism, after all, could be taken as a given. If the Textile Workers Union had repeatedly charged Frank Ix & Sons with being antiunion, for instance, it is hard to imagine that this would have had any effect on either the employer or the employees. This aspect of District 65's campaign says a great deal about the special nature of both its opposition and the employees it was seeking to organize.

District 65's primary motivation for using this antiunion charge was to keep the university at least neutral during its organizing effort. As the union recognized, its membership drive would more likely meet with success if NYU remained silent than if the university came out strongly against the union.

Therefore, District 65 attempted to intimidate the university into keeping quiet by threatening to smear it with an antiunion label. That such a tactic was even feasible was due to the special nature of NYU as an employer. In addition to being a nonprofit, quasi-public institution, which, presumably, made its attitude towards unions more benign than that of antiunion employers in the private sector, NYU also prided itself, as the union claimed, on its "liberal public image."[121] As an example, NYU's Law School, with the approval of university president Hester, canceled classes and postponed finals in May 1970 to allow students and professors to participate in antiwar protests.[122] Inherent in this liberal image was support for workers' right to organize. Even the most strident critics of unions found it necessary to qualify their criticism with the disclaimer that they were not antiunion. How much more so, then, did an institution that wanted to be seen as progressive, strive to not appear intrinsically opposed to organized labor.

Although District 65's attempt to intimidate the university into a neutral stance was ultimately unsuccessful, it did seem to achieve its purpose during the early stages of the campaign. For instance, NYU did not campaign against the union during the May 1970 election. It even went to some pains to point out "that New York University has recognized and worked amiably with labor unions in other areas for over thirty years."[123] Therefore, according to the university, the charge of being antiunion was unfair. By the time of the June 1971 election, however, despite the union's continued use of the antiunion accusation, NYU no longer felt any constraints in its campaign against the union.

The other aspect of District 65's use of the antiunion label was its effort to generate sympathy for the union, both among workers and the university faculty, who could bring pressure to bear on the administration to not oppose the union's organizing drive. Pamphlets included titles such as "Union busting is a non-credit course at NYU" or shouted in bold letters, "NYU is trying to break our union."[124] These were clearly designed to tap into whatever sympathy the public still felt for organized labor in the early 1970s and to rally workers and public opinion to the side of the union. The university's location in Greenwich Village, one of the most heavily unionized and politically liberal communities in the United States, no doubt made this tactic more likely to succeed. In the end, however, District 65 was unable to overcome the suspicions that many workers harbored about unions, despite their support for organized labor in the abstract.

* * *

District 65's failed effort to organize the clerical workers at New York University is remarkable for several reasons. Despite the wide gulf that separated the workers at NYU from those at Frank Ix & Sons, the similarities in these campaigns greatly outweighed the differences. Both employers sought to capitalize on the widespread impression that unions were bureaucratic, work-rule bound organizations that would regiment working life instead of providing the flexibility workers wanted. Though to differing degrees, both employers claimed that this would mean that "close personal contact [would] give way to the requirements of a formal union relationship."[125] In both campaigns the employers played up the possibilities of strikes occurring and what they would mean for lost pay. In the case of NYU, however, the threat of firing striking workers was never mentioned. On the other hand, both Ix and NYU drew on the widespread belief that unions were undemocratic organizations to warn employees that they would have little role "apart from paying dues, manning picket lines and following the dictates of the union leadership."[126] And in what was a standard part of any union campaign, both employers tried to fend off the union by claiming that employees were already receiving wages equivalent to union pay scales and would end up paying union dues for no monetary gain whatsoever if they unionized.

Despite these similarities, the campaign at NYU differed from that at Ix in two significant ways. First, NYU's campaign, though intense, never descended to the level of threats and intimidation resorted to by Ix. Never did the nonprofit university claim that it would be forced to shut down because of the lower profitability a union contract might cause. And at no time did the university threaten to fire anyone for union activities or tighten up on work discipline because of the organizing drive. Instead, NYU confined itself to letters, bulletins, and meetings with employees.

The second major difference was the organized nature of employee opposition to the union at NYU. Although many workers opposed the union at Ix, they did so mostly as individuals. The closest approach to concerted antiunion activity was one worker's efforts to get her coworkers to sign a letter to their senators and representatives complaining about the labor board being biased in favor of the union. At NYU, on the other hand, in addition to individual initiative, such as that by JR, a group of workers created a formal organization to oppose unionization.

This last point is perhaps most surprising considering the location of NYU in the heart of one of the most politically liberal and most heavily unionized cities in all of America. Although District 65, tried to draw on the favorable, pro-union environment in New York to bolster its position, even in this citadel of organized labor there were workers who were so bitterly opposed to unionism that they actively sought, in an organized fashion, to dissuade their fellow employees from voting for a union. Although it is impossible to say exactly what the source of this antiunionism was, it seems probable that America's antiunion culture played an important role in turning these workers against the union. Even if the origins of this antiunionism cannot be ascertained with absolute certainty, however, what is clear is that both NYU and the No-Union Committee drew on the images of this antiunion culture to bolster their case against District 65.

6

The Union that Wasn't
Organizing White-Collar Professionals

If there was any segment of the work force for which America's anti-union culture had its greatest impact in impeding organized labor's ability to expand it was among white-collar professionals. In addition to the general stereotypes about labor, which were applicable to everyone—its oppression of workers, its violation of the norms of meritocracy, its affinity for straight-jacketing work routines with rigid union rules and job classifications, and so on—there was the more specific image of unions as being unsuited for white-collar workers. For instance, most Americans believed that by joining a union a white-collar worker would suffer a drastic loss in prestige. In addition, unionism, with its worker-centered focus on improving wages and working conditions, was seen to violate the ethic of selflessness embodied in the ideology of professionalism, in which the needs of the client came first. Furthermore, it was precisely these workers who were the bearers of the "dominant culture," as C. Wright Mills put it.[1] Thus, a study of how one group of professionals, in this case public school teachers, responded to union organizing drives can provide a better understanding of how unions' place in American culture has affected their ability to organize.

In the context of this study, the teachers' situation was unique, not just because of their position as professionals, but also because of their nominally high rate of unionization. Unlike union density in the private sector, which entered into a period of sustained decline beginning in the 1950s, public employee unionism grew spectacularly starting in the 1960s. A significant portion of this growth was among public school teachers. In 1960 the American Federation of Teachers (AFT) and the National Education Association

(NEA)—the two major groups representing teachers—had about 775,000 members between them; by 1970 this figure had grown to over 1.3 million. By 1985, the AFT claimed over 600,000 members, and the NEA boasted of 1.7 million members.[2] Even these numbers, however, understate the growth of unionism among teachers. In 1960 only a handful of school districts had collective bargaining agreements with their employees. Moreover, the NEA of the early '60s, whose membership of 715,000 dwarfed the AFT's 60,000, specifically eschewed collective bargaining and would have been appalled if anyone had referred to it as a union.[3]

One significant reason for the divergent trajectories followed by unions for public employees and unions in the private sector was the high degree of tolerance federal and state governments had for collective bargaining. In 1962, with the promulgation of Executive Order 10988 (Employee-Management Cooperation in the Federal Service), federal policy shifted from one of "tolerance and benign neglect . . . to an activist and decisive policy encouraging the formation of unions and the commencement of collective bargaining." This shift in policy, according to Leo Troy, was then "emulated by many states and local governments."[4] Thus, whereas employers in the private sector engaged antiunion consultants to advise them on how to avoid unionization, employers in the public sector, who in many cases were forced to seek the votes of the very people they employed, were largely silent, if not accommodating, when unions sought to organize their workers.

In addition, much of this unionization resulted from the transformation of preexisting employee associations into formal unions. The NEA, for instance, had been around since 1886 and until 1971 had enrolled principals and school administrators as well as teachers. Even those organizations that did identify themselves as unions, such as the AFT and the American Federation of State, County and Municipal Employees (AFSCME) eschewed strikes and collective bargaining agreements, two of organized labor's most basic tools, and concentrated instead on lobbying. Unlike organized labor's efforts to gain membership in the private sector, then, a large portion of these "new" union members were already organized by extant associations that either were opposed to unionism (as in the case of the NEA) or were unions in name only (until, that is, the 1960s). Leo Troy has referred to this process as "organizing the organized," which he contrasts with the history of private sector unions which were forced to organize the unorganized.[5]

Because of these differences, when teachers voted for a union representative, explicit "no union" votes were minuscule. The absence of such votes during these elections, however, does not mean that they were especially receptive to unionism. (It is no doubt revealing that the "no union" option was listed on ballots as "no representative.") Therefore, unlike in previous cases, where the competition for worker loyalty was between employer and union, here the contest is between two unions. Yet even though it was two unions facing off against each other, this does not mean that an antiunion position was absent. Instead, the pro-NEA position during the mid-1970s became a stand-in for the antiunion sentiment that would have been expressed as a "no union" vote in a private sector bargaining election. As the NEA explained, the fundamental difference between the NEA and the AFT is that the Association "is a professional organization" whereas the AFT "is a labor-oriented union."[6] In effect, the NEA, which is now the nation's largest single union, attempted to fend off the challenge of the AFT by appealing to teachers' antiunion sentiments.

It is instructive to see not only the NEA's explicit antiunion stance, but also how the AFT played on the popular image of organized labor to either support its own cause or to undermine the position of its opponent. Although the AFT was not ashamed to call itself a union and went so far as to claim that its affiliation with the AFL-CIO was an asset rather than a liability, it was not above drawing on the negative stereotypes of organized labor to smear the NEA. Thus, a study of the rivalry between the NEA and the AFT may be at least suggestive of the extent to which unions themselves were responsible for propagating and making use of the many negative attitudes Americans held with respect to organized labor.

"Professionals Do Not Belong with Workers"

In contests between the AFT and the NEA for teacher support, two issues were of central importance: professionalism and the question of which organization was better able to advance the welfare of its members. The issue of organizational effectiveness will be dealt with in a later section. In this section, the issue of professionalism will be examined to see how it affected teachers' response to both the NEA and the AFT. Both organizations were conscious of the desire of teachers to be seen and treated as professionals; they crafted their appeals accordingly. In addition, each organization developed along differing trajectories based on their changing understanding of how best to represent professionals.

Until the 1960s the NEA had been strictly a professional association with a membership that encompassed teachers, principals, and school superintendents, that is, both workers and management. Were it not for the challenge by the AFT during the 1960s, it is doubtful the NEA would have ever developed into a full-fledged union. In an effort to preserve and expand its membership, however, the NEA gradually came to embrace the idea of collective bargaining. At first, collective bargaining was referred to euphemistically as "professional negotiations."[7] By 1971, with the exit of school superintendents from the association, who were increasingly wary of the NEA's move towards outright acceptance of collective bargaining and the propriety of teacher strikes, the NEA's transformation into a recognizable union was well advanced. This recognition became official when the association was forced by the government to register with the Department of Labor in 1980 as a labor organization under the terms of the Landrum-Griffin Act. As Wayne Urban notes, the transformation of the NEA from professional organization to trade union did not simply stop with the adoption of collective bargaining for its members. Instead, the association had gone so far down the union path that Robert Chase was elected president in 1996 on a platform of "'new unionism' in which the NEA would attend to teachers' professional needs as well as to their salaries and benefits."[8]

Whereas the NEA went from professional association to militant trade union, the AFT trod the opposite path. From its founding in 1916 the AFT had made no bones about its trade union goals, and early on became affiliated with the AFL. As David Selden, president of the AFT from 1968 to 1974, put it, "We are a union first, then an educational association."[9] Following the ascendency of Albert Shanker to the presidency in 1974, however, the strictly trade union orientation of the AFT began to change. More and more the AFT came to concern itself with professional issues such as teacher certification and education reform. According to Urban, by the mid-1980s the AFT came to be perceived as more concerned with professional issues than the NEA.[10] In 1983, for instance, the AFT boasted that a "Rand report recently analyzed the strength and weaknesses of NEA and AFT. AFT was found to be the most professional organization of the two. AFT not only negotiates increased salaries and benefits for teachers but negotiates more items in their contracts dealing with curriculum changes, special classes for students of varying abilities, innovative teaching ideas, provisions for teacher/pupil, principal/parent committees, etc."[11]

The 1970s, then, were a time of transition for both organizations. In appealing to teachers for support, the NEA could draw on its long history as a professional association to generate trust and goodwill. As Phil Kugler, AFT assistant to the president for the organization, explained in a letter to the president of the California Federation of Teachers, "one of the difficulties we all have in building our union . . . is the almost blind faith in the Association as the 'professional organization' that exists in the minds of many teachers."[12] The AFT, on the other hand, found it difficult to overcome the "strong, irrational . . . bias against unions" on the part of teachers, as Raoul Teilhet, president of the California Federation of Teachers, wrote in a 1982 letter.[13] As expressed in a newsletter by the Sarasota County (FL) Teachers Association advocating the affiliation of the local association with the AFT, many teachers feel "a tremble in [their] stomach when [they] hear the word 'union.'"[14]

This "strong, irrational bias," this "tremble in the stomach," was based on teachers' fears that membership in a union would threaten their middle-class status. In the cultural universe of teachers, "professionals d[id] not belong with workers," as one local union newsletter summarized the attitude of many teachers.[15] Although "the AFL-CIO is good for tradesmen and industrial workers," an NEA representative intoned, the association was the proper organization for "educators."[16] "If I had wanted to be a member of the AFL-CIO, I would have picked another line of work," was how one teacher put it.[17] Selden summarized this attitude among teachers in his memoirs, "Professionals were upper class; nonprofessionals were working class. Professionals received salaries or fees; nonprofessionals worked for wages. Professionals worked with their brains; nonprofessionals used their hands and bodies. Professionals were clean; nonprofessionals were dirty. In short, professionals belonged to professional associations, and nonprofessionals belonged to unions."[18] Thus, the fact that the AFT made no pretense that it was anything other than a union was enough to turn off many teachers.

The popular terms used for the two organizations showed the NEA's linguistic advantage over the AFT in this regard. The NEA was referred to as the "association," whereas the AFT was called the "union." This terminology was reflected not only in both NEA and AFT literature, but also in scholarly writing about the two organizations.[19] As an example of how this terminology could be employed in the context of a representation election, in a 1976 campaign in Cincinnati the local association invariably referred to its AFT opponent as "local 1520" or even "AFL-CIO local 1520."[20] If this were not enough to drive home the point, the NEA affiliate put out one flyer that made the contrast explicit: "The basic difference between CTA [Cincinnati Teachers Association] and Local 1520 is that the Association is a professional organization. . . . By comparison, Local 1520 is a labor-oriented union."[21] Even the local newspapers pointed to this difference. For instance, the *Cincinnati Post* described the CTA as "a non-union association," and the *Cincinnati Enquirer* noted that "[v]ictory for the CFT [Cincinnati Federation of Teachers] marks the first time ever teachers in the Cincinnati school district have been formally represented by a union affiliated with the AFL-CIO."[22] (By the mid-1980s, however, reflecting the NEA's gradual transformation, the association would come to openly embrace the "union" label, not only in an urban school district like Washinton, D.C., but also in a rural setting like Lake County, Florida.[23])

Although its self-identification as a labor union hurt the AFT's appeal for teacher support, its affiliation with the AFL-CIO was an even greater detriment. All of these references to the AFL-CIO rather than the AFT were, of course, no accident. By talking about the AFL-CIO rather than the AFT, the NEA greatly reinforced the identity between the AFT and unionism. But the federation's ties to the AFL-CIO did more than just strengthen its image as a "labor-oriented union." If the AFT had been an independent union, teachers' response to its overtures would have been much less skeptical. Instead, affiliation raised the specter that this "teachers' union" was controlled by the AFL-CIO, with its "blue-collar orientations, values, and status."[24] William Carr, executive director of the NEA during the 1950s and '60s, gave voice to this fear when he warned the 1964 convention that if "the AFL-CIO . . . triumphed over the NEA, teachers could expect to live under an 'Iron Curtain' of labor control." As Marjorie Murphy notes, "In keeping with NEA tradition, Carr never mentioned the AFT [in this speech], which was, after all, the actual source of the challenge to the NEA. The NEA always treated the AFT as though it were a satellite, independent in name only."[25] A cartoon entitled "You Compare," included in an NEA handout, provides a graphic example of this tendency. The AFT is shown as a child next to the fat and ignorant AFL-CIO; as a local union rep exclaims "meet my union bosses." The NEA, on the other hand, is represented by clean-cut lobbyists in suits, who are carrying that ultimate symbol of professionalism, the briefcase.[26]

The issue of AFL-CIO domination was constantly raised by the NEA and continually refuted by the AFT. For instance, one NEA representative claimed that "[o]ne man dominates the AFL-CIO . . . George Meany . . . makes the big decisions, runs the convention with an iron hand and sets the tone and the image of the organization."[27] The implication, of course, was that none of the unions affiliated with the AFL-CIO had a voice in setting their own policies, much less those of the federation. One teacher was especially forceful in his denunciation of AFL-CIO domination: "If I had wanted to be a member of the AFL-CIO, I would have picked another line of work. I didn't—and the idea of some lackey from the office of a union boss issuing directives to me, just doesn't sell."[28] In addition, affiliation with the AFL-CIO meant that

Professionalism versus unionism. "You Compare," 1980, box 8, folder Fact Booklet, Papers of the AFT Southern Region.

AFT—and by implication its membership—suffered from the same unappealing image as that organization.

The AFT, naturally, attempted to counter such claims. One fact sheet distributed by the union asserted, "If the fear of control explains the NEA's objection to affiliation . . . we can offer proof that organizations affiliated with the AFL-CIO are independent." It then went on to show how several unions in the federation had taken stances on various issues in opposition to AFL-CIO policy.[29] As another example, the Sarasota County (FL) Teachers Association, in addressing the fears its members might have about their local association affiliating with the AFT, rhetorically asked: "Can the AFT or the AFL-CIO force us to do anything?" Its categorical answer: "No."[30]

Along with the concern about domination by "union bosses" was the related fear that teachers' interests would be submerged within the predominantly blue-collar AFL-CIO. A flyer used by the NEA in the 1976 Cincinnati campaign reminded teachers that, "[t]he AFT is an affiliate of the AFL-CIO which is not controlled by teachers." As a result, "[w]hen the interests of teachers do not coincide with those of organized labor, teachers take second place."[31] In another instance, an NEA spokesman claimed, "The more than 100 AFL-CIO affiliates with workers in the private sector have more in common with one another than they have with one affiliate of school-teachers."[32] In contrast, "NEA is run by and for teachers and other school employees. . . . We in the NEA believe that teachers deserve an organization of their own— an organization that puts teachers first, foremost and always."[33]

Teachers did not just "take second place" within the AFL-CIO, however. According the NEA, the federation was positively antiteacher. A flyer entitled "Straight talk about . . . AFL-CIO" put out by the Wichita, Kansas, affiliate of the NEA, for instance, claimed, "Many AFL-CIO leaders are virulently anti-teacher. . . . The AFL-CIO not only condemns teachers: it often fights against teacher goals. . . . the AFL-CIO often opposes more money for the public schools."[34] In another instance, a fact sheet by the NEA, more moderate in tone but with a similar message, answered the question, "Why isn't NEA in the AFL-CIO?" with the assertion that, "many of the interests, programs and goals of the AFL-CIO are in conflict with those of the NEA and its members."[35] Another, cruder, example of this attitude is seen in the "You Compare" cartoon examined previously, in which the figure of the AFL-CIO blurts out "What's education?"

More troublesome for teachers than the AFL-CIO's attitude towards education, however, was its poor public image, which, it was believed, would rub off on them should they join its affiliate, the AFT. According to one report by the union, "NEA propaganda portrays the labor movement as a collection of gangsters, goons, and illiterates, ruled over by dictatorial, know-nothing leaders who are opposed to the cause of public education."[36] For instance, at the 1972 convention, Sam Lambert, the NEA's executive secretary, claimed that the only way to become the president of a union was to be the son of a president, and that once elected most union leaders would have a lifetime tenure because of the lack of democracy in the labor movement.[37] Another NEA spokesman claimed that the AFL-CIO "lacks commitment to social change . . . There has been very little motion within the organization to assist minorities and other groups and individuals who have been left out of real participation."[38] (The charge that the AFL-CIO and, especially, the AFT, which had led the controversial Ocean Hill–Brownsville strike, were "racist" and unwilling to "assist minorities" was an issue that would surface in many contests between these two unions; it will be examined in more detail in following sections.) The implication of these sorts of accusations, of course, was that unions were perhaps appropriate for the Archie Bunkers of the world, but were not appropriate for middle-class professionals.

The poor public image of the AFL-CIO would do more than just tarnish the claim of teachers to be professionals, however. It had pragmatic, bread-

and-butter consequences as well. As one NEA leaflet pointed out to teachers, "Even if it were true that belonging to the AFL-CIO would give us 'allies,' it would also alienate many other people."[39] The NEA cited polling data to show that "the public doesn't like the AFL-CIO . . . By contrast, the NEA scores very high. . . . 'NEA is one of the two most respected and popular unions' in the country."[40] Allying with the AFL-CIO, then, would damage the NEA's ability to get favorable legislation passed, both at the state and federal level. For example, "[i]f being part of the AFL-CIO meant anything at all," pointed out a leaflet from the Wichita affiliate of the NEA, "it would mean something in New York, which has the largest of all the state AFL-CIO's. . . . But AFT and AFL-CIO have been entirely unable to repeal New York's anti-strike law— the harshest in the nation—which penalizes teachers two days' pay for each day they're on strike." Indeed, according to the same flyer, the NEA actually had more political clout than the federation. "In Washington," it went on to explain, "NEA and AFL-CIO went head-to-head on the Department of Education. NEA won; AFL-CIO lost."[41] (The AFT and the AFL-CIO had opposed the creation of a cabinet level Department of Education, whereas this had been one of the NEA's goals since the early part of the twentieth century. The AFL-CIO and, to an even greater extent, the AFT had been worried that such a position could be used by conservatives to attack education, which quickly proved to be the case when President Reagan appointed William Bennett as his secretary of education.[42])

To counter such attacks, the AFT claimed that the AFL-CIO was "100 percent on teachers issues versus the NEA's 30 percent." It highlighted various education issues that the AFL-CIO supported and the NEA opposed.[43] In addition, the AFT continually reminded teachers that organized labor had been one of the earliest supporters of public education.[44] It also asserted that its membership in the AFL-CIO gave it political "allies." As we have just seen, however, this assertion was easily countered by the NEA.

The AFT did more than simply try to assure teachers that it was not dominated by AFL-CIO "union bosses," or that the AFL-CIO was not antieducation. It went to some length to show that it could represent teachers as professionals. The union liked to remind teachers that both John Dewey and Albert Einstein had been members.[45] It also sponsored workshops on teaching issues, such as "Classroom Management" and "Teaching the Learning Disabled Child," to "convince teachers that the AFT is, indeed, a professional organization."[46] Among the campaign slogans considered for a 1976 Cincinnati campaign were such choices as "CFT, the professionals"; "CFT, the professional organization"; and "CFT, making the profession secure."[47] By 1983 the union could point to a Rand report purporting to show that the

AFT was "the most professional organization of the two."[48] And in response to the charge that the AFL-CIO was for "tradesmen and industrial workers," the AFT pointed out that among those represented by AFL-CIO unions were "professional actors, artists, airline pilots, musicians (including the New York Philharmonic . . .), television and radio personalities, engineers, doctors, dentists, lawyers, college professors and other professionals."[49]

The AFT also began to focus more on the problems facing the teaching profession as a profession, not just bread-and-butter issues. For instance, in the early 1980s, in response to a government report criticizing the state of education in America, the union came out in support of teacher competency tests. As President Albert Shanker put it, "We require physicians, attorneys and others to pass exams before they are licensed. We should hold our own profession to the same high standards."[50] Such a stance was prefigured in statements made by AFT organizers during the 1970s, countering the NEA's assertion that affiliation with the AFL-CIO meant the AFT was unprofessional. According to one such organizer, "to those teachers who say that professionals do not belong with workers, I say that we should foster a professionalism of competence, not snobbery."[51] Teacher competency tests were obviously a step in this direction. By contrast, the NEA came out against such tests. Its position on this issue was based on its concern about the impact competency tests would have on minorities. In fact, it pointed to the AFT's support of such tests as evidence for its claim that the AFT was racist.[52] Nevertheless, this stance seemed to contradict the association's previous assertion that "the fundamental goal of associational activity was the assurance for teaching of its 'rightful place among the professions.'"[53]

Although nonmonetary issues, such as competency tests and teacher workshops, may have played a role in a teacher's understanding of what made an occupation a profession, the issue of pay was an equally, if not more, significant component. As the AFT claimed in one flyer, "Professionalism is measured as much by economic status as by anything else." Although this flyer listed the AFT's support for such "professional" goals as "a well-ordered school environment with full administrative support for student discipline; enforceable class size maxima; adequate guidance and psychological services for all pupils; and fully-funded programs in art, music and physical education," as reasons why teachers should vote for the union, it went on to assert that "a bargaining agent's job is to . . . win salaries and benefits that reflect teachers' professional status."[54] (Of course, these seemingly nonmonetary issues had as much to do with working conditions and job security as they did with abstract professional standards.)

Thus, the AFT could claim that the trade union focus on higher pay for its membership was compatible with professionalism. It could also blame the NEA for failing to support teachers' status as professionals. For instance, in the 1976 Cincinnati campaign, one AFT flyer compared teachers' salaries with those of other local occupations. According to this flyer, Cincinnati teachers made less than mail carriers, assembly line workers at General Motors, parking meter enforcement officers, supermarket cashiers, and maintenance workers in City Hall—occupations that most people would not consider professions. Such a state of affairs, according to the AFT, was one reason teachers should turn against the NEA and support the union.[55] The NEA could also use this line of attack. In a 1985 Washington, D.C., campaign, for instance, the NEA attacked the local AFT affiliate in much the same manner. According to a flyer distributed by the association during this campaign, "Teachers should stand proud, among the ranks of physicians and dentists—those professionals who help students grow into responsible and healthy adults. Yet, due to a failure of aggressive leadership on our behalf, the WTU [Washington Teachers' Union] has allowed us to be treated with indignity; WTU officials have hurt us in our pocketbooks."[56]

To defend against such attacks, the incumbent bargaining representative would invariably accuse its opponent of making "fantastic promises"[57] in much the same way private sector employers would accuse union organizers of making promises they knew they could not keep to win a bargaining election. During the 1976 Cincinnati campaign, for instance, the Cincinnati Teachers' Association (CTA) accused the Cincinnati Federation of Teachers (CFT) of "wishful thinking;" of promoting "pipe dreams;" of promising "pie in the sky;" and of "throwing reason and responsibility to the winds."[58] That same year in Terre Haute the Vigo County Teachers' Association responded to an AFT challenge with the message that "[a]ny Tom, Dick or Harry can promise you anything but the VCTA believes responsible action means more than words."[59]

Such accusations, when employed by one teachers union against another, may have been more effective than in a private sector organizing campaign because they implied that the union making the promises was acting in an unprofessional manner. Professionals were expected to take into account all sides to an issue and to refrain from adopting a narrow, partisan stance. This attitude was demonstrated in an editorial in the *Cincinnati Enquirer* that praised the CTA for the way in which it negotiated with the school board. "The *Enquirer* believes that the bargaining approach taken by CTA and its new president, Mrs. Ruth Clephane, indicates a most encouraging sign of professional deportment in Cincinnati. . . . In fact, over the long run, we can only believe that this policy of professionalism and prudent understanding will pay salary dividends that would not be forthcoming through the coercive tactics of the militant opposition."[60] "Throwing reason and responsibility to the winds," as the CTA reminded teachers, was totally contrary to a professional approach toward bargaining. Indeed, "responsible leadership" became the campaign slogan for the CTA in its ultimately unsuccessful defense against the CFT challenge.[61]

According to many teachers (and newspaper editors), professionals did not just avoid adopting narrow, one-sided positions, they actively cooperated with school boards and superintendents in striving for the best interests of the children they taught. Appeals to a "community of interest," as we have seen, were commonly used by employers in private sector bargaining campaigns. Yet this appeal had special relevance to professionals. As Dave Selden, one-time president of the AFT, commented on association policy during the 1960s, "NEA policy makers conceded that raw collective bargaining might be all right for blue collar workers, but teachers, they thought, were part of a professional team to which everyone in the educational structure belonged: teachers, principals, superintendents and staff specialists such as psychologists and guidance counselors. 'The profession' would negotiate—not bargain—with board of education representatives, and the superintendent would act as advisor to both sides."[62]

This belief in a community of interest presented major problems for both the NEA as it struggled to become a collective bargaining agent, and for the AFT as it tried to sway teachers wary of its openly confrontational tactics. As Urban has observed, "[t]he major difficulty for opponents of collective bargaining was that it embodied a trade union approach of adversarialism that deviated strongly from the cooperation between teachers and school administrators that had underlain the NEA's commitment to professionalism since the 1920s."[63] This hesitancy about adopting "a trade union approach" can be seen in the NEA's first formal resolution endorsing the concept of collective bargaining, euphemistically referred to as "professional negotiations." The opening sentence of this resolution, adopted in 1961, stated, "Since boards of education and the teaching profession have the same ultimate aim of providing the best possible educational opportunity for children and youth, relationships must be established which are based upon this community of interest and the concept of education as both a public trust and a professional calling." It went on to conclude, "The National Education Association believes, therefore, that professional education associations should be accorded the right, through democratically elected representatives, using appropriate professional channels, to participate in the determination of policies of common concern, including salary and other conditions for professional service."[64] By the 1970s, however, the association had overcome this initially hesitant attitude to become an unabashed and militant trade union. In part, this was because, as Urban comments, within the NEA's understanding of professionalism "was a notion of consultation of teachers by administrators and school board members that was not abandoned but was often institutionalized in formal negotiations conducted and agreements reached under collective bargaining. Thus, advocates of collective bargaining within the NEA could and did argue that adoption of collective bargaining was not a repudiation of professionalism but rather the road to its meaningful accomplishment."[65] Selden had made this same argument in defense of the AFT's professionalism. According to Selden, "teachers must participate in the policy-making process if they are to be truly professional."[66]

Nevertheless, for many teachers—as well as for much of the general public—the concept of professionalism precluded an openly confrontational stance towards school boards and administrators. In his study of teachers in the early 1970s, Ronald Corwin noted, "many citizens and educators . . . tend to confuse being 'professional' with being an obedient employee. In effect, they emphasize the teachers' obligations to their students and to their colleagues—for example, to stay late to work with students, to cooperate with the administration, to come to work on time, or to obey school rules."[67] This, of course, is merely a restatement of the notion that professionals ought to be client-centered rather than self-centered. This understanding of what it meant to be a professional could be seen even among those associated with the labor movement. For instance, Selden recalled that one AFL-CIO representative continually "marveled at the fierce militancy of the teacher delegates. Invariably he would exclaim after a meeting, 'God damn, Dave! These don't sound like college graduates. They sound like coal miners!'"[68] Because of attitudes like these, the AFT's Cincinnati affiliate, for example, felt it necessary to defend itself against charges that it was "too outspoken and critical" by claiming that, "[w]hile CFT cooperates with administrators, it does not cater to them."[69] Thus, even as the NEA moved to openly embrace a union ideology, many of its own members continued to hold to the less militant and confrontational ideal of a professional association.

This opposition to a confrontational approach to bargaining was driven not only by concerns about professionalism, however. It had a gendered component as well. Implicit in collective bargaining, as Urban notes, is a "masculine ideology."[70] This is demonstrated most clearly in surveys done during the early 1970s that showed that male teachers leaned towards the AFT whereas female teachers tended to favor the less militant NEA. Indeed, many observers attribute the rise of teacher unionism to the increase in the number of male secondary school teachers, whose numbers rose from 69 percent to 76 percent between 1955 and 1970.[71] The AFT itself was apparently cognizant of this wariness on the part of female teachers towards its more militant stance. For instance, during the Cincinnati campaign, the president of the CFT wrote to the president of the New York State United Teachers explicitly asking that he send some women representatives to help during that organizing drive.[72] And despite historian Marjorie Murphy's claim in 1990 that, "Collective bargaining is no longer seen as a masculine pursuit," as late as 1998 one could still find objections within the NEA to unionism because of its connection with masculinity.[73] For instance, one article in *NEA Today* asserted, "For some NEA members, the AFL-CIO seems a male world."[74] For teachers, then, the ideology of professionalism was intertwined with notions of gender, much in the same way that Daniel Walkowitz has found was the case for social workers.[75]

The changing attitudes of teachers towards collective bargaining, as could be seen in their increased willingness to adopt a confrontational rather than cooperative stance in negotiations with local school boards, were reflected in their changed attitude towards strikes as well. Corwin, for instance, cites survey data that show the following:

> Whereas only 1 out of 2 teachers surveyed by the NEA in 1965 supported the right to strike, by 1970, 9 out of 10 teachers supported some type of group action, and 3 out of 4 believed that at least in some circumstances teachers should strike. In 1972, 7 out of 10 teachers who approved of strikes said that striking is justified to remedy unsafe conditions for pupils, obtain higher salaries, achieve satisfactory teaching conditions, improve the instructional program, or obtain a negotiation agreement. In 1965, the majority of teachers considered none of these reasons justifications to strike with the exception of the remedy of unsafe conditions.[76]

This change was reflected in the NEA's evolving attitude towards strikes. In its initial resolution endorsing collective bargaining in the 1960s, the NEA declared, "The seeking of consensus and mutual agreement on a professional basis should preclude the arbitrary exercise of unilateral authority by boards of education and the use of the strike by teachers as a means for enforcing economic demands."[77] By 1980, however, an NEA fact sheet was not only claiming that the association was as militant as the AFT, but was even pointing out that its affiliates staged more strikes than AFT affiliates.[78]

This brochure, however, seems to have been an exception. Although teachers may have been more willing to strike by the end of the 1970s, and may have been leery of any organization that unconditionally foreswore the use of the strike, like most workers, they were hardly "strike happy." Just as in private sector bargaining campaigns, charges that one union or the other was likely to precipitate a strike if elected were frequent. In the Cincinnati campaign, for instance, the CFT felt it necessary to defend itself against charges that it would force a strike, in much the same way many a private sector union did. One leaflet claimed that the "CFT would strike only if its membership overwhelmingly authorized a strike and it had the support of related unions," and another handout claimed that AFT affiliates in other cities achieved "good contracts without striking."[79] At the same time, the CFT put together a leaflet that included a copy of a newspaper article about a previous CTA strike; "Who Strikes?!" was written next to the article.[80] Similar leaflets could be found from other campaigns during the 1970s and '80s.[81] So, although teachers came to accept that professionalism did not preclude striking, they also felt it was a tactic that should be used only in extremis.

Despite the amount of ink spent on the issue of professionalism and the NEA's repeated emphasis on its own status as the "professional organization," the AFT was able to overcome teachers' concerns and to defeat the association in several elections. In the Cincinnati campaign, for instance, the CFT outpolled the CTA 1747 to 1125 (with only 22 votes for no representative).[82] Likewise, the AFT displaced the incumbent NEA affiliate in the 1976 campaign in Terre Haute. At the national level, the union grew from a mere 60,000 members in 1960 to over 600,000 by 1985.[83] There can be no doubt that teachers were vitally concerned with how these two organizations would affect their status as professionals. The AFT's success in these elections, then, indicates that it was able to allay the doubts of enough teachers so that other issues became decisive when they went to the polls. In addition, the NEA's eventual embrace of the "union" label indicates that many teachers came to accept that professionalism and unionism were not incompatible.

"Which One Would You Choose?"

The most important of these other issues was the question of which organization could more effectively represent teachers. Although the NEA tried to portray itself as a "non-union association," its role as a bargaining representative caused it to adopt appeals similar to those used by any trade union in its efforts to recruit teachers. This section considers the issue of organizational effectiveness. More than simply tracing how this issue played out in contests between the NEA and the AFT, however, the goal here is to examine how popular attitudes towards unions were either echoed in this debate, or, in a few cases, how these unions' arguments about their respective merits diverged sharply from how the public thought organized labor ought to conduct itself.

As might be expected when an outside union challenged an incumbent organization, charges that the current representative had "sold out" its membership were common. In the 1976 Cincinnati campaign, for instance, the AFT challenger charged, "Rather than suggesting ways of improving declining schools, *CTA has taken the Board's position:* there is no money; nothing more can be done."[84] According to the CFT, "[t]he problem with teachers' salaries is not the size of the budget—it's the competence of the bargaining agent."[85] The CTA responded in kind by pointing to AFT failures in other districts. For instance, the CTA pointed to New York City where a list of AFT "accomplishments" included: "loss of 20,000 jobs; an additional cut of 4500 to 6000 teaching positions this month; loss of tenure for all professionals who went on strike; loss of sabbaticals for all teaching professionals; reduction of minority staff from 15 percent to 4 percent."[86] They also pointed to Terre Haute, Indiana, where "after four months of negotiations, the union local announced . . . that it had bargained, 'as good an agreement as they could get.' Teachers were told that the team had negotiated away their longstanding salary index, had expanded the elementary working day from seven to seven and one-half hours, and that the bargaining team 'felt good' with the board's final salary offer of 2.8 percent." This leaflet went on to assert that the AFT affiliate had to resort to underhanded parliamentary tactics to ram the contract down teachers' throats, even after a majority of those that attended the meeting to vote on the contract rejected it.[87] Also in 1976, the Terre Haute association accused its AFT challenger of having "sold out" its membership in a nearby district.[88] And in a Washington, D.C., campaign in 1985 the NEA asserted that "[t]eachers . . . worry about the school board's heavy handed control of WTU," that "WTU accepts what the school board gives it," and that the WTU was like an overseer employed by the "Big House" on a plantation.[89]

The assertion that corrupt and self-seeking union bosses regularly "sold out" their memberships was often found in media portrayals of organized labor. In contests between the AFT and the NEA, however, the charge usually was not that one union or the other was corrupt, but rather that it was either incompetent or identified too closely with the local school board.

Nevertheless, echoes of the popular idea that self-serving union bosses had negotiated "sweet heart contracts" could occasionally be found. For instance, in the Washington campaign, the NEA claimed that, "WTU put[s] what's good for the union and its leaders ahead of the well-being of teachers—[it has] the largest payroll of any local teachers union."[90]

If talk about "selling out" echoed popular notions of how unions operated, the NEA's and AFT's positions on political involvement ignored the popular belief that unions ought to stay out of politics. Indeed, a major source of contention between these two organizations was which one had more political clout. Initially, many teachers may have been as leery as the general public about labor's involvement in politics. Such is the implication of one AFT leaflet that commented that "it [is] interesting that CTA has followed CFT's lead in collective bargaining tactics (including striking) and now in political action, after originally calling such endeavors 'unprofessional.'"[91] By 1976, however, this initial reluctance had been overcome. In fact, according to one AFL-CIO organizer involved in the Cincinnati campaign, "the question of which organization could more effectively push for pro-public employee legislation and build greater community support for education was [a] key" issue in that campaign.[92] This was reflected in CTA leaflets and newsletters that touted the association's successes. Two separate handouts reminded teachers that the Ohio teacher retirement plan was the result of association lobbying.[93] Another newsletter article featured pictures from a party hosted by the local association, showing state representatives and senators as well as the school superintendent in attendance, implying, of course, that the association was politically influential.[94] Yet another leaflet claimed that the NEA lobbying was responsible for a congressional override of a veto by President Ford of an appropriation bill for the Department of Health, Education, and Welfare (HEW).[95] Likewise, in Wichita, Kansas, the local association put together a handout that asserted, "The fact is: It was Kansas-NEA, not the Kansas AFL-CIO, which won the money that guaranteed us a minimum nine percent pay hike this year. The AFL-CIO didn't even testify—much less lobby—for our education bills. The fact is also: In Washington, NEA and AFL-CIO went head-to-head on the Department of Education. NEA won; AFL-CIO lost."[96]

That teachers, as public employees, were keen to have a politically influential bargaining representative is to be expected. Their salaries and working conditions, unlike those of workers in the private sector, were wholly and visibly determined through the political process. Teachers' attitudes about labor involvement in politics, then, should be seen as something of an exception. There is ample evidence that workers in the private sector, including many union members, held to the position, so prominently promoted in the media, that unions should stay out of politics.[97] Even some teachers, as the CFT pamphlet mentioned previously indicates, apparently believed that labor's involvement in politics was unprofessional.

Teachers' views on organizational size and, presumably, organizational power vis-à-vis employers also ran counter to the generally held belief that large, national unions were threatening. In almost every bargaining campaign, the NEA affiliate would invariably point to the large size of the association compared to the AFT as one reason to vote for it.[98] An organization's size not only contribute to its power, both political and economic, it also demonstrated that it had achieved widespread legitimacy. As one NEA newsletter put it, "Two million NEA members must be right!"[99] This bandwagon effect could be seen even at the local level. One CFT leaflet, for instance, tried to allay teachers' doubts about joining because "CFT's membership is too small to win" by claiming that "CFT . . . has a growing membership of 801, its highest ever."[100] Subsequent pamphlets continued to tout the CFT's growing number of members.[101] Occasionally, a kind of reverse bandwagon approach was used, as with one NEA leaflet that rhetorically asked, "What do teachers in 62 districts across the country have in common?" The answer: "They've dumped AFT."[102] This leaflet is reminiscent of some of those used by Frank Ix & Sons that featured newspaper articles about workers who had voted against unionization. And, of course, NYU used a similar argument to convince its clerical workers to reject District 65. In all of these cases, workers, whether at a textile mill, a private university, or a public school, wanted the extra assurance of having chosen a "proven winner."[103]

Based on this evidence, it would seem that workers were of two minds when they thought about the implications of union size. When considering whether to join or vote for a union, the greater its power vis-à-vis the employer, the better, at least up to a certain point. At Ix, for instance, the ACTWU's apparent weakness probably deterred many workers from supporting the union. Larger unions, as in the case of the NEA, were also able to demonstrate the acceptability of the union alternative to those who were concerned about whether unionization was appropriate for workers like themselves.

At the same time, larger unions had a problem showing that they would be responsive to their members' needs. Even if the union were the very model of a democratic organization, its sheer size could create the impression that individual workers would have little say in shaping its policies. At the Dupont

Corporation, for instance, independent, plant-based unions survived well into the 1990s, because the workers were unwilling to affiliate with larger international unions, such as the Steel Workers. Yet by threatening such affiliation they could draw on the power of these large internationals to force Dupont into offering concessions that the local was unable to obtain on its own. Once such concessions were granted, however, the drive for affiliation faltered and died. Thus, these workers could both have their cake (i.e., local control) and eat it too (i.e., take advantage of the benefits that a larger union could offer).[104] Large unions could also suffer from the impression that they were too diverse in membership to adequately represent a particular type of worker. Thus, as was noted previously, the NEA made much of its independent status: "NEA is run by and for teachers . . . an organization that puts teachers first, foremost and always."[105]

Trade Union Antiunionism

We have examined the ways in which ideas about professionalism affected teachers' response to organized labor, and how issues unique to inter-union competition either echoed popular notions about unions, or, in some cases, were dealt with in a way that ran counter to how the public generally felt unions should behave. This final section examines how these two unions drew on popular notions about organized labor to smear their opponent in much the same way a private sector employer might try to dissuade his employees from joining or voting for a union. As will quickly become apparent, both of these unions were not above drawing on popular antiunion sentiment when they thought it could be beneficial.

For example, charges that one union or the other was undemocratic were common during contests between the AFT and the NEA. Such charges were applied against the local as well as the national organizations. For instance, in Cincinnati the CFT pointed to its respect for "non-member rights" as a reason to vote for it. "If you are not a member of either organization," declared one leaflet, "and believe that you have a right to vote on a contract that affects you as a teacher, VOTE CFT. CFT POLICY: All teachers have the right to vote on the contract, and no contract will be ratified until all teachers have had that opportunity."[106] Another handout claimed that, "CFT pursues cautious, sensible actions based upon the wishes of its total balanced membership (not just its building representatives, as in CTA)."[107] The CTA countered by pointing to the AFT's actions in Terre Haute, where, to intimidate teachers into accepting a contract, union officers required that, "[t]o register a strike vote, teachers were required to sign their ballots." When teachers voted to strike anyway, "union negotiators decided a second ratification vote was required—this time disallowing all non-members a vote and requiring a standing vote for 'ratification of a strike.' Although 456 of 600 teachers present voted to strike, union leaders claimed that a simple majority of all teachers in the bargaining unit had not voted to strike and the Federation president announced the contract ratified."[108] Likewise, in Washington, D.C., the NEA challenger claimed that its AFT opponent was "clique-run, and guilty of nepotism and cronyism. A tiny group of people, not the rank-and-file, set union goals, policies and programs in secrecy."[109] The most remarkable example of this type of charge was an NEA leaflet that could have been lifted directly from a private sector organizing campaign. This leaflet reads just like those put out by unions trying to overcome employees' fear that their boss might find out they had signed a union card. In this case, however, the incumbent union was substituted for the employer:

> According to the law, teachers have the right to choose the union of their choice without interference, coercion, or restraint by any representative of the school board or the DC government—*that right includes protection from any union harassment.*
>
> The law also prevents *the union* from seeing or knowing anything about who signs a petition to call for a representation election. Signing a petition doesn't mean you have to vote for NEA, AFT or anyone else. It just means that:
>
> —you support the democratic representation process
> —you want to hear more facts about your representation
> —you want to exercise your right to vote for or against one of the competing unions
>
> Signing a petition is not a vote. It's not a decision or comment against any one or any union. It's your legal means to exercise your right to hear all the facts and cast your ballot. Don't allow anyone to intimidate you on these issues.[110]

At the national level, both organizations accused each other of being run by their staffs rather than their members. According to the AFT, "the NEA staff and its supporters oppose" merger because a merged organization would place more power in the hands of the elected leaders. "And since the elected leadership would have greater authority, the organization itself would be more accountable and responsive to the will of the membership. It is this which the NEA staff opposes."[111] The NEA, not to be outdone, claimed that the AFT was guilty of the same sin. As a consequence, "a union controlled by its own staff employees is going to do what's good for its staff first, and what's good for its members only secondly—if at all."[112] And despite the fact that teachers wanted to be represented by a large, powerful organization, they too apparently shared the concerns expressed in the media that, "unless careful safeguards are established, an organization can grow large, bureaucratic, and arrogant," as Albert Shanker put it. Unlike the NEA, where "The views and the needs of the members are seen as little more than troublesome intrusions," however, "[t]he AFT is structured around the basic principle of democratic accountability."[113]

The most serious issue dividing the NEA and the AFT in this regard was their respective interpretations of how best to achieve "democratic accountability." In addition to the AFT's affiliation with the AFL-CIO, the union's policy of public voting became a major sticking point whenever these two organizations discussed merger.[114] According to the NEA, within the association, "[i]ssues are debated and acted upon by secret ballot. This insures that all ballots are cast in an atmosphere of free choice." In contrast, within the AFT, "to register dissatisfaction through the voting process is to publicly identify oneself or one's local as a dissident since its has long been the practice that all votes are publicly exposed."[115] What the AFT viewed as a method whereby members could hold their representatives accountable, the NEA saw as a way for the union "boss" to identify and punish his opposition.

Another similarity to private sector campaigns was a concern about "outsiders." For instance, a south Florida affiliate of the AFT ran a radio ad during one campaign to defend itself from the charge that it was run by "outsiders." According to this ad, "AFT contracts are not settled by outsiders. AFT has won strong contracts throughout South Florida by building strong local teacher organizations and building strong community support. You don't need outsiders to settle contracts when the community is supporting you."[116] In another instance, a Wichita, Kansas, affiliate of the AFT put out a flyer entitled "WFT Our Homegrown Organization" that traced the history of the local union back to 1942.[117] And in another Florida contest, this time between the NEA and the Service Employees International Union (SEIU), the local association published a leaflet that showed the letterheads for both organizations. The NEA letter had a local postmark, while that for the SEIU had a postmark from a more distant locale. As this leaflet concluded, "One of these unions offers experienced representation right here in Lake County."[118]

Union dues were another occasional item of contention. In the Cincinnati campaign, for instance, one CFT handout boasted that the union's dues were $51.27 less annually than those for the CTA, though it went on to note, "we are really not in the discount business. We represent teachers. And we want to represent you."[119] The CTA countered by asking teachers to "[t]ake a long, hard look at what has happened to Union dues in urban [school districts] in this part of the country when the Union has become the bargaining agent. . . . In the cities [listed] above, the smallest dues increase took place in Chicago where Union dues DOUBLED after the Union got a foothold."[120] And in Terre Haute, the local association pointed to the job losses and other give backs suffered by the AFT in New York City and intoned, "New York City's union dues were $178. Ineffectiveness comes at a high price in this case."[121] In addition, just as in any number of private sector campaigns, both unions prominently touted the various benefits members received in return for their dues, such as various types of insurance and interest-free loans for unusual circumstances.[122] Such flyers were reminiscent of the Retail Clerks slogan during the 1950s, "It doesn't cost—it pays to belong to the union."[123] For teachers, just as with textile workers, university secretaries, and department store clerks, the cost of union membership was an issue of some concern that these unions tried to assuage by pointing to the benefits they provided.

Finally, the one issue that the NEA was able to exploit and the AFT found difficult to counter was the union's responsibility for the Ocean Hill–Brownsville strike, which had done so much to cast an image of organized labor as racist. Though the NEA itself had only integrated its state organizations during the late 1960s and early '70s, by 1976 it was already pointing with pride to its policy of "ethnic-minority guaranteed representation" and castigating the New York City AFT affiliate for allowing a "reduction of minority staff from 15 percent to 4 percent."[124] In 1980 an NEA fact sheet claimed that the association had fought the Department of Labor's effort to classify it as a union, not because it was opposed to being labeled as such or because it did not want to comply with the reporting requirements of the Landrum-Griffin Act, but because it wished to preserve its minority set aside for staff and executive positions.[125] According to Wayne Urban, one of the major obstacles to merger between the NEA and the AFT in 1998 was the NEA's continuing fear that a merged organization would not aggressively address issues of concern to minorities.[126]

Perhaps the NEA's most concerted employment of the race issue, however, was during the 1985 bargaining campaign in Washington, D.C.—a district with a majority African American population. Several handouts asserted "AFT hires very few Blacks as staffers."[127] One leaflet showed a picture of the president of the NEA with the caption "Mary Hatwood Futrell is the Third Black President of the NEA" and claimed "NEA's civil rights record is second to none!" This same leaflet likened the local AFT affiliate to an overseer on a plantation, hired by the "big house"—that is, the school board—to do its dirty work.[128] Yet another handout was devoted entirely to the issue of the AFT's racism and specifically pointed to the Ocean Hill–Brownsville strike as an example.

> AFT's national president, Albert Shanker, protests that the term "racist" is thrown about too freely these days. What he means is that the label is often attached to him. There's good reason:
>
> - Shanker is also president of AFT's New York City local—and he led the bitter 1968 strikes against the black community in Ocean Hill–Brownsville.
> - Though the student population in New York City is over 40% black, fewer than 12% of the city's teachers are black. The reason is a discriminatory "exam"—and AFT supports that test.
> - AFT is vehemently opposed to affirmative action.
> - Being very cozy with Ronald Reagan, Al Shanker got one of his personal aides named executive director of the US Civil Rights Commission.[129]

Although the Washington, D.C., campaign may have been a somewhat unique case, it is nevertheless apparent that the racist image organized labor had acquired during the 1960s continued to affect it well into the '80s. On the other hand, as with African Americans generally, it seems that the teachers in Washington either were not persuaded of the validity of this charge or believed that this issue was not crucial, electing to remain with the AFL-CIO affiliate by a margin of 3,647 to 1,127.[130]

* * *

On balance, teachers came to accept that professionalism and unionism were not incompatible. The popular image of unions did affect and slow their willingness to adopt this position. Yet by the 1980s even the NEA, which had portrayed itself as the nonunion alternative, had come to openly advertise itself as a trade union. This acceptance of unionism, however, needs a good deal of qualification. For instance, even as the NEA came to moderate its antiunionism, the AFT moved to enhance its position as a professional organization concerned with educational issues beyond just the pay and working conditions of teachers. In addition, the AFT's strength continued to be concentrated in urban districts in the Northeast. The NEA's strength, by contrast, lay in the suburbs and in the South and West.[131] This distribution not only reflected the relative prevalence of unionization in general, but the cultural background of the residents of these areas: NEA members were less likely to be exposed to other unions and were more likely to be of Anglo descent, the group most likely to have been influenced by the antiunion culture. In addition, a significant portion (19 percent) of the NEA's membership lay in states (particularly in the South) where public employees were not permitted to engage in collective bargaining. In such cases, the association continued to operate as a professional organization rather than as a trade union.[132]

The failed attempt of the AFT and NEA to merge in 1998, however, provides the clearest evidence that antiunion sentiment still ran deep within the NEA at the close of the twentieth century. One of the primary reasons the NEA's rank-and-file rejected this merger effort was because the new organization would be affiliated with the AFL-CIO. As one convention delegate told the *New York Times*, "We'd go along with it if there wasn't affiliation with the AFL-CIO. It's the unionization part. We don't consider ourselves a union. We're not into the boycotting and rioting." According to the *Times*, "Many [delegates] voiced discomfort with joining the labor federation because they see it as blue-collar and confrontational."[133] The *Washington Post's* reporter also noted that "Many teachers who belong to the NEA view themselves more as professionals in an organization akin to the American Medical Association rather than a labor union."[134] One NEA member, arguing against the merger in the pages of *NEA Today*, claimed, "Formal affiliation with AFT and the AFL-CIO threatens both our membership and our mission. . . . If we are forced to affiliate with the AFL-CIO, those of us who work in 'right-to-work' states—where we have to go out and earn our members one by one—stand to lose those very members. Believe me, there are plenty of 'professional' organizations out there literally salivating at the prospect of swooping in and taking away members *who aren't willing to wear the union label.*" And, like so many other critics of unions, she went to some length to claim that her antiunion message did not mean that she was antiunion: "I grew up in a pro-union household. In fact, my father was president of his local unions. [*sic*] I wholeheartedly support unions and value the countless contributions they've made to this country over the years. But I didn't become a school teacher to strengthen the American union movement. And that, I fear, is the real purpose behind the proposed merger between NEA and the American Federation of Teachers."[135] As Peter Shrag, writing in the *New Republic* about the proposed merger, noted:

[T]eacher unionism has always been an uncomfortable fit, producing no end of ambivalence among the rank and file . . . Are teachers just another collection of blue-collar working stiffs, like steel workers or auto workers or coal miners? Or are they professionals whose responsibilities transcend the limitations of negotiated hours, working conditions, and seniority rules? That is, are they not properly subject to collective bargaining, rigid salary structures, grievance procedures, and so on? And, if they insist on the prerogatives and status of professionals, can they also behave like assembly-line unionists— hitting the bricks and trying to shut down the enterprise, even as they claim to have only the children's interests at heart?[136]

So although many teachers came to accept the idea of belonging to a trade union, large segments of the profession continued to view organized labor with a jaundiced eye.[137]

Conclusion

Despite the diversity of cases presented here, from blue-collar workers in a mass production setting to white-collar semiprofessionals, there are many striking commonalities in workers' concerns about what unionization would mean. References to strikes, to a lack of union democracy, and to the self-serving nature of union leaders can be found in each of these cases. These stereotypes were drawn from and make up America's antiunion culture. The fact that unions quite often prepared literature in advance to refute these images is a testament to the strength and pervasiveness of this culture as well as the impact it had in making at least some workers wary of organized labor.

Perhaps the greatest worry workers harbored about organized labor concerned the perceived consequences unionization would have for their relationships with their employers. Both Frank Ix & Sons and New York University, to varying degrees, warned workers that unionization would create a regimented and impersonal work environment, one in which workers could no longer deal directly with their managers but would have to go through the union instead. Likewise, many teachers felt that professionalism implied consulting with school boards, not confronting them. The NEA's first resolution endorsing (albeit tentatively) collective bargaining embraced this concept of professionalism: "Since boards of education and the teaching profession have the same ultimate aim of providing the best possible educational opportunity for children and youth, relationships must be established which are based upon this community of interest and the concept of education as both a public trust and a professional calling."[1] In time, teachers came to accept the idea that collective bargaining was not only compatible with professionalism, but, as Wayne Urban has observed, "the road to its meaningful accomplishment."[2] Nevertheless, teachers, like clerical workers and blue-collar textile workers, continued to view organized labor's supposed dedication to confrontational tactics as anathema to their preference for working with their bosses, not against them.

Instead of seeing their interests as generally opposed to those of their employers, workers focused on those which they had in common. They accepted, for instance, the claim that a company must make a profit to continue in business. As a result, they agreed that there were limits to how much they could expect to be paid, and that employers should have a certain degree of flexibility in how they ran their businesses. As Sidney Hillman, president of the Amalgamated Clothing Workers, put it, labor should "give its full cooperation to further industrial efficiency, recognizing that the improvement in the living standards of the workers must, in the main, come from increased productivity."[3]

Perhaps even more important, workers wanted a work environment characterized by cooperation, not confrontation. They valued their jobs as much for the people they worked with as for the pay they received. Creating and maintaining a friendly work environment was a vital component in their considerations about how a union would affect their working conditions.[4] These attitudes explain why 85 percent of workers, when asked in a 1999 survey what form an employee representation plan should take, responded that it should be run jointly by workers and management.[5] They also explain why the presence of preexisting employee representation plans have had the greatest impact in dissuading workers from voting for a union, more so than captive audience meetings, firings, wage increases, or the presence of an antiunion committee.[6] To the extent that workers wanted collective representation, they preferred that their representative work with management rather than against it.

Thus, the cultural portrayal of organized labor as being dedicated to confrontational tactics presented a serious obstacle to unions when they sought to win over workers. According to the cultural ideal, unions would work with management to increase productivity, and thus increase profits and pay. Yet this ideal, most people believed, was hardly ever attained. The focus on strikes, burdensome work rules, and union leaders who were only interested in their own power and enrichment conveyed the impression that unions, by and large, were "outsiders" dedicated to conflict no matter what the cost for the company. When workers considered whether to vote for or against a union, these stereotypes played an important role in making them believe that unions would worsen rather than improve working conditions.

It is this perception of unions, I believe, that also explains why, as Joel Rogers and Richard Freeman observe, such unions as "the National Education Association, the Association of University Professors, and various police organizations often defeat AFL-CIO affiliates in elections for union representation." As they put it, these organizations "are seen as something different from a union."[7] That "something" appears to be workers' perceptions of their willingness to put cooperation with the employer ahead of confrontation. The NEA, for instance, could draw on its origins and long history as a professional association to bolster this feeling that it was more interested in consultation than conflict. Another factor may be that the nonaffiliated status of such organizations gave workers a greater sense of being able to control these organizations. Affiliation with the AFL-CIO would raise the specter of being submerged within a large organization that had little concern for the particular needs of one segment of the workforce.

This embrace of the cooperative ideal points to a basic problem organized labor had to deal with in the postwar period: its inability to reshape the public's understanding of the nature of capitalism and labor's place within it. Unions are organized to represent workers' interests, particularly in cases where those interests diverge from those of management. They represent a counterweight to employers' power to hire, fire, and set the pay and conditions of work. Unions, by their very nature, must, to some degree, work against management and not just with it. It is hardly remarkable then that the public would view unions as confrontational. What is remarkable is that this was seen as a negative by large numbers of workers.

There are some signs, however, that the cultural and ideological milieu within which unions now operate is becoming more favorable. This is reflected in polling data as it relates to attitudes towards organized labor. Whereas in the 1970s and '80s, 60 percent of workers surveyed said they would vote against a union and only 30 percent said they would vote for one, in the latest poll conducted by the AFL-CIO, taken in 2002, 53 percent of workers responded that they would vote for a union and 43 percent said they would vote against one. This number has been trending in favor of unions since the 1980s.[8] Likewise, the number of people who "approve" of unions has recently seen an increase from its nadir in the 1980s (see chapter 3). Overall, it would seem that attitudes towards organized labor are becoming more positive.

These changes, I believe, are the result of the intensified drive towards globalization. Job loss due to foreign competition is no longer confined to the blue-collar, manufacturing sector. Increasingly, white-collar workers are facing the prospect of seeing their jobs sent overseas—what is now euphemistically referred to as "outsourcing." Corporations have already made strides in offshoring accountancy, software programming, and legal research. Even if this phenomenon has not yet been of decisive importance, their awareness that such a fate may await them may cause some white-collar workers to rethink the basic premises of free market capitalism.

In terms of America's antiunion culture, this change in perception may be contributing to a rejection of the new cooperative ideal. In the 1970s when one of the major challenges American workers faced was foreign competition, the commonality of interests between employees and employers seemed readily apparent. Indeed, this era may have marked the height of the acceptance of the idea of the mutuality of interests between workers and employers. Both parties were threatened by the loss of business resulting, on the one hand, in fewer jobs and, on the other, diminished profits. In the current climate, by contrast, the threat seems to originate not from foreign *companies,* but from foreign *workers.* Whereas in the 1970s and '80s a factory might close or a business go under because of foreign competition, now the factory or the business is likely to be sent overseas. Instead of seeing a job disappear, workers now see it being directly transferred to someone else; only the workers suffer while the company continues to profit. Under these circumstances, the divergent interests of workers and capitalists becomes more apparent, undermining the cooperative ideal. In turn, organized labor's adversarial image becomes an asset rather than a liability. Globalization, in other words, has revived the "us versus them" mentality that fueled the organizing drives of the 1930s.

Job loss and wage stagnation are also leading to a change in political priorities, particularly among progressives. The Port Huron Statement, a founding document of the New Left, was written by a "generation, bred in at least modest comfort" whose main concerns would, by the end of the 1960s, come to be called "identity politics."[9] So-called social issues eclipsed economic issues in the Affluent Society. This appears to be changing as progressives focus more on economic issues again. Almost inevitably, this shift is leading to a renewed focus on organized labor as a vital institution for ensuring economic justice.[10]

Taking advantage of these changes, labor leaders have had some success rehabilitating the union image. Consider the UPS strike of 1997, for instance. This strike had the potential to revive one of the oldest and most negative images of unions, pitting the interests of a limited number of workers against the interests of the larger society. Yet Ron Carey, president of the Teamsters union, was able to define the goals of the strike as part of a larger struggle to improve the lives of part-time and contingent workers, a segment of the workforce that was steadily growing. Thus, rather than considering it a self-seeking money grab by a special interest, a large segment of the public saw the strike as a fight for the underdog.[11] The campaign for a minimum wage increase in 1996, "America Needs a Raise," led by John Sweeny, president of the AFL-CIO, also highlighted how labor was fighting for the interests of poorly paid workers, not just its own members.[12] Campus-based, antisweat-shop movements and the enactment of living wage laws have also helped revitalize labor's legitimization myth.[13]

Although in some respects these are positive developments, the success they have had in improving labor's standing rests on labor's old legitimization myth—the notion that unions are supposed to represent the interests of the underprivileged. As has been demonstrated, however, this is a very shaky foundation on which to build. As it has in the past, this idea can reinforce the perception of the labor movement as a special interest. A more productive strategy for identifying labor's interests with the public interest would be to highlight the inherent conflicts of interest between capital and labor, now so evident, and to position labor as the workingman's representative in this conflict. Such a strategy would highlight the need for collective action for all workers, not just for those who felt themselves to be underpaid or mistreated. Reviving the concept of industrial democracy would be one path toward accomplishing this goal.

One interesting development in the last few years that could aid the promotion of this strategy has been the reemergence of the bourgeoisie. Whereas, by the 1950s the public's attention had shifted from the "Leisure Class" to "Café Society," the super-rich are once again becoming more visible. Although the attention paid to celebrities has hardly waned since the 1950s, many of the haute bourgeoisie have themselves become celebrities. Donald Trump, Tommy Hilfiger, and Paris Hilton have all been the stars of network reality shows. This renewed celebration of the super-rich is somewhat reminiscent of the 1920s. As happened before, of course, this increased visibility can have a negative impact on the interests of capitalists when the economy turns sour. Already in recent congressional debates, opponents of repealing the estate tax were able to exploit this increased visibility by labeling the proposal "the Paris Hilton tax cut." Whether these highly visible members of the bourgeoisie are simply setting up themselves and their class for a fall remains to be seen, but the protection of its class interests was the reason the bourgeoisie tried to lessen its visibility during the 1930s.

None of these changes, by themselves, will easily be translated into a resurgent union movement. The obstacles employers create to avoid unionization—aided and abetted by a legal regime that makes it extremely difficult for workers to realize their supposed right to organize—have become especially daunting. Nevertheless, the legal regime that allows employers to fire union activists with almost no penalties, that allows "captive audience" meetings, and so on, can be changed. Such a change, of course, can only come about through a change in the political calculus, that is, the election of more representatives who are favorable to organized labor. If voters begin seeing support for unions as not only a positive, but a priority, then more politicians will support them. The improving image of unions in the last few years, then, has at least some potential for improving the political climate in favor of organized labor and reviving an almost moribund labor movement.

Notes

Introduction

1. Larry Reibstein, "Score Another for Japan Inc.," *Newsweek*, Aug. 7, 1989, 44; Timothy Minchin, *Fighting against the Odds: A History of Southern Labor since World War II* (Gainesville: University Press of Florida, 2005), 152–55.

2. On racial divisions, see Rick Halpern, *Down on the Killing Floor: Black and White Workers in Chicago's Packing Houses, 1904–54* (Urbana: University of Illinois Press, 1997); Roger Horowitz, *Negro and White, Unite and Fight! A Social History of Industrial Unionism in Meatpacking, 1930–90* (Urbana: University of Illinois Press, 1997); Robert Korstad, *Civil Rights Unionism: Tobacco Workers and the Struggle for Democracy in the Mid-Twentieth-Century South* (Chapel Hill: University of North Carolina Press, 2003); Michael Honey, *Southern Labor and Black Civil Rights: Organizing Memphis Workers* (Urbana: University of Illinois Press, 1993); and Cliff Brown, *Racial Conflict and Violence in the Labor Market: Roots in the 1919 Steel Strike* (New York: Garland Publishing, 1998). On ethnic divisions, see Lizabeth Cohen, *Making a New Deal: Industrial Workers in Chicago, 1919–1939* (New York: Cambridge University Press, 1990); Gary Gerstle, *Working-Class Americanism: The Politics of Labor in a Textile City, 1914–1960* (New York: Cambridge University Press, 1989); John Bodnar, *Immigration and Industrialization: Ethnicity in an American Mill Town, 1870–1940* (Pittsburgh: University of Pittsburgh Press, 1977); Ewa Morawska, *For Bread with Butter: The Life-Worlds of East Central Europeans in Johnstown Pennsylvania, 1890–1940* (New York: Cambridge University Press, 1985); and Gwendolyn Mink, *Old Labor and New Immigrants in American Political Development: Union, Party, and State, 1875–1920* (Ithaca: Cornell University Press, 1986).

On divisions created by levels of skill, see David Montgomery, *The Fall of the House of Labor: The Workplace, the State, and American Labor Activism, 1865–1925* (New York: Cambridge University Press, 1987); David Brody, *Steelworkers in America: The*

Nonunion Era (New York: Russell and Russell, 1970); and Stephen Meyer, *"Stalin over Wisconsin": The Making and Unmaking of Militant Unionism, 1900–1950* (New Brunswick: Rutgers University Press, 1992).

3. For obstacles from employers, see Sanford Jacoby, *Modern Manors: Welfare Capitalism since the New Deal* (Princeton: Princeton University Press, 1997); Gerald Zahavi, *Workers, Managers, and Welfare Capitalism: The Shoeworkers and Tanners of Endicott Johnson, 1890–1950* (Urbana: University of Illinois Press, 1988); Howell Harris, *The Right to Manage: Industrial Relations Policies of American Business in the 1940s* (Madison: University of Wisconsin Press, 1982); Sidney Fine, *"Without Blare of Trumpets": Walter Drew, the National Erectors Association, and the Open Shop Movement, 1903–57* (Ann Arbor: University of Michigan Press, 1995); and Howell Harris, *Bloodless Victories: The Rise and Fall of the Open Shop in the Philadelphia Metal Trades, 1890–1940* (New York: Cambridge University Press, 2000). Discussions of obstacles from the state appear in Christopher Tomlins, *The State and the Unions: Labor Relations, Law, and the Organized Labor Movement, 1880–1960* (New York: Cambridge University Press, 1985); William Forbath, *Law and the Shaping of the American Labor Movement* (Cambridge: Harvard University Press, 1991); Melvyn Dubofsky, *The State and Labor in Modern America* (Chapel Hill: University of North Carolina Press, 1994); and Daniel Ernst, *Lawyers against Labor: From Individual Rights to Corporate Liberalism* (Urbana: University of Illinois Press, 1995).

4. Stephen Norwood, *Strikebreaking and Intimidation: Mercenaries and Masculinity in Twentieth-Century America* (Chapel Hill: University of North Carolina Press, 2002); Robert Michael Smith, *From Blackjacks to Briefcases: A History of Commercialized Strikebreaking and Unionbusting in the United States* (Athens: Ohio University Press, 2003).

5. Horowitz, *Negro and White, Unite and Fight*, 65; Halpern, *Down on the Killing Floor*, 39, 51–53; Harvard Sitkoff, *A New Deal for Blacks: The Emergence of Civil Rights as a National Issue: The Depression Decade* (New York: Oxford University Press, 1978), 169–70.

6. Meyer, *"Stalin over Wisconsin,"* ch. 5.

7. Jacquelyn Dowd Hall et al., *Like a Family: The Making of a Southern Cotton Mill World* (1987, repr. New York: W. W. Norton, 1989), 340–47.

8. Brody, *Steelworkers in America;* John Bodnar, *The Transplanted: A History of Immigrants in Urban America* (Bloomington: Indiana University Press, 1985) ch. 1.

9. Timothy Minchin, *What Do We Need a Union For? The TWUA in the South, 1945–1955* (Chapel Hill: University of North Carolina Press, 1997); Minchin, *Fighting against the Odds;* see also Barbara Griffith, *The Crisis of American Labor: Operation Dixie and the Defeat of the CIO* (Philadelphia: Temple University Press, 1988). Although Griffith points to the opposition of many southern workers to the CIO's postwar organizing drive, she can only speculate about why these workers were against unionization.

10. Seymour Martin Lipset, "The Future of Private Sector Unions in the U.S.," in

The Future of Private Sector Unionism in the United States, edited by James Bennet and Bruce Kaufman (Armonk: M. E. Sharpe, 2002), 10.

11. Barry Hirsch and Edward Schumacher, "Private Sector Union Density and the Wage Premium: Past, Present, and Future," in *The Future of Private Sector Unionism in the United States,* edited by Bennet and Kaufman, 96–97.

12. Charles Craver, *Can Unions Survive? The Rejuvenation of the American Labor Movement* (New York: New York University Press, 1993), 47–51; Richard Freeman and James Medoff, *What Do Unions Do?* (New York: Basic Books, 1984), 230–39; Richard Freeman, "Why Are Unions Faring Poorly in NLRB Representation Elections?" in *Challenges and Choices Facing American Labor,* edited by Thomas Kochan, 45–65; Hirsch and Schumacher, "Private Sector Union Density and the Wage Premium"; Morris Kleiner, "Intensity of Management Resistance: Understanding the Decline of Unionization in the Private Sector," in *The Future of Private Sector Unionism in the United States,* edited by Bennet and Kaufman, 292–316.

13. Freeman, "Why are Unions Faring Poorly in NLRB Representation Elections?" 53.

14. Michael Goldfield, *The Decline of Organized Labor in the United States* (Chicago: University of Chicago Press, 1987); Gary Fink, "Labor Law Revision and the End of the Postwar Labor Accord," in *Organized Labor and American Politics, 1894–1994: The Labor-Liberal Alliance,* edited by Kevin Boyle (Albany: State University of New York Press, 1998), 239–53. Although Elizabeth Fones-Wolf's study *Selling Free Enterprise: The Business Assault on Labor and Liberalism, 1945–1960* (Urbana: University of Illinois Press, 1994) would appear to fit into this category, it is unclear from her analysis just what impact the "great free enterprise campaign" of the 1950s had on people's images of unions. She does not delve into the content and message of this campaign, so it is difficult to know what, if anything, employers and the NAM were saying about unions. Related to this difficulty is the fact that a campaign directed at selling the virtues of free enterprise is not the same as one meant to denigrate unions. Opinion leaders had many negative things to say about specific union practices, but no one after the war would have publicly claimed that unions had no place in a capitalist economy. Indeed, even the most rabid critics of unions would take pains to emphasize that they were not "antiunion."

15. Jack Fiorito, "Human Resource Management Practices and Worker Desires for Union Representation," in *The Future of Private Sector Unionism in the United States,* edited by Bennet and Kaufmann, 205–26; Jacoby, *Modern Manors.*

16. Craig Becker, "Democracy in the Workplace: Union Representations and Federal Labor Law," *Minnesota Law Review* 77 (Feb. 1993): 495; Paul Weiler, "Promises to Keep: Securing Workers' Rights to Self-Organization under the NLRA," *Harvard Law Review* 96 (June 1983): 1769; Joel Rogers, "In the Shadow of the Law: Institutional Aspects of Postwar U.S. Union Decline," in *Labor Law in America: Historical and Critical Essays,* edited by Christopher Tomlins and Andrew King (Baltimore: Johns Hopkins University Press, 1992), 283–302; David Brody, *Labor Embattled: His-*

tory, Power, Rights (Urbana: University of Illinois Press, 2005); Kate Bronfenbrenner, "Employer Behavior in Certification Elections and First-Contract Campaigns: Implications for Labor Law Reform," in *Restoring the Promise of American Labor Law,* edited by Sheldon Friedman et al. (Ithaca: ILR Press, 1994), 89. For a contrasting opinion see Julius Getman et al., *Union Representation Elections: Law and Reality* (New York: Russell Sage Foundation, 1976). Getman and his colleagues argue that an election campaign by employers (or unions) makes no difference on how employees eventually vote. By the time the campaign begins, according to Getman, workers have already made up their minds about whether to vote for or against a union. See also Laura Cooper, "Authorization Cards and Union Representation Election Outcome: An Empirical Assessment of the Assumption Underlying the Supreme Court's *Gissel* Decision," *Northwestern University Law Review* 79 (June 1984): 87–141. Cooper shows that unfair labor practices by employers have no statistical impact on the outcome of union elections. That agrees with Bronfenbrenner's finding that unfair labor practice charges have no impact on elections. Although the idea is widespread that unions lose many elections because employers' unfair labor practices intimidate employees, that has not been shown to be the case. It is not employers' illegal practices that have proven most effective against organizing drives but the practices allowed by the "free speech" provisions of the Taft-Hartley Act that permit employers to wage vigorous campaigns against unions (e.g., captive audience meetings, letters to employees, and one-on-one meetings with supervisors).

17. Janice Klein and David Wanger, "The Legal Setting for the Emergence of the Union Avoidance Strategy," in *Challenges and Choices Facing American Labor,* edited by Kochan, 75–88; James Gross, *Broken Promise: The Subversion of U.S. Labor Relations Policy, 1947–1994* (Philadelphia: Temple University Press, 1995); see also Dubofsky, *The State and Labor in Modern America,* for an overview of the varying fortunes of organized labor, which, he argues, are sensitive to state action.

18. Mike Davis, *Prisoners of the American Dream* (London: Verso Press, 1986); Kim Moody, *An Injury to All: The Decline of American Unionism* (London: Verso Press, 1988).

19. Nelson Lichtenstein, *The Most Dangerous Man in Detroit: Walter Reuther and the Fate of American Labor* (New York: Basic Books, 1995).

20. Freeman and Medoff, *What Do Unions Do?* 228–30; Freeman, "Why Are Unions Faring Poorly in NLRB Representation Elections?"; Hirsch and Schumacher, "Private Sector Union Density and the Wage Premium."

21. Craver, *Can Unions Survive?* 40–42; Henry Farber, "The Extent of Unionization in the United States," in *Challenges and Choices Facing American Labor,* edited by Kochan, 15–44; Freeman, "Why Are Unions Faring Poorly in NLRB Representation Elections?"; Leo Troy, "Twilight for Organized Labor," in *The Future of Private Sector Unionism in the United States,* edited by Bennet and Kaufman, 59–76; Hirsch and Schumacher, "Private Sector Union Density and the Wage Premium"; Edward Potter, "Labor's Love Lost? Changes in the U.S. Environment and Declining Private Sector

Unionism," in *The Future of Private Sector Unionism in the United States,* edited by Bennet and Kaufman, 188–204.

22. Farber, "The Extent of Unionization in the United States"; Potter, "Labor's Love Lost?"

23. Seymour Martin Lipset, "North American Labor Movements: A Comparative Perspective," in *Unions in Transition: Entering the Second Century,* edited by Lipset (San Francisco: ICS Press, 1986), 421–54; Lipset, "The Future of Private Sector Unions in the U.S."

24. Craver, *Can Unions Survive?* 51–55.

25. Richard Freeman, "Spurts in Union Growth: Defining Moments and Social Processes," National Bureau of Economic Research Working Paper 6012, April 1997.

26. Forbath, *Law and the Shaping of the American Labor Movement;* Christopher Tomlins, *Law, Labor, and Ideology in the Early American Republic* (New York: Cambridge University Press, 1993); Brody, *Labor Embattled.*

27. C. Wright Mills, *White Collar: The American Middle Classes* (1951, repr. New York: Oxford University Press, 1953), 306.

28. Jacoby, *Modern Manors,* 42; Dubofsky, *The State and Labor in Modern America,* 206–7.

29. In 1976 only 33 percent of nonsupervisory, nonself-employed persons not already in a union indicated they would vote for a union. Thomas Kochan, "How American Workers View Labor Unions," *Monthly Labor Review* (April 1979): 30. Since 1984 the AFL-CIO has conducted polls asking if nonunion employees would vote for a union. In 1984, 65 percent of respondents said they would vote against a union, and only 30 percent indicated they would vote for one. Since then, the number saying they would vote for a union has steadily risen. In 2002, for the first time, more respondents indicated they would vote for a union than not; fifty percent said they would vote for a union, and 43 percent said they would vote against one (polling data conducted by Lou Harris in 1984 and by Peter Hart since then; AFL-CIO Web page, http://www.aflcio.org/media center/upload/LaborDay2002Poll.ppt, accessed Dec. 5, 2007). See also Joel Rogers and Richard Freeman, *What Workers Want* (Ithaca: ILR Press, 1999), 69. As Henry Farber has noted about such numbers, "Clearly, if the nonunion workers who desire union representation are not concentrated in particular establishments but are randomly spread throughout the nonunion workforce, then unions are going to have problems winning very many representation elections" ("The Extent of Unionization in the United States," 39).

30. Rogers and Freeman, *What Workers Want,* 150.

31. Kochan, "How American Workers View Labor Unions," 30.

Part I: America's Antiunion Culture

1. The definition of a "cultural image" used here is somewhat different from that of a "cultural model" of which cognitive anthropologists speak and which Daniel Gold-

hagen uses in his study of the Holocaust. Goldhagen, *Hitler's Willing Executioners: Ordinary Germans and the Holocaust* (New York: Vintage Books, 1996). A cultural model is, as its name implies, a model of how a particular cultural pattern operates. Dorothy Holland and Debra Skinner for instance describe a model of gender relations among American women of college age, as follows:

> There is a standard, taken-for-granted way in which close male/female relationships—both romantic and friendship—come about. The male demonstrates his appreciation of the female's personal qualities and accomplishments by concerning himself with her needs and wants, and she, in turn, acts on her attraction to him by permitting a close, intimate relationship and by openly expressing her admiration and affection of him.
>
> In the prototypical relationship, the two parties are equally attractive and equally attracted to one another. However, if the discrepancy in relative attractiveness is not too great, adjustments are possible. A relatively unattractive male can compensate for his lesser standing by making extraordinary efforts to treat the woman well and make her happy. A relatively unattractive female can compensate by scaling down her expectations of good treatment.

Women then deploy this model to classify men based on how they fit into this "taken-for-granted" standard. Those who are attractive but do not treat women well are "playboys" or "Don Juans"; those who are unattractive and do not treat women well are "creeps" and "assholes." Dorothy Holland and Debra Skinner, "Prestige and Intimacy: The Cultural Models behind Americans' Talk about Gender Types" in *Cultural Models in Language and Thought,* edited by Dorothy Holland and Naomi Quinn (New York: Cambridge University Press, 1987), 89–90, 104.

In the case of a cultural image, the focus is the picture that comes to mind, the associations formed when someone is asked to describe a particular cultural object—in this case, unions. It seems likely that unions fit into a cultural model of employment relations rather than constituting a model of their own. Thus, it may be that a person's response to a union's overtures are conditioned by how they perceive their current employment relationship with regard to the cultural standard. The further their own situation negatively diverges from the cultural model of employment relations, the more likely they will be to support unionization.

The other significant difference between the concept of a cultural model as used by Goldhagen and the idea of a cultural image as used here is the extent of its acceptance. For Goldhagen, the German cultural model of Jews is totalizing. It encompasses practically all Germans and conditions their behavior to a greater or lesser extent in the same direction. I do not see the cultural image of unions as being so all-encompassing. Someone may be raised in America's antiunion culture and be aware of its many nuances, but that does not predetermine whether the person would, for example, vote against a union if presented with such a choice.

2. Antonio Gramsci, *The Antonio Gramsci Reader*, edited by David Forgacs (New York: New York University Press, 2000), 323–62. In many ways this study could be viewed as a Gramscian project; it is motivated by much the same concern that motivated Gramsci. Why were workers not more responsive to socialism and communism in his case, and why are they not more responsive to unions in the case of this study? The answer presented here, similar to Gramsci, involves the cultural hegemony of the ruling class. By "hegemony," Gramsci does not intend to imply an uncontested and absolute position of control. Rather, hegemony is negotiated by acknowledging some of the working class's concerns and incorporating them into the ruling ideology. The discussion in this volume presents an example of such incorporation in the widespread agreement that to be antiunion is wrong and that unions are a legitimate part of the capitalist system. At the same time, the overwhelmingly negative image of unions, especially the limited scope of their activities that are culturally permissible (e.g., the assumption that unions should only be involved in negotiating wages, benefits, and hours of work and should steer clear of politics), serve the ruling-class's interests in discouraging workers from joining unions and limiting their power.

3. Lipset, "The Future of Private Sector Unions in the U.S."

4. Derek Bok and John Dunlop, *Labor and the American Community* (New York: Simon and Schuster, 1970), 22; Seymour Martin Lipset, "Labor Unions in the Public Mind," in *Unions in Transition: Entering the Second Century,* edited by Lipset (San Francisco: ICS Press, 1986), 304.

5. Seymour Martin Lipset and William Schneider, *The Confidence Gap: Business, Labor, and Government in the Public Mind* (Baltimore: Johns Hopkins University Press, 1983), 219, 218.

6. Bok and Dunlop, *Labor and the American Community,* 22; Lipset, "Labor Unions in the Public Mind," 304.

7. Elizabeth Perse, *Media Effects and Society* (Mahwah: Erlbaum Associates, 2001); Melvin De Fleur and Sandra Ball-Rokeach, *Theories of Mass Communication,* 3d ed. (1966, 1970, repr. New York: D. McKay, 1975); Todd Gitlin, *The Whole World Is Watching: Mass Media in the Making and Unmaking of the New Left* (Berkeley: University of California Press, 1980); Denis McQuail, *Mass Communication Theory: An Introduction,* 3d ed. (1983, 1987, repr. London: Sage, 1994).

8. John Heidenry, *Theirs Was the Kingdom: Lila and DeWitt Wallace and the Story of* Reader's Digest (New York: W. W. Norton, 1993), 235, 272.

9. Heidenry, *Theirs Was the Kingdom,* 235; James Paysted Wood, *The Curtis Magazines* (New York: Ronald Press, 1971), 63, 231.

10. Heidenry, *Theirs Was the Kingdom;* Wood, *The Curtis Magazines;* Carl Ryant, *Profit's Prophet: Garet Garret (1878–1954)* (Selinsgrove, Pa.: Susquehanna University Press, 1989); W. A. Swanberg, *Luce and His Empire* (New York: Scribner, 1972); Jan Cohn, *Creating America: George Horace Lorimer and the* Saturday Evening Post (Pittsburgh: University of Pittsburgh Press, 1989).

11. Heidenry, *Theirs Was the Kingdom*, 120.

12. Tom Zaniello, *Working Stiffs, Union Maids, Reds and Riffraff: An Organized Guide to Films about Labor* (Ithaca: Cornell University Press, 1996).

13. William Puette, *Through Jaundiced Eyes: How the Media View Organized Labor* (Ithaca: ILR Press, 1992), ch. 3.

14. C. Wright Mills, *The New Men of Power: America's Labor Leaders* (1948, repr. Urbana: University of Illinois Press, 2001), 34.

15. E. P. Thompson, *The Making of the English Working Class* (New York: Vintage Books, 1963).

16. Bok and Dunlop, *Labor and the American Community*, 22; Lipset, "Labor Unions in the Public Mind," 304.

17. George Lipsitz, *Rainbow at Midnight: Labor and Culture in the 1940's* (Urbana: University of Illinois Press, 1994), 261.

18. Kochan, "How American Workers View Labor Unions," 25.

19. David Witwer, *Corruption and Reform in the Teamsters Union* (Urbana: University of Illinois Press, 2003). Witwer traces the association of the Teamster Union with corruption from the early part of the twentieth century through the McClellan hearings of the 1950s.

20. Puette, *Through Jaundiced Eyes*, 50.

21. Tomlins, *The State and the Unions*, 4–5.

22. Walter Lippmann, *Public Opinion* (New York: Harcourt Brace, 1922), 218–22.

Chapter 1: The Union Image in the Age of Industrialization

1. Eric Hobsbawm, *Age of Revolution, 1789–1848* (1962, repr. New York: Vintage Books, 1996), 198.

2. Dorothy Ross, *The Origins of American Social Science* (New York: Cambridge University Press, 1991)

3. Louis Adamic, *Dynamite: The Story of Class Violence in America*, rev. ed. (Glouster, Mass.: Peter Smith, 1934), 36.

4. John Higham has argued that Haymarket was the key event in the upsurge in nativist sentiment in the late nineteenth century. Higham, *Strangers in the Land: Patterns of American Nativism, 1860–1925* (New Brunswick: Rutgers University Press, 1955), 54–55.

5. Edward Bellamy, *Looking Backward, 2000–1887* (1888, repr. Cleveland: World Publishing, 1945), 54, 56.

6. Jacob Riis, *How the Other Half Lives: Studies among the Tenements of New York* (1890, repr. New York: Penguin Books, 1997), 196.

7. Bellamy, *Looking Backward*, 57.

8. Higham, *Strangers in the Land*, 89.

9. Frederick Lewis Allen, *Only Yesterday: An Informal History of the Nineteen-Twenties* (New York: Harper and Brothers, 1931), 46–49, 54; see also Gary Gerstle,

American Crucible: Race and Nation in the Twentieth Century (Princeton: Princeton University Press, 2001), 99.

10. Higham, *Strangers in the Land,* ch. 5; Michael Kazin, *Barons of Labor: The San Francisco Building Trades and Union Power in the Progressive Era* (Urbana: University of Illinois Press, 1987), 285.

11. Sheldon Stromquist, *Reinventing "The People": The Progressive Movement, the Class Problem, and the Origins of Modern Liberalism* (Urbana: University of Illinois Press, 2006).

12. Herbert Croly, *The Promise of American Life* (1909, repr. Boston: Northeastern University Press, 1989), 128.

13. Walter Lippmann, *Drift and Mastery: An Attempt to Diagnose the Current Unrest* (1914, repr. Englewood Cliffs, N.J.: Prentice-Hall, 1961), 60–63, 65.

14. Montgomery, *The Fall of the House of Labor,* 61.

15. Jack London, *War of the Classes* (New York: Macmillan, 1905), x.

16. Adamic, *Dynamite,* 187–253.

17. Interchurch World Movement, Commission of Inquiry, *Report on the Steel Strike of 1919* (New York: Harcourt, Brace and Howe, 1920), 150–55.

18. For more on the great Red Scare see William Preston, *Aliens and Dissenters: Federal Suppression of Radicals, 1903–1933* (1963, repr. Urbana: University of Illinois Press, 1994), esp. chs. 8 and 9.

19. Nancy Maclean, *Behind the Mask of Chivalry: The Making of the Second Ku Klux Klan* (New York: Oxford University Press, 1994), xi, 4, 182.

20. Adamic, *Dynamite,* 325.

21. Albert Jay Nock, "If We Must Have a Revolution," *American Mercury* (Sept. 1932): 75–82; George Sokolsky, "Will Revolution Come?" *Atlantic Monthly* (Aug. 1932) 184–91; George Soule, "Are We Going to Have a Revolution?" *Harpers,* (Aug. 1932): 277–86; Charles Walker, "Relief and Revolution," *Forum* (Aug. 1932): 73–78.

22. Nelson Lichtenstein and Howell John Harris, eds., *Industrial Democracy in America: The Ambiguous Promise* (New York: Cambridge University Press, 1993), chs. 1–3; Joseph McCartin, *Labor's Great War: The Struggle for Industrial Democracy and the Origins of Modern American Labor Relations, 1912–1921* (Chapel Hill: University of North Carolina Press, 1997), ch. 1.

23. Kazin, *Barons of Labor,* 237.

24. McCartin, *Labor's Great War,* 174, 214.

25. Barry Cushman, *Rethinking the New Deal Court: The Structure of a Constitutional Revolution* (New York: Oxford University Press, 1998), 120.

26. Allen, *Only Yesterday,* 76.

27. Irving Bernstein, *The Lean Years: A History of the American Worker, 1920–1933* (Boston: Houghton Mifflin, 1960), 434.

28. Whiting Williams, "The Hopeful American Worker," *Saturday Evening Post,* June 17, 1933, 8+, emphasis added.

29. Gerstle, *American Crucible,* 138–39.

30. Matthew Frye Jacobson, *Whiteness of a Different Color: European Immigrants and the Alchemy of Race* (Cambridge: Harvard University Press, 1998), chs. 3 and 8; David Roediger, *Working Toward Whiteness: How America's Immigrants Became White: The Strange Journey from Ellis Island to the Suburbs* (New York: Basic Books, 2005), ch. 6.

31. Roy Rosenzweig, "Organizing the Unemployed: The Early Years of the Great Depression, 1929–1933," *Radical America* 10, no. 4 (1976): 37–60.

32. Walker, "Relief and Revolution," 73–78.

33. "'Stick to End!' Watchword at Buddies' Camps," *Washington Herald,* June 5, 1932, 3.

34. Floyd Gibbons, "War on Vets a Shock, Says Floyd Gibbons," *Washington Herald,* July 31, 1932, 1.

35. Rosenzweig, "Organizing the Unemployed," 52.

36. Lucy Barber, *Marching on Washington: The Forging of an American Political Tradition* (Berkeley: University of California Press, 2002), 90.

37. Floyd Gibbons, "Congress Dog Really Bitten by Bonus Flea," *Washington Herald,* June 7, 1932, 4.

38. "The Human Side of the Bonus Army," *Literary Digest,* June 25, 1932, 29–30.

39. *The Great Depression: The Road to Rock Bottom* (PBS video, 1993).

40. Sokolsky, "Will Revolution Come?"

41. Quoted in "Nation-Wide Press Comment on Expulsion of the Veterans from the Capital," *New York Times,* July 30, 1932, 4.

42. Rexford G. Tugwell, *The Brains Trust* (New York: Viking Press, 1968), 352–53.

43. Paul Anderson, "Tear-Gas, Bayonets, and Votes: The President Opens His Reelection Campaign," *The Nation,* Aug. 17, 1932, 138–40.

44. *Golddiggers of 1933* (Warner Brothers, 1933).

45. "What's the Bonus Army's Next Move?" *Literary Digest,* Aug. 13, 1932, 31–32.

46. Jay Franklin, "Why This Political Apathy?" *Current History,* June 1, 1932, 265–69.

47. Allen, *Only Yesterday,* 355.

48. Tugwell, *The Brains Trust,* 359.

49. Lillian Symes, "Blunder on the Left: The Revolution and the American Scene," *Harpers,* Dec. 1, 1933, 90–101.

50. Williams, "The Hopeful American Worker," 8+.

51. Symes, "Blunder on the Left," 90–101. See also Alvin Johnson, "The Coming American Revolution," *Yale Review* (June 1934): 649–61; Archibald MacLeish, "Preface to an American Manifesto," *Forum* (April 1934): 195–98; and Max Ascoli, "Notes on Roosevelt's America," *Atlantic Monthly* (June 1934): 654–65.

52. MacLeish, "Preface to an American Manifesto," 195–98.

53. Symes, "Blunder on the Left," 90–101.

54. Irving Bernstein, *Turbulent Years: A History of the American Worker, 1933–1941* (Boston: Houghton Mifflin, 1971), 217, see also 238, 285, 287–90.

55. "Homer Martin and the Communists," *New Republic,* Feb. 16, 1938, 30.

56. Garet Garrett, "Closed during Altercations," *Saturday Evening Post,* May 14, 1938, 25.

57. Max Lerner, "Meeting the Blitz on Labor," *New Republic,* April 28, 1941, 598.

58. Harry Conn, "Communist-Led Unions and U.S. Security," *New Republic,* Feb. 18, 1952, 16; Lester Velie, "Red Pipe Line into Our Defense Plants," *Saturday Evening Post,* Oct. 18, 1952, 19; Charles Kersten, "We Are Protecting Spies in Defense Plants!" *Reader's Digest* (Jan. 1953): 27; Lester Velie, "Red Pipeline into Our Uranium Sources," *Reader's Digest* (June 1955): 81.

59. Max Zaritsky, "Can Labor Prosper under Free Enterprise?" *Saturday Evening Post,* Jan. 30, 1943, 24.

60. Philip Murray, "The CIO Looks at 'Labor Laws,'" *Reader's Digest* (April 1947): 29.

61. Philip Murray, "If We Pull Together," *Reader's Digest* (Aug. 1948): 10.

62. Gary Gerstle, *Working-class Americanism.*

63. Jonathan Rieder, "The Rise of the Silent Majority," in *Rise and Fall of the New Deal Order, 1930–1980,* edited by Steve Fraser and Gary Gerstle (Princeton: Princeton University Press, 1989), 246–47; Michael Kazin, *The Populist Persuasion: An American History* (New York: Basic Books, 1995), ch. 7.

64. Tom Englehardt, *The End of Victory Culture: Cold War America and the Disillusioning of a Generation* (New York: Basic Book, 1995), 96–100, 113–132, quotation on 98.

65. Joseph Alsop and Stewart Alsop, "Will the CIO Shake the Communists Loose?" *Saturday Evening Post,* March 1, 1947, 26; Joseph Alsop and Stewart Alsop, "Will the CIO Shake the Communists Loose?" *Saturday Evening Post,* Feb. 22, 1947, 15: J. C. Rich, "How the Garment Unions Licked the Communists," *Saturday Evening Post,* Aug. 9, 1947, 23; Donald Robinson, "How Our Seamen Bounced the Commies," *Saturday Evening Post,* Dec. 25, 1948, 14; Raymond Hilliard, "We Threw the Commies Out," *Saturday Evening Post,* June 30, 1951, 20.

66. Peter Levy, *The New Left and Labor in the 1960s* (Urbana: University of Illinois Press, 1994), ch. 1.

67. James Foreman, *The Making of Black Revolutionaries* (Seattle: University of Washington Press, 1972), 369.

68. Robert Novak, "Reagan's New Coalition," *National Review,* Aug. 22, 1980, 1023; Robert Novak, "Fiasco, '76," *National Review,* Dec. 24, 1976, 1396.

69. Gerstle, *American Crucible,* 129–80.

70. Interchurch World Movement, *Report on the Steel Strike of 1919.*

71. Robert Brooks, *As Steel Goes . . . : Unionism in a Basic Industry* (New Haven: Yale University Press, 1940)

72. "Strikes Ahead," *Life,* Dec. 12, 1945, 34.

73. C. Wright Mills, "The Trade Union Leader: A Collective Portrait," *Public Opinion Quarterly* 9 (Summer 1945): 160.

74. Warner Bloomberg Jr., Joel Seidman, and Victor Hoffman, "New Members, New Goals," *New Republic*, July 6, 1959, 9; see also Robert Zieger, *The CIO, 1935–1955* (Chapel Hill: University of North Carolina Press, 1995), 227–41, in particular the picture on 203.

75. Steve Fraser, *Labor Will Rule: Sidney Hillman and the Rise of American Labor* (Ithaca: Cornell University Press, 1991), 526–38.

76. *Gabriel over the White House* (MGM, 1933).

77. Allen, *Only Yesterday*, 177–81, quotation on 179.

78. John T. Flynn, "American Revolution, 1933," *Scribners* (July 1933): 1–6.

79. Edward Aswell, "The Social Revolution: A Young Man Looks at His World," *Forum* (July 1933): 30–34.

80. John K. Galbraith, *The Affluent Society* (New York: Mentor Books, 1958), 79; C. Wright Mills, *The Power Elite* (1956, repr. New York: Oxford University Press, 2000), 117.

81. "Moses and Wheeler Clash in Senate on Demands to Feed Marchers," *Washington Herald*, June 10, 1932, 3.

82. "Behind the Bonus Battlefront," *Literary Digest*, Oct. 1, 1932, 11.

83. James Auerbach, *Labor and Liberty: The La Follette Committee and the New Deal* (Indianapolis: Bobbs-Merrill, 1966), 2.

84. Auerbach, *Labor and Liberty*, 114–15, 99n7. See also Smith, *From Blackjacks to Briefcases*, 92–96.

85. Auerbach, *Labor and Liberty*, 49–50; Edward Levinson, *I Break Strikes! The Technique of Pearl L. Bergoff* (New York: Arno Press, 1969).

86. Adamic, *Dynamite*, 35–37, 42, 44, 60, 66, 83, 85, 95, 111, 130, 132, 143, 174, 319, 321, 361–62, 364, 376, 380, 383, 394, 396.

87. Clete Daniel, *Culture of Misfortune: An Interpretive History of Textile Unionism in the United States* (Ithaca: ILR Press, 2001), 167; see also Klein and Wanger, "The Legal Setting for the Emergence of the Union Avoidance Strategy."

88. "Labor: Era of Change," *Business Week*, Sept. 4, 1954, 83.

89. Mills, *White Collar*, 306.

90. Alice Kessler-Harris, *In Pursuit of Equity: Men, Women, and the Quest for Economic Citizenship in Twentieth-Century America* (New York: Oxford University Press, 2001), 67–74.

91. Kazin, *The Populist Persuasion*, ch. 6.

92. Walter Reuther, "GM v. the Rest of Us," *New Republic*, Jan. 14, 1946, 41.

93. In using the word *myth*, I am not questioning the truth—or falsehood—of this idea. Rather, I wish to emphasize how the idea came to have a life of its own, detached from historical grounding. Instead of representing *history*, the myth became part of Americans' collective *memory*.

94. William Hard, "Whites and Blacks Can Work Together," *Reader's Digest* (March 1944) 17; "The Labor Movement Moves," *New Republic*, Dec. 2, 1940, 742.

95. "Ford Strike," *New Republic*, Sept. 23, 1967, 7; Irving Ives, "The Truth about the

New Labor Law," *Reader's Digest* (Oct. 1947): 13; Lester Velie, "When a Fellow Needs a Front," *Reader's Digest* (May 1957): 135; Wellington Roe, "Workers Must Fight," *Reader's Digest* (Jan. 1947): 61; "Labor Day, 1951," *Life*, Sept. 3, 1951, 22; Westbrook Pegler, "But What of Soulless Unions?" *Reader's Digest* (Dec. 1937): 57.

96. For the first quotation, see Stuart Chase, "The Twilight of Communism in the U.S.A.," *Reader's Digest* (Sept. 1941): 25; see also James Mitchell, "Help Wanted: Skilled Blue-collar Workers," *Reader's Digest* (July 1958): 124. For the second quotation see "Labor Day, 1951."

97. Harold Martin, "Has Success Spoiled Big Labor?" *Saturday Evening Post,* Dec. 8, 1962, 75; for second quotation, see "'New Unionism' Demands New Laws," *Saturday Evening Post,* July 13, 1946, 124.

98. Lipset and Schneider, *The Confidence Gap,* 219.

99. *Norma Rae* (Twentieth Century-Fox, 1979).

100. Warner Bloomberg Jr., Joel Seidman, and Victor Hoffman, "Bureaucrats and Idealists," *New Republic,* Sept. 14, 1959, 10.

101. "Labor Day, 1951."

102. Lipset and Schneider, *The Confidence Gap,* 219.

103. "What Really Ails the Unions," *Reader's Digest* (Jan. 1960): 55.

104. Max Lerner, "Our Strike Dilemma: What to Do about It," *Reader's Digest* (July 1963): 75.

105. "'New Unionism' Demands New Laws'"; "It's Time to Stop Coddling Unions; They're on Top Now!" *Saturday Evening Post,* Feb. 7, 1959, 10.

106. "Another Kind of Public Enemy," *Life,* Sept. 9, 1957, 34.

107. Shift in Public Perceptions About Union Strength, Influence, Gallup website: http://www.gallup.com/poll/18040/Shift-Public-Perception-About-Union-Strength-Influence.aspx, accessed Dec. 12, 2007.

108. Gilbert Gall, *The Politics of Right to Work: The Labor Federations as Special Interests* (New York: Greenwood Press, 1988), 107–21. Also of note is the recent failure of a ballot initiative in California that would have restricted the rights of unions to participate in politics.

109. William Hard, "Labor and National Unity," *Reader's Digest* (Nov. 1939): 1; William Hard, "The Typographical Union—Model for All," *Reader's Digest* (June 1943): 1; Cecil B. DeMille, "Must Union Members Give Up Their American Rights?" *Reader's Digest* (July 1945): 93; Merlyn Pitzele, "What Can We Do about Strikes?" *Saturday Evening Post,* Sept. 7, 1946, 22; "A Connecticut Housewife Asks: 'Where Are the Lobbyists for America?'" *Life,* June 3, 1946, 32; David Lawrence, "The End of Labor Monopoly Is Near," *Reader's Digest* (Feb. 1947): 18; Donald Richberg, "Labor Should Live within the Law" *Reader's Digest* (March 1947): 65; Kersten, "We Are Protecting Spies in Defense Plants!"; "Is Congress Boss, or Hoffa?" *Life,* June 1, 1959, 30; Barry Goldwater, "Who Speaks for Labor?" *Reader's Digest* (Nov. 1960): 83; John McClellan, "These Labor Abuses Must Be Curbed," *Reader's Digest* (Dec. 1962): 97; George Denison, "Where Labor Gets Its Political Muscle," *Reader's Digest* (June 1971): 98;

Glenn Stahl, "The Case against Strikes," *Reader's Digest* (Oct. 1971): 128; William F. Buckley Jr., "Beware: Common Situsitis," *National Review,* Dec. 5, 1975, 1436.

Chapter 2: The Postwar Offensive against Organized Labor

1. Puette, *Through Jaundiced Eyes,* 12.
2. Fones-Wolf, *Selling Free Enterprise.*
3. First quotation in Bloomberg, Seidman, and Hoffman, "Bureaucrats and Idealists," 10; second quotation in "What Really Ails the Unions," 55.
4. Roe, "Workers Must Fight," 61.
5. Dubofsky, *The State and Labor in Modern America,* 206–7, emphasis added. See also Jacoby, *Modern Manors,* 42.
6. "It's Time to Stop Coddling Unions; They're on Top Now!"
7. Ed Marciniak, "Are We Condoning Union Tyranny?" *New Republic,* Jan. 10, 1955, 12.
8. "A United America," *New Republic,* Jan. 10, 1949, 6.
9. Dubofsky, *The State and Labor in Modern America,* 207.
10. Lipset, "Labor Unions in the Public Mind," 321.
11. "It's Time to Stop Coddling Unions; They're on Top Now!"
12. "A United America."
13. Murray, "If We Pull Together," 10.
14. Mills, *The New Men of Power* John Kenneth Galbraith, *American Capitalism: The Concept of Countervailing Power* (Boston: Houghton Mifflin, 1952).
15. Lerner, "Our Strike Dilemma."
16. "Is the Wagner Labor Law Unfair?" *New Republic,* Aug. 4, 1937, 348; Garet Garrett, "Putting the Law on the Boss," *Saturday Evening Post,* June 26, 1937, 5; Beverly Bowie, "Let's Get This Settled," *New Republic,* April 6, 1938, 267; Leonard Boudin, "How to Amend the Wagner Act," *New Republic,* Aug. 9, 1939, 7; Garet Garrett, "Labor at the Golden Gate," *Saturday Evening Post,* March 18, 1939, 12; Leo Huberman, "Is the Wagner Act One Sided?" *New Republic,* March 1, 1939, 91; "The Anti-Labor Drive," *New Republic,* April 7, 1941, 467; "A Connecticut Housewife Asks"; "Labor and the Law," *Life,* Dec. 9, 1946, 32; "'New Unionism' Demands New Laws," ; "The Experts in Congress Know Their Public," *Saturday Evening Post,* May 31, 1947, 136; Ives, "The Truth about the New Labor Law"; John Knox, "There Is a Way Out," *Ladies Home Journal* (March 1947): 45.
17. Ives, "The Truth about the New Labor Law."
18. "A Connecticut Housewife Asks: 'Where Are the Lobbyists for America?'"
19. Goldwater, "Who Speaks for Labor?".
20. "It's Time to Stop Coddling Unions; They're on Top Now!"
21. M. Stanton Evans, "Push-Button Unionism?" *National Review,* March 17, 1978, 348; see also William F. Buckley Jr., "The New Labor Bill," *National Review,* March 3, 1978, 298.

22. Lipset, "Labor Unions in the Public Mind," 310.

23. Lester Velie, "Our Union-Labor Collegians," *Reader's Digest* (Aug. 1955): 117.

24. The quotation is from "New Affluence, Unity for Labor," *Life,* Dec. 12, 1955, 26; see also "Labor's View from a Plateau," *Life,* Dec. 15, 1952, 36; Martin, "Has Success Spoiled Big Labor?" ; and "Rugged Ascent of U.S. Unionism," *Life,* Dec. 26, 1960, 56.

25. The quotation is from A. H. Raskin, "The Squeeze on the Unions," *Reader's Digest* (July 1961): 81; see also "New Affluence, Unity for Labor"; Warner Bloomberg Jr., Joel Seidman, and Victor Hoffman, "Paradoxes of Union Democracy," *New Republic,* Sept. 21, 1959, 10; Warner Bloomberg Jr., Joel Seidman, and Victor Hoffman, "How Far Has Merger Gone?" *New Republic,* June 29, 1959, 9; and Martin, "Has Success Spoiled Big Labor?" *Saturday Evening Post.*

26. Martin, "Has Success Spoiled Big Labor?"

27. "New Affluence, Unity for Labor."

28. Croly, *The Promise of American Life,* 127.

29. Tomlins, *The State and the Unions,* 65–67; see also Kazin, *Barons of Labor,* 116–17, 153.

30. Richberg, "Labor Should Live within the Law," 65.

31. George Gallup, *The Gallup Poll: Public Opinion, 1935–1971* (New York: Random House, 1972), 3: 2025.

32. Thurman Arnold, "Labor's Hidden Holdup Men," *Reader's Digest* (June 1941): 136. See also Thurman Arnold and Walton Hamilton, "Thoughts on Labor Day," *New Republic,* Sept. 2, 1946, 252; and Thurman Arnold, "Labor against Itself," *Reader's Digest* (Jan. 1944): 37.

33. "End of a Taboo," *Life,* June 10, 1946, 38.

34. Bloomberg, Seidman, and Hoffman, "How Far Has Merger Gone?"

35. Garrett, "Labor at the Golden Gate."

36. Bloomberg, Seidman, and Hoffman, "How Far Has Merger Gone?"

37. W. L. White, "Should Unions Have Monopoly Powers?" *Reader's Digest* (Aug. 1955): 33.

38. "Steel: How Inflationary?" *Life,* Jan. 18, 1960, 26.

39. Kochan, "How American Workers View Labor Unions," 24.

40. As quoted in Marciniak, "Are We Condoning Union Tyranny?"

41. Goldwater, "Who Speaks for Labor?" ; McClellan, "These Labor Abuses Must Be Curbed," 97.

42. George Denison, "Where Labor Gets Its Political Muscle," *Reader's Digest* (June 1971): 98.

43. Gallup, *The Gallup Poll,* 3: 1667.

44. Lipset, "Labor Unions in the Public Mind," 307–8.

45. S. Lubell, "How Taft Did It," *Saturday Evening Post,* Feb. 10, 1951, 32.

46. Roe, "Workers Must Fight," 61.

47. Cyrus Ching, "Can Labor Live Down Dave Beck?" *Saturday Evening Post,* Aug. 24, 1957, 31.

48. David Witwer, *Corruption and Reform in the Teamsters Union* (Urbana: University of Illinois Press, 2003), 186.

49. Bok and Dunlop, *Labor and the American Community*, 15.

50. Arthur M. Whitehill, "Is Labor Ready for the Buyers' Market Which May be Looming on the Horizon?" *Saturday Evening Post*, March 19, 1949, 12.

51. Lester Velie, "What Shall We Do about the Power-Hungry Union Leader?" *Reader's Digest* (April 1958): 49.

52. Mills, *The New Men of Power*, 108.

53. "Truman's Labor Advisers Weave a Tangled Web," *Saturday Evening Post*, March 5, 1949, 10; see also Mills, *The New Men of Power*, 107.

54. Marciniak, "Are We Condoning Union Tyranny?"

55. Brock Brower, "Bullheaded Leader of Aerospace Labor," *Life*, Jan. 19, 1968, 60.

56. Arnold "Labor's Hidden Holdup Men"; John Patric, "Remove Union Restrictions and Increase Shipyard Production by One Third," *Reader's Digest* (June 1943): 114; Frank Taylor and John Patric, "'Featherbedding' Hampers the War Effort," *Reader's Digest* (March 1943): 25; J. Mack Swigert, "The Taft-Hartley Law: Does It Really Hurt Labor?" *Saturday Evening Post*, Oct. 25, 1947, 23; "Truman's Labor Advisers Weave a Tangled Web"; James Kilpatrick, "And Must We Lose This Freedom?" *Reader's Digest* (April 1965): 221.

57. "The Experts in Congress Know Their Public."

58. Taylor and Patric, "'Featherbedding' Hampers the War Effort."

59. "Truman's Labor Advisers Weave a Tangled Web."

60. Warner Bloomberg Jr., Joel Seidman, and Victor Hoffman, "The Role and Training of Leaders," *New Republic*, Aug. 24, 1959, 15.

61. Warner Bloomberg Jr., Joel Seidman, and Victor Hoffman, "The State of the Unions: Labor on the Defense," *New Republic*, June 22, 1959, 12.

62. Lester Velie, "How a Labor Leader Went Wrong," *Reader's Digest* (Nov. 1957): 74.

63. Nicholas von Hoffman, "The Last Days of the Labor Movement," *Harper's*, Dec. 1978, 22.

64. Davis, *Prisoners of the American Dream*; Kim Moody, *An Injury to All: The Decline of American Unionism* (London: Verso Press, 1988).

65. Martin, "Has Success Spoiled Big Labor?"

66. Marciniak, "Are We Condoning Union Tyranny?"

67. "Organized Labor's Ten Years Together," *New Republic*, Dec. 11, 1965, 7.

68. Bloomberg, Seidman, and Hoffman, "The Role and Training of Leaders."

69. Mills, *The New Men of Power*, 103.

70. von Hoffman, "The Last Days of the Labor Movement."

71. J. Mack Swigert, "Should We Repeal the Taft-Hartley Law?" *Saturday Evening Post*, Oct. 30, 1948, 15.

72. Velie, "How a Labor Leader Went Wrong."

73. "Auto Strike," *National Review,* Sept. 19, 1967, 1002; see also Felice Swados, "Waterfront," *New Republic,* Feb. 2, 1938, 361; Eric Johnston, "Frank Warning to Labor and Management," *Reader's Digest* (April 1944): 20; Victor Riesel, "Labor Is Big Business," *Reader's Digest* (Feb. 1946): 118; "Truman's Labor Advisers Weave a Tangled Web"; "If Taft-Hartley Enslaves Anybody, Its Critics Ought to Tell Us How!" *Saturday Evening Post,* Nov. 21, 1953, 12; Lester Velie, "Robber Barons with Union Cards," *Reader's Digest* (July 1954): 37; "New Affluence, Unity for Labor"; Marciniak, "Are We Condoning Union Tyranny?"; Velie, "How a Labor Leader Went Wrong"; "The Subject of Ike's Jibe," *Life,* March 2, 1959, 36; Bloomberg, Seidman, and Hoffman, "The Role and Training of Leaders"; Bloomberg, Seidman, and Hoffman, "Paradoxes of Union Democracy"; Bloomberg, Seidman, and Hoffman, "How Far Has Merger Gone?"; A. H. Raskin, "The Squeeze on the Unions," 81; and Martin, "Has Success Spoiled Big Labor?"

74. Velie, "Robber Barons with Union Cards"; "If Taft-Hartley Enslaves Anybody, Its Critics Ought to Tell Us How!"

75. Marciniak, Are We Condoning Union Tyranny?"

76. "Truman's Labor Advisers Weave a Tangled Web."

77. "The Subject of Ike's Jibe."

78. Swados, "Waterfront"; "If Taft-Hartley Enslaves Anybody, Its Critics Ought to Tell Us How!"; Velie, "Robber Barons with Union Cards"; "New Affluence, Unity for Labor."

79. Elizabeth Faue, *Community of Suffering and Struggle: Women, Men, and the Labor Movement in Minneapolis, 1915–1945* (Chapel Hill: University of North Carolina Press, 1991), 73–83; see also Sam Keen, *Faces of the Enemy: Reflections on the Hostile Imagination* (San Francisco: Harper and Row, 1986).

80. Puette, *Through Jaundiced Eyes,* 85.

81. Quoted in von Hoffman, "The Last Days of the Labor Movement."

82. Adamic, *Dynamite,* 439.

83. Lipset and Schneider, *The Confidence Gap,* 219.

84. Lipset, "Labor Unions in the Public Mind," 296.

85. Ibid., 295.

86. Ibid., 297.

87. "What Really Ails the Unions."

88. Roe, "Workers Must Fight," 61.

89. Ibid.

90. Donald Richberg, "The Rights and Wrongs of Labor," *Reader's Digest* (Jan. 1954): 88.

91. Roe, "Workers Must Fight," 61.

92. "Is Congress Boss, or Hoffa?" 30.

93. Robert Wilkin, "Why Are Strikes above the Courts?" *Saturday Evening Post,* Sept. 14, 1946, 164; see also "Let Right-to-Work Remain a Right," *Life,* Oct. 8, 1965, 8.

94. William Hard, "Regulating Unions for the Common Good," *Reader's Digest*

(Sept. 1942): 43; Hard, "The Typographical Union—Model for All," 1; Johnston, "Frank Warning to Labor and Management"; Walter Cenerazzo, "Labor Reform by Labor," *Reader's Digest* (Nov. 1944): 56; "Who Wins by Stabbing America?" *Saturday Evening Post*, June 22, 1946, 132; "Why Weaken the Taft-Hartley Law When the Voters Seem to Endorse It?" *Saturday Evening Post*, Sept. 26, 1953, 12; John Dos Passos, "What Union Members Have Been Writing Senator McClellan," *Reader's Digest* (Sept. 1958): 25; W. L. White, "The Right to Work: Our Hottest Labor Issue," *Reader's Digest* (Aug. 1958): 32; Oswald Garrison Villard, "Why Unions Must Be Regulated," *Reader's Digest* (Aug. 1944): 27; Wilkin, "Why Are Strikes above the Courts?"; Richberg, "The Rights and Wrongs of Labor"; Marciniak, "Are We Condoning Union Tyranny?"; Richberg, Labor Should Live Within the Law"; Lester Velie, "When a Fellow Needs a Front," 135; John McClellan, "What We Learned about Labor Gangsters," *Saturday Evening Post*, May 3, 1958, 22; Knox, There Is a Way Out"; Roe, "Workers Must Fight."

95. Puette, *Through Jaundiced Eyes*, 64.

96. Mills, *The New Men of Power*, 102–3.

97. Lipset, "Labor Unions in the Public Mind," 296, 316.

98. Lester Velie, "Wanted: A Bill of Rights for the Union Man," *Reader's Digest* (Jan. 1955): 33.

99. Roe, "Workers Must Fight."

100. "Democracy in Unions," *New Republic*, June 3, 1957, 7.

101. Lester Velie, "How Can We Restore Unions to Their Members?" *Reader's Digest* (June 1958): 58.

102. Roe, "Workers Must Fight."

103. Velie, "Wanted: A Bill of Rights."

104. Arnold, "Labor's Hidden Holdup Men."

105. "The Purge in the CIO," *New Republic*, Nov. 14, 1949, 5.

106. Garrett, "Labor at the Golden Gate."

107. Velie, "Wanted: A Bill of Rights."

108. "This Time the People Wrote Their Own Labor Law," *Saturday Evening Post*, Oct. 17, 1959, 10.

109. Hard, "Regulating Unions for the Common Good."

110. Roe, "Workers Must Fight."

111. "Another Kind of Public Enemy," 34.

112. Marciniak, "Are We Condoning Union Tyranny?"

113. For the connection between closed shop agreements and racketeering see Pegler, "But What of Soulless Unions?" 57; "A 'Right to Work' Law Might Help Rid Unions of Goons," *Saturday Evening Post*, Sept. 28, 1955, 10; "Those 'Bad' Union Leaders Were Created by Law," *Saturday Evening Post*, July 13, 1957, 10; "This Time the People Wrote Their Own Labor Law"; and Goldwater, "Who Speaks for Labor?" For the connection between closed-shop agreements and communism see "Labor Can't Afford Obtuse Leadership," *Saturday Evening Post*, Aug. 15, 1942, 104, and "Blueprint for Conquest of a Labor Union," *Saturday Evening Post*, July 3, 1948, 104.

114. "The Anti-Labor Act," 811.

115. Leo Huberman, *The Truth about Unions* (New York: Pamphlet Press, 1946), 139.

116. "A 'Right to Work' Law Might Help Rid Unions of Goons."

117. "Law or No Law, There Is a Right to Work!" *Saturday Evening Post,* July 12, 1958, 10.

118. "Blueprint for Conquest of a Labor Union."

119. William Hard, "Should Labor Have Glass Pockets?" *Reader's Digest* (Jan. 1942): 1.

120. Bloomberg, Seidman, and Hoffman, "Paradoxes of Union Democracy."

121. Swigert, "The Taft-Hartley Law"; Roe, "Workers Must Fight"; Velie, "Wanted: A Bill of Rights"; "Shall the People Govern?" *Life,* Aug. 17, 1959, 33; "Is Congress Boss, or Hoffa?"; "This Time the People Wrote Their Own Labor Law"; Evans, "Push-Button Unionism?"

122. "Truman's Labor Advisers Weave a Tangled Web."

123. Swigert, "The Taft-Hartley Law."

124. "The Experts in Congress Know Their Public."

125. Richberg, "Labor Should Live within the Law."

126. "Many Union Men Resent Forced Campaign 'Giving,'" *Saturday Evening Post,* Dec. 29, 1956, 6. See also Villard, "Why Unions Must Be Regulated"; Cenerazzo, "Labor Reform by Labor"; DeMille, "Must Union Members Give Up Their American Rights"; Swigert, "The Taft-Hartley Law"; "There Isn't Any Republican 'War against Labor,'" *Saturday Evening Post,* Jan. 28, 1956, 10; "Should Unions Back Democrats with Money from GOP Members?" *Saturday Evening Post,* Dec. 14, 1957, 10; W. L. White, "Why Should Labor Leaders Play Politics with the Workers' Money?" *Reader's Digest* (Oct. 1958): 157; Goldwater, "Who Speaks for Labor?"; William Schulz, "Labor Drives for a 'Veto-Proof' Congress," *Reader's Digest* (Oct. 1974): 97; Denison, "Where Labor Gets Its Political Muscle"; William Lambert, "Ex-Con Who Spends Big on Candidates," *Life,* July 26, 1968, 42A; John Davenport, "The Bigger Coverup," *National Review,* Aug. 2, 1974, 867; Ralph de Toledano, "Labor's Free Ride," *National Review,* Aug. 4, 1978, 959; Evans, "Push-Button Unionism?"; and William F. Buckley Jr., "Harry Beck, Hero," *National Review,* Nov. 14, 1980, 1417.

127. Denison, "Where Labor Gets Its Political Muscle."

128. Davenport, "The Bigger Coverup."

129. Huberman, *The Truth about Unions,* 151; Robert Griffin, "The Right-to-Work Fight Misses the Point," *Saturday Evening Post,* Feb. 26, 1966, 12.

130. Garet Garrett, "One to Make a Bargain," *Saturday Evening Post,* Sept. 23, 1939, 14.

131. Richberg, "The Rights and Wrongs of Labor."

132. "Why Don't Unions Want a Vote on 'Right to Work' Laws?" *Saturday Evening Post,* Oct. 20, 1956, 10.

133. Kilpatrick, "And Must We Lose This Freedom?"

134. Villard, "Why Unions Must Be Regulated."

135. "Labor Can't afford Obtuse Leadership"; "Antistrike Laws Miss the Point," *Saturday Evening Post,* March 2, 1946, 100; White, "Should Unions Have Monopoly Powers?"; Ching, "Can Labor Live Down Dave Beck?"; "Those 'Bad' Union Leaders Were Created by Law"; "It's Time to Stop Coddling Unions; They're on Top Now!"; de Toledano, "Labor's Free Ride."

136. "Antistrike Laws Miss the Point."

137. de Toledano, "Labor's Free Ride."

138. White, "Should Unions Have Monopoly Powers?"

139. "Labor Can't afford Obtuse Leadership."

140. Stanley High, "Rehearsal for Revolution," *Reader's Digest* (June 1941): 89.

141. Eugene Schneider, *The Rank-and-File Leader* (New Haven: College and University Press, 1963), 146.

142. Bernstein, *The Lean Years,* 146–57.

143. Andrew Kopkind, "Congress and the 'Right to Work,'" *New Republic,* June 5, 1965, 11.

144. Goldwater, "Who Speaks for Labor?"

145. Gallup, *The Gallup Poll,* 1: 159, 347, 519, 621.

146. Gallup, *The Gallup Poll,* 2: 1505.

147. Gallup, *The Gallup Poll,* 3: 1506.

148. Gall, *The Politics of Right to Work,* 107–21.

149. Gallop, *The Gallup Poll,* 3: 1944, 3: 1965, 3: 1992.

150. Lipset, "Labor Unions in the Public Mind," 315.

151. James Dworkin and Marian Extejt, "The Union-Shop Deauthorization Poll: A New Look after Twenty Years," *Monthly Labor Review* (Nov. 1979): 36.

152. "Taft-Hartley Change," *New Republic,* Sept. 3, 1951, 7.

153. Garet Garrett, "Whose Law and Order?" *Saturday Evening Post,* March 25, 1939, 8.

154. William Green, "Does the U.S. Want a Labor Dictator?" *Reader's Digest* (Dec. 1937): 104.

155. Pegler, "But What of Soulless Unions?"; Oliver Pilat, *Pegler: Angry Man of the Press* (Westport: Greenwood Press, 1963), 171.

156. Velie, "Wanted: A Bill of Rights."

157. Huberman, *The Truth about Unions,* 148.

158. "The 'Long Nose' of Government," *New Republic,* Jan. 25, 1954, 5.

159. "A United America."

160. Puette, *Through Jaundiced Eyes,* 179.

161. Randy Fitzgerald, "We'll Get Those Scabs!" *Reader's Digest (Aug. 1981): 130.*

162. Puette, *Through Jaundiced Eyes,* 174–75, 178, 184–85.

163. "The Wonderland of Strikes," *Life,* June 3, 1946, 34.

164. Puette, *Through Jaundiced Eyes,* 177–78.

165. Ibid., Appendix D.

166. Adamic, *Dynamite*, 1, 94, 60.

167. Harold Seidman, *Labor Czars: A History of Labor Racketeering* (New York: Liveright Publishing, 1938); Pilat, *Pegler,* 171.

168. "A Bold Stroke for Labor," *New Republic,* Nov. 10, 1941, 607.

169. Huberman, *The Truth about Unions*, 141.

170. Gallup, *The Gallup Poll,* 1: 271.

171. Bloomberg, Seidman, and Hoffman, "The State of the Unions: Labor on the Defense."

172. David Witwer has shown how the term *union corruption* was used to cover a wide variety of union practices, many of which were legal. "Critics of organized labor wielded a broad definition of corruption, one that involved more than simply acts of bribery or extortion and at times included union activities that were technically legal. This broad, antiunion sense of the word corruption referred to cases where union leaders used aggressive organizing techniques that appeared to give them authority over the economy and society at large. In this way the label of corruption often amounted to a charge of irresponsible power." Witwer, *Corruption and Reform in the Teamsters Union,* 2. These other union practices are treated separately here because it is my contention that all of these issues together made up the cultural image of unions. Thus, the idea that unions cause inflation, and the issue of "union racketeering," although analytically distinct, could easily flow together in peoples' thinking about organized labor.

173. Velie, "When a Fellow Needs a Front," 135.

174. "Shall the People Govern?" 33.

Chapter 3: The Postwar Boom and Organized Labor's Lost Legitimacy

1. Galbraith, *The Affluent Society,* 72.

2. William Whyte, *The Organization Man* (1956, repr. Philadelphia: University of Pennsylvania Press, 2002).

3. Michael Harrington, *The Other America: Poverty in the United States* (New York: MacMillan, 1962).

4. Andrew Levison, *The Working-Class Majority* (New York: Coward, McCann and Geoghegan, 1974).

5. Mills, *The Power Elite,* esp. ch. 4; see also Galbraith, *The Affluent Society,* 78–81.

6. Davis, *Prisoners of the American Dream*; Kim Moody, *An Injury to All: The Decline of American Unionism* (London: Verso Press, 1988).

7. Lipset, "Labor Unions in the Public Mind," 321 (emphasis added).

8. "Another Kind of Public Enemy," 34.

9. Martin, "Has Success Spoiled Big Labor?" 75.

10. "Auto Strike," 1002.

11. "Ford Strike," 7.

12. "Organized Labor's Ten Years Together," 7.

13. As quoted in "What Really Ails the Unions," 55.

14. Bloomberg, Seidman, and Hoffman, "Bureaucrats and Idealists," 10.

15. Alan Reynolds, "Unions: Scapegoat for Inflation," *National Review*, Dec. 31, 1971, 1463.

16. Alan Reynolds, "What Strikes Do to the Innocent Bystander," *National Review*, Sept. 29, 1972, 1057.

17. Freeman and Medoff, *What Do Unions Do?*

18. Hard, "Whites and Blacks Can Work Together," 17; Villard, "Why Unions Must Be Regulated," 27; Swigert, "The Taft-Hartley Law, 23.

19. James Youngdahl, "Unions and Segregation," *New Republic*, July 9, 1956, 14; Mitchell, "Help Wanted, 124; "Jim Crow in Building Unions," *Life*, Nov. 12, 1966, 4; Earl Gottschalk, "Suit against the Unions," *New Republic*, March 12, 1966, 7; Griffin, "The Right-to-Work Fight Misses the Point," 12.

20. Judith Stein, *Running Steel, Running America: Race, Economic Policy, and the Decline of Liberalism* (Chapel Hill: University of North Carolina Press, 1998), 105–6.

21. Jerald Podair, *The Strike That Changed New York: Blacks, Whites, and the Ocean Hill–Brownsville Crisis* (New Haven: Yale University Press: 2002); Maurice Berube and Marilyn Gittell, eds., *Confrontation at Ocean Hill–Brownsville: The New York School Strikes of 1968* (New York: Praeger, 1969); Marvin Hoffman, "Conflict in a Counterfeit Community: The Ocean Hill School Crisis," *New Republic*, Nov. 9, 1968, 19.

22. Robert Cassidy, "Strikes against Government," *New Republic*, March 18, 1972, 31.

23. "Why Tolerate the Excesses of Unions?" *Life*, Aug. 26, 1966, 4.

24. Peggy Flint, "Florida's Anti-Labor Drive," *New Republic*, June 18, 1945, 842.

25. Timothy Minchin, *Hiring the Black Worker: The Racial Integration of the Southern Textile Industry, 1960–1980* (Chapel Hill: University of North Carolina Press, 1999), ch. 8.

26. "The Battle of the Grapes," *Reader's Digest* (Oct. 1969): 88; John Gregory Dunne, "Strike!" May 6, 1967, *Saturday Evening Post*, 32.

27. von Hoffman, "The Last Days of the Labor Movement," 22.

28. Leon Fink and Brian Greenberg, *Upheaval in the Quiet Zone: A History of Hospital Workers' Union, Local 1199* (Urbana: University of Illinois Press, 1989), ch. 7.

29. Gall, *The Politics of Right to Work*, 142–43.

30. Minchin, *Hiring the Black Worker*, ch. 8.

31. Kochan, "How American Workers View Labor Unions," 25.

32. One need only consider the vastly different reactions of whites and blacks to the O. J. Simpson verdict to realize that the cultural universe of African Americans differed from that of whites.

33. Edwin Lahey, "What's Ahead of American Labor?" *New Republic*, July 26, 1943, 106.

34. Lichtenstein and Harris, eds., *Industrial Democracy in America,*; Martin, "Has Success Spoiled Big Labor?"

35. Gerald Johnson, "The Superficial Aspect," *New Republic,* April 11, 1955, 19.

36. Willard Shelton, "Labor's Failure," *New Republic,* May 19, 1947, 37.

37. "The Coming Together of Organized Labor," *New Republic,* Feb. 21, 1955, 3.

38. "Labor at a Crossroad," *Life,* Jan. 26, 1959, 24.

39. Martin, "Has Success Spoiled Big Labor?"

40. Croly, *The Promise of American Life,* 126–31, esp. 131; Thorstein Veblen, *Engineers and the Price System* (New York: B. W. Huebsch, 1921), 88–90; Adamic, *Dynamite,* 436, 439.

41. Reuther, "GM v. the Rest of Us," 41.

42. Lichtenstein, *The Most Dangerous Man in Detroit,* 297.

43. Lizabeth Cohen, *A Consumers' Republic: The Politics of Mass Consumption in Postwar America* (2003, repr. New York: Random House: 2004), ch. 1; Fraser, *Labor Will Rule,* 330.

44. "Red or Reactionary, We Must Produce!" *Saturday Evening Post,* Dec. 28, 1946, 84; "Bystanders Guide to the Labor Argument," *Saturday Evening Post,* Dec. 22, 1945, 112; "Who Wins by Stabbing America?" *Saturday Evening Post,* June 22, 1946, 132; "The Public and the Strikers," *New Republic,* Oct. 8, 1945, 486; "The Wonderland of Strikes," 34; Thompson, Dorothy, "Wanted: A Federal Labor Policy," *Ladies Home Journal,* Feb. 1947, 6; "Both Sides See Need for Avoiding Strikes," *Life,* Feb. 3, 1947, 24.

45. "Antistrike Laws Miss the Point," 100.

46. "Loafing Creates No Purchasing Power," *Saturday Evening Post,* Nov. 17, 1945, 136.

47. "Loafing Creates No Purchasing Power," 126; "What's Back of the GM Strike," *New Republic,* Dec. 31, 1945, 884; "The Wonderland of Strikes," 34; "Both Sides See Need for Avoiding Strikes," 24; John Knox, "There Is a Way Out," 45; Thompson, "Wanted: A Federal Labor Policy," 6.

48. "Is Congress Boss, or Hoffa?" 30.

49. "It's Serious, Mr. President," *New Republic,* April 2, 1951, 5.

50. "Where Society Steps In," *New Republic,* Oct. 26, 1959; "Labor at a Crossroad"; "A New Kind of Steel Strike," *Life,* Aug. 10, 1959, 38; Joseph Block, "Steel Executive Blasts the Union's Demands," *Life,* Nov. 9, 1959, 38; Bloomberg, Seidman, and Hoffman, "Bureaucrats and Idealists"; "It's Time for a 'Work Break,'" *Reader's Digest,* Dec. 1960, 118; "Steel: How Inflationary?" 26; Harry Wellington, "Labor Disputes: When Should Government Intervene?" *New Republic,* Jan. 11, 1960, 11.

51. "Auto Strike"; "Strike or Boycott What?" *National Review,* Dec. 16, 1969, 1256; "See Them Strike," *New Republic,* Sept. 26, 1970, 7; Paul London, "Wage Restraint Pro Quo: A Program for Solidarity Day," *New Republic,* Oct. 7, 1981, 15; Reynolds, "Unions"; Novak, "Reagan's new Coalition," 1023.

52. Gallup, *The Gallup Poll,* 3: 1619.

53. Gallup, George, *The Gallup Poll: Public Opinion, 1972–1977* (Willimington: Scholarly Resources, 1978), 1:298.

54. London, "Wage Restraint Pro Quo," 15.

55. Nicholas von Hoffman, "Stee-rike!: The Owners' Squeeze Play," *New Republic,* July 4, 1981, 9.

56. "A New Kind of Steel Strike," 38; "Steel," 26.

57. Michael Piore and Charles Sabel, *The Second Industrial Divide: Possibilities for Prosperity* (New York: Basic Books, 1984), 115; Lawrence Mishel and Paula Voos, *Unions and Economic Competitiveness* (Armonk: M. E. Sharpe, 1992).

58. Samuel Kornhauser, "Why Can't Wage Disputes Be Settled Like Other Controversies—By Law?" *Saturday Evening Post,* July 16, 1949, 12; Karl Detzer, "The Citizens Themselves Prevent Strikes," *Reader's Digest,* Dec. 1941, 33.

59. Stahl, "The Case Against Strikes," 128.

60. Edward Zwick, "Hollywood Diarist," *New Republic,* Oct. 4, 1980, 43.

61. W. L. White, "Strike Without End—The Kholer Story," *Reader's Digest,* Oct. 1957, 91; Ralph Martin, "The CIO Takes a Long Lease in the South," *New Republic,* Jan. 13, 1947, 19.

62. George Soule, "Panic over Labor," *New Republic,* June 23, 1937, 175.

63. "General Strike," *Life,* Dec. 16, 1946, 38; "Violence Breaks Out as Nation's Strikes Spread," *Life,* Jan. 28, 1946, 34; "Allis-Chalmers Strike Has Been Long, Costly," *Life,* Feb. 3, 1947, 22; "The Meat Strike," *Life,* May 3, 1948, 30; "'High Noon' in a Strikebound Town," *Life,* April 13, 1953, 61; "Old Style Labor War Explodes in Indiana," *Life,* Oct. 17, 1955, 46; "Sugar Strike Turns Bitter," *Life,* July 18, 1955, 42; "New Affluence, Unity for Labor," 26.

64. "Letter to the Middle Class," *New Republic,* Jan. 21, 1946, 67; Samuel Rosenman, "A Better Way to Handle Strikes," *Reader's Digest,* Oct. 1967, 106; "See Them Strike," 7; "Labor and the Law," 32; Knox "There Is a Way Out," 45.

65. Knox, "There Is a Way Out," 45.

66. Stahl, "The Case Against Strikes," 128.

67. Rosenman, "A Better Way to Handle Strikes," 106.

68. "Labor and the Law," 32; Stahl, "The Case Against Strikes," 128; Kornhauser, "Why Can't Wage Disputes Be Settled Like Other Controversies—By Law?" 12.

69. "Letter to the Middle Class," 67.

70. Mills, *The New Men of Power,* 119.

71. Reinhold Niebuhr, *Moral Man and Immoral Society: A Study in Ethics and Politics* (1932, repr. Louisville: Westminster John Knox Press, 2001), 129–30.

72. Knox, "There Is a Way Out," 45.

73. Puette, *Through Jaundiced Eyes,* 50.

74. Knox, "There Is a Way Out," 45.

75. Huberman, *The Truth about Unions,* 146, 148.

76. "What Goeth before a Fall," *Saturday Evening Post,* Dec. 27, 1941, 24; "Why Tolerate the Excesses of Unions?"; Tomlinson, Kenneth, "Can Public-Employee Unions Be Controlled?" *Reader's Digest,* April 1977, 141.

77. Soule, George, "Are Unions Too Strong?" *New Republic,* June 17, 1946, 860.

78. Murray, "The CIO Looks at 'Labor Laws,'" 29.

79. Arnold, "Labor's Hidden Holdup Men," 136.

80. "Truman's Labor Advisers Weave a Tangled Web," 10.

81. "Titler, M'Tigue Explain Benefits to DuPont Workers," *District 50 News,* July 15, 1942, 4.

82. Huberman, *The Truth about Unions,* 131.

83. "Who Wins by Stabbing America?" 132.

84. Reynolds, "What Strikes Do to the Innocent Bystander."

85. "Letter to the Middle Class," 67; "It's Time to Stop Coddling Unions; They're on Top Now!" 10; "What Is the Kennedy Solution for Strikes?" *Saturday Evening Post,* Oct. 22, 1960, 10; "The Spectacle New Yorkers Hope Never to See Again," *Life,* Jan. 21, 1966, 62D; "Transit Union Gets a Half-Nelson on New York," *Life,* Jan. 14, 1966, 28; "An Intolerable Strike," *Life,* Jan. 14, 1966, 4; Stahl, "The Case against Strikes," 128; James Kilpatrick, "They Struck a Blow for Tyranny, *National Review,* Oct. 2, 1981, 1132; "Letter to the Middle Class," 67; "Temporarily Out of Order," *Life,* April 21, 1947, 40; Evan Hill, "City of Silence," *Saturday Evening Post,* June 8, 1957, 32; Stahl, "The Case against Strikes," 128. Oswald Garrison Villard, "A Letter F.D.R. Ought to Have Written," *Reader's Digest,* Sept. 1937, 63; "Kansas City Has Surprise Blackout," *Life,* Sept. 29, 1941, 34. "Say It With Flowers," *National Review,* April 7, 1970, 340; Tomlinson, "Can Public-Employe Unions Be Controlled?" 141.

86. "Second Class Citizens," *New Republic,* May 17, 1943, 655.

87. Murray, "The CIO Looks at 'Labor Laws.'"

88. Johnson, "The Superficial Aspect."

89. Lipset, "Labor Unions in the Public Mind," 303.

90. Lipset and Schneider, *The Confidence Gap,* 219, 218.

91. Daniel Bell, *The Coming of Post-Industrial Society: A Venture in Social Forecasting* (1973, repr. New York: Basic Books, 1999), 129, 164, 125.

92. Willard Shelton, "Featherbedding" *New Republic,* July 28, 1947, 30; "Stuck with Obsolete Bedding," *Life,* March 23, 1953, 36; "And Then There's Featherbedding," *Life,* June 1, 1959, 30; "If We Want Growth, Just Cut Down on Strikes," *Saturday Evening Post,* Nov. 28, 1959, 10; Gerald Johnson, "Time to Get Up," *New Republic,* Nov. 9, 1959, 11; Stahl, "The Case against Strikes," 128; Rosenman, "A Better Way to Handle Strikes," 106.

93. Chase, "The Twilight of Communism in the U.S.A.," 25.

94. "Stuck with Obsolete Bedding," 36.

95. "And Then There's Featherbedding," 30; Garrett, "The Labor Mask," 18.

96. Huberman, *The Truth about Unions,* 134.

97. Ives, "The Truth about the New Labor Law," 13.

98. Piore and Sabel, *The Second Industrial Divide,* 115. See also Mike Parker, "Industrial Relations Myth and Shop-Floor Reality: The 'Team Concept' in the Auto Industry," in *Industrial Democracy in America: The Ambiguous Promise,* edited by Lichtenstein and Howell, 270.

99. Mills, *White Collar,* 248–49, 313.

100. Edward Gibson, interview with the author, Aug. 2000.

101. Jacoby, *Modern Manors,* 44.

102. Bloomberg, Seidman, and Hoffman, "New Members, New Goals," 9.

103. Everett Kasslow, "Organization of White-Collar Workers," *Monthly Labor Review* (March 1961), 234–38; Goldstein, Bernard and Bernard Indik, "Unionism as a Social Choice: The Engineers' Case," *Monthly Labor Review* (April 1963), 365–69.; Albert Blum, "Prospects for Organization of White-Collar Workers," *Monthly Labor Review* (Feb. 1964), 125–29.; George Strauss, "Dilemma for Engineers: Union or Professional Society?" *Monthly Labor Review* (Aug. 1964), 1026–28; Irving Brotslaw, "Attitude of Retail Workers toward Union Organization," *Labor Law Journal* (March 1967); Roger Manley and Charles McNichols, "Attitudes of Federal Scientists and Engineers Toward Unions," *Monthly Labor Review* (April 1975), 57–60; Kochan, "How American Workers View Labor Unions."

104. Puette, *Through Jaundiced Eyes,* 54–55.

105. Bell, *The Coming of Post-Industrial Society,* 362.

106. Mills, *White Collar,* 138.

107. Bloomberg, Seidman, and Hoffman, "New Members, New Goals."

108. Mills, *White Collar,* 312.

109. Leonard Sayles and George Strauss, *The Local Union: Its Place in the Industrial Plant* (New York: Harper, 1953), 225.

110. Mills, *White Collar,* 248–49, 312; see also Jurgen Kocka, *White Collar Workers in America, 1890–1940: A Social-Polithite Collar Workers in America, 1890–1940* (London: Sage Publications, 1980), 132.

111. David Selden, *The Teacher Rebellion* (Washington, D.C.: Howard University Press, 1985), 82.

112. Manley and McNichols, "Attitudes of Federal Scientists and Engineers Toward Unions," 57–60.

113. "Antistrike Laws Miss the Point," 100.

114. Kochan, "How American Workers View Labor Unions," 30.

115. Faue, *Community of Suffering and Struggle,* quotation on 74, picture on 75.

116. Blum, "Prospects for Organization of White-Collar Workers," 125–29.

117. Manley and McNichols, "Attitudes of Federal Scientists and Engineers Toward Unions," 57–60.

118. Murray, "The CIO Looks at 'Labor Laws,'" 29.

119. Blum, "Prospects for Organization of White-Collar Workers," 125–29.

120. Donald Richberg, *Labor Union Monopoly: A Clear and Present Danger* (Chicago: H. Regnery, 1957), 97; Maurice Franks, *What's Wrong with Our Labor Unions!* (Indianapolis: Bobbs-Merrill, 1963), 136, 209, 218, 233, 235.

121. Kessler-Harris, *In Pursuit of Equity,*esp. 16.

122. Faue, *Community of Suffering and Struggle.*

123. Wayne Urban, *Gender, Race, and the National Education Association: Professionalism and its Limitations* (New York: RoutledgeFalmer, 2000), 254–45.

124. Ching, "Can Labor Live Down Dave Beck?" 31. See also White, "Should Unions Have Monopoly Powers?" 33; "Why Tolerate the Excesses of Unions?"

125. Arnold and Hamilton, "Thoughts on Labor Day."

126. Shelton, "Featherbedding."

127. Hillman, "The Promise of American Labor," 62.

128. Patric, "Remove Union Restrictions."

129. Arnold and Hamilton, "Thoughts on Labor Day."

130. Donald Richberg, "Will Labor Lose the War?" *Saturday Evening Post,* April 18, 1942, 19.

131. Patric, "Remove Union Restrictions."

132. Robert Bellah, et al., *Habits of the Heart: Individualism and Commitment in American Life* (1985, repr. Berkeley: University of California Press, 1996), 175–76. The reference to being paid for not working refers to Supplemental Unemployment Benefits. Also, note the initial disclaimer that the speaker is "not against unions" per se.

133. Kenneth Gilmore, "The Scandal of Our Missile Program," *Reader's Digest,* Aug. 1961, 25.

134. McClellan, "These Labor Abuses Must Be Curbed," 97.

135. Blum, "Prospects for Organization of White-Collar Workers," 125–29.

136. Strauss, "Dilemma for Engineers, 1026–28.

137. "This Is One Way Not to Get More Skilled Workers," *Saturday Evening Post,* March 15, 1958, 10.

138. Frank Taylor, F. "This Union Prospers by Producing," *Reader's Digest,* July 1953, 118; Karl Detzer, "This Union Found the Best Way to Raise Wages," *Reader's Digest,* Feb. 1957, 153. See also Charles Coates, "The Union of Tomorrow," *Reader's Digest,* Nov. 1938, 48; Hillman, "The Promise of American Labor," 62; Joseph Gollomb, "Sidney Hillman," *Reader's Digest,* July 1939, 104; Frank Taylor, "Getting Along with Eighteen Unions," *Reader's Digest,* Feb. 1939, 59; Cenerazzo, "Class Struggle Isn't the Answer," 27; Ives, "The Truth about the New Labor Law"; Victor Riesel, "Come the Revolution," *Reader's Digest,* Oct. 1948, 119; Murray, "If We Pull Together," 10; Martin McIntyre, "A Labor Editor Says," *Reader's Digest,* June 1953, 16; Blake Clark, "Meet a New Kind of Labor Secretary," *Reader's Digest,* Nov. 1956, 155; Irwin Ross, "Who Wins a Strike?" *Reader's Digest,* Aug. 1967, 101.

139. Hard, "The Typographical Union—Model for All," 1.

140. Fraser, *Labor Will Rule.*

141. Sydney Hillman, "The Promise of American Labor," *New Republic,* Nov. 8, 1939, 62.

142. Cenerazzo, "Class Struggle Isn't the Answer," 27.

Part II: Antiunion Culture at Work

1. Nelson Lichtenstein, *State of the Union: A Century of American Labor* (Princeton: University of Princeton Press, 2002), 267.

2. Bernstein, *Turbulent Years,* 481.

3. Stephen Waring, *Taylorism Transformed: Scientific Management Theory since 1945* (Chapel Hill: University of North Carolina Press, 1991), 15.

Chapter 4: Union Outsiders versus the Ix Family

1. The TWUA's effort to organize J. P. Stevens had began in the mid-1960s. It was not until 1976, however, that it was able to win its first representation election at any of Stevens' numerous plants. The movie *Norma Rae* is based on this effort by the TWUA to organize Stevens. Whereas the movie ends with the union winning the election, in real life the union was not able to negotiate a contract until 1980. Winning this first contract, in fact, proved to be as fraught with difficulty as had the union's effort to win an election in the first place. Timothy, *"Don't Sleep With Stevens!": The J. P. Stevens Campaign and the Struggle to Organize the South, 1963–80* (Gainesville: University Press of Florida, 2005).

2. "John Todd to Mr. E. A. Thomas," 29 Oct. 1980, box 79, folder 3, Papers of Frank Ix & Sons, Special Collections, University of Virginia (hereafter cited as PIx). Copies of most of the letters, brochures, etc., referred to here were sent by John Todd, the plant manager at the Charlottesville facility of Frank Ix & Sons, to E. A. Thomas, apparently a senior company official located at the corporate headquarters in New York. Thus, most of the citations reference "John Todd to Mr. E. A. Thomas." Dates and locations within the collection are given to help differentiate among these PIx items. See also, Minchin, *Don't Sleep With Stevens!* 173.

3. "Wayne Dernoncourt to Sol Stein," 11 Dec. 1979, box 179, Papers of the Amalgamated Clothing and Textile Workers of America, Kheel Center, Cornell University (hereafter cited as PACTWU).

4. Agre, Louis, "Frank Ix and Sons," 10 Nov. 1980, box 830, PACTWU.

5. "John Todd to Mr. E. A. Thomas," 5 Feb. 1981, box 79, folder 3, PIx.

6. "John Todd to Mr. Paul Thompson," 15 Oct. 1980, box 79, folder 3, PIx.

7. See boxes 79 and 80, PIx.

8. See box 79, folder 8, PIx.

9. For an excellent historiographical essay about this literature, see Robert Zieger, "From Primordial Folk to Redundant Workers: Southern Textile Workers and Social Observers, 1920–1990," in *Southern Labor in Transition, 1940–1995,* edited by Robert Zieger (Knoxville: University of Tennessee Press, 1997).

10. Clete Daniel, *Culture of Misfortune: An Interpretive History of Textile Unionism in the United States* (Ithaca: ILR Press, 2001), 167.

11. Minchin, *What Do We Need a Union For?*; Minchin, *Don't Sleep with Stevens!;* Minchin, *Hiring the Black Worker;* Minchin, *Fighting Against the Odds;* Daniel, *Culture of Misfortune;* Daniel Clark, *Like Night and Day: Unionization in a Southern Mill Town* (Chapel Hill: University of North Carolina Press, 1997).

12. Minchin, *What Do We Need a Union For?*

13. Sam Crawford, interview with the author, May 2000. Tapes of these interviews are in the author's possession and available to interested researchers.

14. Tammy H., interview with the author, Apr. 2000. Throughout this text, a last name abbreviated to a single letter indicates the use of a pseudonym.

15. Charlotte Dudley, interview with the author, Apr. 2000.

16. Henry Peregoy, interview with the author, Aug. 2000.

17. Sam Crawford interview.

18. Henry Peregoy interview.

19. John Todd, "Dear Fellow Employee," 31 Jan. 1981, box 79, folder 3, PIx.

20. "John Todd to Mr. E. A. Thomas," 31 Jan. 1981, box 79, folder 3, PIx.

21. "John Todd to Mr. E. A. Thomas," 5 Feb. 1981.

22. "John Todd to Mr. E. A. Thomas," 29 Oct. 1980.

23. "John Todd to Mr. E. A. Thomas," 5 Feb. 1981.

24. "Retirement at Frank Ix," 29, Sept. 1980, box 79, folder 3, PIx.

25. "John Todd to Mr. E. A. Thomas," 5 Feb. 1981.

26. Data for this analysis is taken from box 79, folder 1, PIx, where employee data such as name, department, supervisor, shift, pay, race, and hire date are listed, as well as tabulations on how employees were expected to vote. Gender and age data were gleaned from the personnel files. Start dates were also confirmed from the personnel files, because some employees would leave for a while only to return later. In this case, the earliest start date was used to test against long-term connection to the company. The dependent variable used here is support for the union (prounion = 1; antiunion = 0).

independent variables	impact	significance
same last name as supervisor (same = 1)	−.818	.014
gender (female = 1)	−.476	.075
race (nonwhite = 1)	.531	.054
pay	−.243	.20
length of service (in years)	−.049	.002
age (in years)	−.037	.001

It should be noted that Ix's "polling data" was not completely accurate. For instance, one worker I interviewed was listed by Ix as being against the union. As it turned out, she had supported the union but had disguised her sympathies out of fear. The magnitude of such discrepancies is not known. Nevertheless, it seems probable that Ix had a fairly accurate picture of how particular employees were going to vote.

27. "John Todd to Mr. E. A. Thomas," 10 Dec. 1980, box 79, folder 3, PIx.

28. "1—The Union Organizer arrived on 8–12–80 at . . . ," 1980, box 79, folder 2, PIx.

29. "From John Todd to Mr. Paul Thompson," 17 Sept. 1980, box 79, folder 3, PIx; "John Todd to Mr. Paul Thompson," 26 Sept. 1980, box 79, folder 3, PIx; "John Todd to Mr. Paul Thompson," 15 Oct. 1980, box 79, folder 3, PIx; "Uncle Sam Is 100% Behind You," 28 Jan. 1981, box 79, folder 3, PIx.

30. "Talking points for members of Management as they discuss the union with employees," 1981, box 79, folder 3, p. 3, PIx.

31. "Are your ready to give up your employees to a labor union?," 1 Dec. 1980, box 79, folder 2, p. 4, PIx.

32. "John Todd to Mr. E. A. Thomas," 5 Feb. 1981.

33. "The Law Says," 1981, box 79, folder 3, PIx.

34. "John Todd to Mr. E. A. Thomas," 5 Feb. 1981.

35. "Are your ready to give up your employees to a labor union?," 1 Dec. 1980.

36. "John Todd to Mr. E. A. Thomas," 5 Feb. 1981.

37. Fred Carey, interview with the author, Aug. 2000.

38. "John Todd to Mr. E. A. Thomas," 5 Nov. 1980, box 79, folder 3, PIx.

39. "John Todd to Mr. Paul Thompson," 26 Sept. 1980, box 79, folder 3, PIx.

40. NLRB case no. 5–CA-13019, box 79, folder 6, PIx; Tammy H. interview.

41. "From John Todd to Mr. E. A. Thomas," 28 Aug. 1980, box 79, folder 3, PIx.

42. "John Todd to Mr. Paul Thompson," 26 Sept. 1980.

43. "John Todd to Mr. E. A. Thomas," 26 Nov. 1980, box 79, folder 3, PIx.

44. Tammy H. interview.

45. "Talking points for members of Management . . . ," 1981, 3.

46. Newspaper clippings, 1981, box 79, folder 3, PIx.

47. "John Todd to Mr. E. A. Thomas," 23 Jan. 1981, box 79, folder 3, PIx.

48. "Are your ready to give up . . . ?," 1 Dec. 1980, 7.

49. "John Todd to Mr. E. A. Thomas," 5 Feb. 1981.

50. Tammy H. interview.

51. Sam Crawford interview.

52. Daniel, *Culture of Misfortune,* 254–55.

53. "Are your ready to give up . . . ?," 1 Dec. 1980, 5; "Talking points for members of Management . . . ," 1981, 2; "John Todd to Mr. E. A. Thomas," 5 Feb. 1981.

54. "Are your ready to give up . . . ?," 1 Dec. 1980.

55. "Uncle Sam is 100% Behind You," 28 Jan. 1981, box 79, folder 3, PIx.

56. "John Todd to Mr. E. A. Thomas," 5 Feb. 1981.

57. "You Have a Right to Organize a Union—The Federal Law Protects You," 3 Nov. 1980, box 79, folder 3, PIx.

58. "John Todd to Mr. E. A. Thomas," 19 Jan. 1981, box 79, folder 3, PIx.

59. Tammy H. interview.

60. See folders 1 and 2, box 79, PIx.

61. NLRB case no. 5–CA-13019, box 79, folder 6, PIx.

62. Sam Crawford interview.

63. Robert Freeman, "Dear Fellow Worker," 10 Mar. 1982, box 79, folder 3, PIx.

64. "John Todd to Mr. E. A. Thomas," 24 Oct. 1980, box 79, folder 3, PIx, emphasis added.

65. Sam Crawford interview.

66. Fred Carey interview.

67. "John Todd to Mr. E. A. Thomas," 5 Feb. 1981.

68. "Talking points for members of Management . . . ," 1981, 5.

69. "Dear Fellow Employee: We have been successful in have a secret ballot election . . . ," 1981, box 79, folder 3, PIx.

70. "John Todd to Mr. E. A. Thomas," 26 Nov. 1980, box 79, folder 3, PIx.

71. "Talking points for members of Management . . . ," 1981, 5.

72. Sam Crawford interview.

73. Ibid.

74. "Job Security?," 1981, box 79, folder 3, PIx, emphasis in original.

75. "John Todd to Mr. E. A. Thomas," 24 Oct. 1980; "Job Security?," 1981.

76. "General Supervisors Meeting—9/8/80," 4 Sept. 1980, box 79, folder 3, PIx.

77. John M., interview with the author, Aug. 2000.

78. Sam Crawford interview.

79. "Mack Patton to Mr. J. Todd," 29 Oct. 1980, box 79, folder 3, PIx.

80. "John Todd to Mr. E. A. Thomas," 24 Oct. 1980; "John Todd to Mr. E. A. Thomas," 10 Dec. 1980, box 79, folder 3, PIx.

81. "1—The Union Organizer arrived on 8-12-80 at . . . ," 1980, box 79, folder 2, PIx.

82. "September 18, 1980—Thursday; 1. Meeting at 8:15 A.M., 3rd shift, Holiday Inn South . . . ," 18 Sept. 1980, box 79, folder 2, p. 14, PIx.

83. John M. interview.

84. About 19 percent of the workforce (87 of 460 workers) was African American.

85. Tammy H. interview.

86. See footnote 26 for polling data.

87. Tammy H. interview; James Morton, Charge #03681–0820, box 80, PIx; *Gregory Brown vs Frank Ix & Sons,* box 80, PIx.

88. James Morton, Charge #03681–0820.

89. *Gregory Brown vs Frank Ix & Sons.*

90. "John Todd to Mr. E. A. Thomas," 24 Oct. 1980.

91. John M. interview.

92. "Comments—1—Shop—Drunk getting more pay per hour than . . . ," 12 Aug. 1980, box 79, folder 2, PIx.

93. "John Todd to Mr. E. A. Thomas," 5 Feb. 1981; see footnote 26 for polling data.

94. Fred Carey interview.

95. "September 18, 1980—Thursday; 1. Meeting at 8:15 A.M., 3rd shift, Holiday Inn South . . . ," 18 Sept. 1980, box 79, folder 2, PIx.

96. "John Todd to Mr. E. A. Thomas," 5 Feb.

97. Giametta, Charles, "Textile Union Organizing Here: Ix Plant is Target," 10 Oct. 1980, *The Daily Progress,* box 79, folder 3, PIx.

98. "John Todd to Mr. E. A. Thomas," 24 Oct. 1980; "John Todd to Mr. E. A. Thomas," 7 Nov. 1980.

99. Sam Crawford interview.

100. "What Is a Union?," 1981, box 79, folder 3, PIx.

101. All quotes taken from "September 18, 1980—Thursday," 18 Sept. 1980.

102. "Norfolk Union Official Indicted," 25 Nov. 1980, box 79, folder 3, PIx, emphasis in original.

103. John Todd, "This was on warp, B. Fox," 29 Oct. 1980, box 79, folder 3, PIx.

104. "Velida Tomlin to Honorable John Warner," 9 June 1981, box 79, folder 3, PIx.

105. Sam Crawford interview; "September 18, 1980—Thursday . . . ," 18 Sept. 1980.

106. Charlotte Dudley interview; Fred Carey interview.

107. "John Todd to Mr. E. A. Thomas," 5 Feb. 1981.

108. Ibid.

109. See footnote 26. It should be said, however, that this trend is only significant at the 7.5 percent level.

110. "John Todd to Mr. E. A. Thomas," 5 Feb. 1981.

111. Sam Crawford interview.

112. "John Todd to Mr. E. A. Thomas," 5 Feb. 1981.

113. John Todd, "Dear Fellow Employee," 31 Jan. 1981.

114. "John Todd to Mr. E. A. Thomas," 5 Feb. 1981.

115. "What Is a Union?," 1981, emphasis in original.

116. "Do You Know These Men?," 1981, box 79, folder 3, PIx.

117. "Are your ready to give up . . . ?," 1 Dec. 1980, 1.

118. "What the Union Has Not Told You," 1981, box 79, folder 3, PIx.

119. "Are your ready to give up . . . ?," 1 Dec. 1980, 4.

120. "John Todd to Mr. E. A. Thomas," 5 Feb. 1981; "What the Union Has Not Told You," 1981, emphasis in original.

121. "Are your ready to give up . . . ?," 1 Dec. 1980, 9.

122. D"Wayne Dernoncourt to Sol Stein," 11 Dec. 1979, box 179, PACTWU.

123. Zieger, *The CIO, 1935–1955*, 227–41. See also the picture on page 203.

124. "John Todd to Mr. E. A. Thomas," 23 Jan. 1981.

125. Sam Crawford interview.

126. "John Todd to Mr. E. A. Thomas," 5 Feb. 1981.

127. "Ask Yourself When Was The Last Time I Got Something for Nothing?," 1981, box 79, folder 3, PIx.

128. "John Todd to Mr. E. A. Thomas," 5 Feb. 1981; John Todd, "Dear Fellow Employee," 31 Jan. 1981.

129. "Talking points for members of Management . . . ," 1981; "Do You Know the A.C.T.W.U.?," 1981, box 79, folder 3, PIx.

130. "John Todd to Mr. E. A. Thomas," 23 Jan. 1981.

131. Ibid.

132. "What the Union Has Not Told You," 1981.

133. "Ask Yourself When Was The Last . . . ?," 1981.

134. "John Todd to Mr. E. A. Thomas," 29 Jan. 1981.

135. "John Todd to Mr. E. A. Thomas," 5 Feb. 1981.

136. Ibid.

137. "John Todd to Mr. E. A. Thomas," 27 Jan. 1981, box 79, folder 3, PIx.

138. "Federal Laws Protect You," 27 Jan. 1981, box 79, folder 3, PIx.

139. "John Todd to Mr. Paul Thompson," 17 Sept. 1980.

140. "John Todd to Mr. Paul Thompson," 26 Sept. 1980.

141. "The U.S. Government Is 100% Behind a Free Labor Movement," 29 Jan. 1981, box 79, folder 3, PIx.

142. "John Todd to Mr. E. A. Thomas," 10 Dec. 1980, box 79, folder 3, PIx.

143. "The U.S. Government Is 100% . . . ," 29 Jan. 1981.

144. "John Todd to Mr. E. A. Thomas," 13 Dec. 1980, box 79, folder 3, PIx.

145. Ibid.

146. "John Todd to Mr. E. A. Thomas," 5 Feb. 1981.

147. "John Todd to Mr. Wayne L. Dernoncourt," 14 Nov. 1980, box 79, folder 3, PIx.

148. "John Todd to Mr. E. A. Thomas," 5 Feb. 1981.

149. Henry Peregoy interview.

150. Charlotte Dudley interview.

151. Ibid.

152. Henry Peregoy interview.

153. "The U.S. Government Is 100% Behind . . . ," 29 Jan. 1981.

154. Cartoon, 1981, box 79, folder 6, PIx.

155. "Are your ready to give up your employees to a labor union?," 1 Dec. 1980, box 79, folder 2, PIx.

156. "John Todd to Mr. E. A. Thomas," 27 Jan. 1981.

157. "John Todd to Mr. E. A. Thomas," 13 Dec. 1980, box 79, folder 3, PIx.

158. Fred Carey interview.

159. Sam Crawford interview; Henry Peregoy interview.

160. "What Is a Union?," 1981, box 79, folder 3, PIx.

161. Edward Gibson interview.

162. Ibid.

163. Charlotte Dudley interview, emphasis added.

164. "Comments—1—Shop—Drunk getting more pay per hour than . . . ," 12 Aug. 1980, box 79, folder 2, PIx.

165. See footnote 26. When department and shift are added as independent variables, no significant trend emerges due to the overwhelming and widespread rejection of the union and because there are simply too many independent variables for the analysis to have any validity. Nevertheless, visual inspection of Ix's polling data does show a tendency for union support to cluster in a few departmental shifts.

166. "September 18, 1980—Thursday . . . ," 18 Sept. 1980.

167. Tammy H. interview.

168. Organizing Department, "Examples of type of information that is vital to organizing," 1979, box 185, PACTWU.

169. "The U.S. Government Is 100% Behind a Free Labor Movement," 29 Jan. 1981.

170. "Famous Americans Praise Unions," 1981, box 79, folder 3, PIx.

171. Sam Crawford interview.

172. Charlotte Dudley interview.

173. "John Todd to Mr. E. A. Thomas," 18 Oct. 1980, box 79, folder 3, PIx.

174. Sam Crawford interview.

175. "John Todd to Mr. E. A. Thomas," 23 Jan. 1981; "Do You Know These Men?," 1981, box 79, folder 3, PIx; "Ask Yourself When Was The Last Time . . . ," 1981; "Do You Know the A.C.T.W.U.?," 1981, box 79, folder 3, PIx.

176. "John Todd to Mr. E. A. Thomas," 14 Jan. 1981.

177. Mack Patton, "Schedule for United Way Film Showing," 8 Sept. 1980, box 79, folder 3, PIx.

178. "John Todd to Mr. E. A. Thomas," 5 Feb. 1981, box 79, folder 3, PIx.

179. John M. interview.

Chapter 5: Antiunionism in the Citadel of Organized Labor

1. Joshua Freeman, *Working-Class New York: Life and Labor since World War II* (New York: New Press, 2000).

2. Walter Kelly, "Local Trying to Form an All-U Union," *Washington Square Journal*, Dec. 10, 1969, 1; NLRB case no. 2–RM-1621, 21 July 1971, box 65, folder 1, James Hester Papers, New York University Archives (hereafter cited as JHP).

3. "Library workers take first step toward union recognition," Mar. 1970, box 65, folder 3, JHP.

4. "Library and placement workers vote to strike," Apr. 1970, box 65, folder 3, JHP.

5. "Monday's latest," Apr. 1970, box 65, folder 3, JHP.

6. "The strike is over!," Apr. 1970, box 65, folder 3, JHP.

7. James Hester, "The University's position on strike," 17 Apr. 1970, box 65, folder 2, JHP.

8. James Hester, "The University Petitions for an Election," 17 Apr. 1970, box 65, folder 2, JHP.

9. Don Holloschutz, "Workers to Strike on Sixth Day," *Washington Square Journal*, April 4, 1970, 1.

10. "NYU Concedes," Apr. 1970, box 65, folder 3, JHP.

11. Kimball Commune, "Rumors . . . Clarifications," May 1970, box 1, folder "NYU's position on the unionization of the workers by District 65 and Local 153" (hereafter cited as NYU's Position), Staff Unionization, Office of the General Counsel, NYU Archives (hereafter cited as OGC).

12. Allan Cartter, "To University Staff in code 101, 104, and code 106," 12 May 1970, box 65, folder 2, JHP.

13. Allan Cartter, "The University's Statement on Last Friday's Election," 19 May 1970, box 65, folder 2, JHP.

14. Irving Berezin, "Status of Union Negotiations," 10 Sept. 1970, box 65, folder 2, JHP.

15. "A contract: not a run-around," Sept. 1970, box 65, folder 3, JHP.

16. "Dreamy University or Nightmare Union," June 1971, box 65, folder 2, JHP.

17. Don Holloschutz, Vandals Smash Loeb Windows as Strike Rolls On," *Washington Square Journal*, Mar. 30, 1971, 1; Don Holloschutz, "Garbage Fire Heats up NYU Workers' March," *Washington Square Journal*, May 6, 1971, 1.

18. "Strike at the Garden by Utility Workers Cancels All Events," *New York Times*, June 7, 1971, 40.

19. Williams Jones, "Salaries at NYU without a union are among the best at private universities and colleges in this area," 24 May 1971, box 65, folder 2, JHP.

20. Joselow, Froma and Don Holloschutz, "Strike Expected Over Bargaining Agent," *Washington Square Journal*, April 13, 1970, 1.

21. "Reply to the University position of 17 April 1970," Apr. 1970, box 1, folder NYU's Position, Staff Unionization, OGC. NYU has been unable to provide any information on the extent of this turnover. Because many of the clerical workers involved were also students, it is reasonable to assume that this figure was indeed high.

22. Malcolm, Andrew, "NYU Loss Put at $4.5 Million," *New York Times*, Dec. 4, 1970, 31.

23. "Memo from Irving Berezin to James Hester," 21 Sept. 1970, folder 1, box 65, JHP; "Memo from Irving Berezin to Cartter Allen," 12 Apr. 12, 1971, folder 1, box 65, JHP.

24. Sonny Kleinfield, "Strike Ends; Workers Return Today," *Washington Square Journal*, 29 Apr. 1970, 1.

25. "We Win!," May 1970, box 65, folder 3, JHP.

26. As an example, during the organizing drive at Frank Ix & Sons, the organizer Louis Agre told the local paper that 80 percent of the workers there had signed union cards. This was a lie. According to a memo written by Agre himself, only 160 out of a possible 460 workers had actually signed cards. See Louis Agre, "Frank Ix and Sons," 10 Nov. 1980, box 830, Papers of the ACTWU; and Charles Giametta, "Textile Union Organizing Here: Ix Plant Is Target," 10 Oct. 1980, *The Daily Progress*, box 79, folder 3, Papers of Frank Ix and Sons.

27. NLRB case no. 2–RM-1621, 21 July 1971, box 65, folder 1, JHP.

28. "The Big Lie," 27 May 1971, box 65, folder 3, JHP.

29. Williams Jones, "The Likelyhood of the Union Ordering You Out on Strike," 1 June 1971, box 65, folder 2, JHP.

30. "Dreamy University or Nightmare Union," June 1971, box 65, folder 2, JHP.

31. Williams Jones, "The Likelyhood of the Union . . . ," 1 June 1971.

32. "Setting the record straight," June 1971, box 65, folder 3, JHP; "Dear Fellow Employee," 7 June 1971, box 1, folder "Promotional materials issued by District 65," (hereafter cited as Promtional of Dist. 65) OGC.

33. "Dear Fellow Employee," 7 June 1971.

34. "Special Meeting," 1971, box 65, folder 3, JHP.

35. "NYU Concedes," Apr. 1970, box 65, folder 3, JHP; "The strike is over!," Apr. 1970, box 65, folder 3, JHP; *NYU Local News*, 25 July 1970, box 65, folder 3, JHP.

36. "Join Us, We Are the NYU Local," 1971, box 65, folder 3, JHP.

37. James Hester, "University's Position on Disruptions," 17 Apr. 1970, box 65, folder 2, JHP.

38. Hugh Davis Graham, *Civil Rights and the Presidency: Race and Gender in American Politics, 1960–1972* (New York: Oxford University Press, 1992), ch. 10.

39. "Questions and answers about the NYU local," Dec. 1970, box 1, folder Promotional of Dist. 65, OGC.

40. "Right on with 153," May 1970, box 65, folder 3, JHP.

41. "The Big Lie," 27 May 1971, box 65, folder 3, JHP.

42. Jones, "The Likelihood of the Union . . . ," 1 June 1971.

43. Holloschutz, "Vandals Smash Loeb Windows . . . ," 1; Holloschutz, "Garbage Fire Heats up NYU Workers' March," 1.

44. Jones, "The Likelihood of the Union . . . ," 1 June 1971.

45. James Hester, "Acts of Violence," 23 Apr. 1970, box 1, folder NYU's Position, Staff Unionization, OGC.

46. Peter Fishauf and Walter Kelly, "NYU to Ask State for Election," *Washington Square Journal,* April 20, 1970, 1.

47. "Your paycheck is trying to tell you a story," 12 Dec. 1969, box 65, folder 3, JHP.

48. Kelly, "Local Trying to Form an All-U Union," 1

49. "Your paycheck is trying to tell you a story," 12 Dec. 1969.

50. "Who's fooling who?" Sept. 1970, box 65, folder 3, JHP; Hester, James, "The University's position on strike," 17 Apr. 1970, box 65, folder 2, JHP.

51. Jones, "Salaries at NYU without a union . . . ," 24 May 1971.

52. Williams Jones, "NYU Employees have a good overall fringe benefit package," 26 May 1971, box 65, folder 2, JHP.

53. "Instead of just talking let's look at facts," June 1971, box 65, folder 2, JHP.

54. Jones, "Salaries at NYU without a union . . . ," 24 May 1971.

55. "Promises . . . Promises," June 1971, box 65, folder 2, JHP.

56. "Right on with 153," May 1970; "The Big Lie," 27 May 1971; "It's your future, look it over," May 1971, box 1, folder "Promotional Material issued by Local 153," OGC.

57. "Who's fooling who?" Sept. 1970.

58. "The bigger the vote the better the salary increase," May 1970, box 65, folder 3, JHP.

59. Jones, "Salaries at NYU without a union . . . ," 24 May 1971.

60. Ibid.

61. Kelly, "Local Trying to Form an All-U Union," 1.

62. "Dear Fellow Employee," 7 June 1971.

63. "What it's all about," 22 Apr. 1970, box 1, folder Promotional of Dist. 65, OGC.

64. "You can't fool all the people all the time," May 1971, box 65, folder 3, JHP.

65. "To all employees at New York University, Tomorrow you will decide . . . ," May 1970, box 65, folder 3, JHP; "Setting the record straight," June 1971, box 65, folder 3, JHP; "It's your future, look it over," May 1971, box 1, folder Promotional material issued by Local 153, OGC.

66. "It's your future, look it over," May 1971.

67. "The facts about the May 15 election," May 1970, box 65, folder 3, JHP.

68. Levy *The New Left and Labor in the 1960's* (Urbana: University of Illinois Press, 1994), 1.

69. Paul Buhle, Mari-Jo Buhle, and Dan Georgakas, eds., *Encyclopedia of the American Left,* 2d ed. (New York: Oxford University Press, 1998), 191–92.

70. "Enough is enough," May 1970, box 65, folder 3, JHP.

71. "Rally at Washington Sq. Park," April 1970, box 65, folder 3, JHP.

72. "Union hits NYU double standard," May 1970, box 65, folder 3, JHP.

73. "NYU Local supports cafeteria workers' demands," April 1970, box 65, folder 3, JHP.

74. "On the line," 2 Dec. 1970, box 1, folder Promotional of Dist. 65, OGC.

75. "Demands for a District 65 contract," May 1970, box 65, folder 3, JHP.

76. "Free . . . And it's just for you," Oct. 1970, box 1, folder Promotional of Dist. 65, OGC.

77. "How the equal rights amendment will affect working women," 8 Oct. 1970, box 1, folder Promotional of Dist. 65, OGC.

78. Graham, *Civil Rights and the Presidency,* ch. 11; Alice Kessler-Harris, *In Pursuit of Equity: Men, Women, and the Quest for Economic Citizenship in 20th-Century America* (New York: Oxford University Press, 2001), ch. 5, 6.

79. "Demands for a District 65 contract," May 1970, box 65, folder 3, JHP.

80. "What it's all about," 22 Apr. 1970.

81. Gary Fink, ed., *Labor Unions* (Westport, Conn.: Greenwood Press, 1977), 256–57.

82. "On Monday morning a group of us employed at New York University, assisted by representatives of Local 153 . . . ," May 1970, box 65, folder 3, JHP.

83. Ibid.

84. "Right on with 153," May 1970; "On Monday morning a group of us . . . ," May 1970; "Setting the record straight," June 1971; "The Big Lie," 27 May 1971.

85. "On Monday morning a group of us . . . ," May 1970; "The Big Lie," 27 May 1971.

86. "A voice in our own affairs," May 1971, box 65, folder 3, JHP; "Reply to the University position of 17 April 1970," April 1970, box 1, folder NYU's position, OGC.

87. "Friday fact sheet," 24 Apr. 1970, box 65, folder 3, JHP; Kleinfield"Strike Ends; Workers Return Today," 1.

88. "Questions and answers about the NYU local," Dec. 1970, ; see also "Wednesday fact sheet," April 1970, box 65, folder 3, JHP.

89. Eileen Hoffman, "Union vs. University," *Washington Square Journal*, 17 Feb. 1971, 2; see also *NYU Local News*, 25 July 1970, box 65, folder 3, JHP.

90. "Union hits NYU double standard," May 1970.

91. "NYU Denies Workers Rights!," Sept. 1970, box 65, folder 3, JHP.

92. "Union busting is a non-credit course at NYU," April 1970, box 65, folder 3, JHP.

93. *NYU Local News*, 25 July 1970.

94. Jones, "Salaries at NYU without a union . . . ," 24 May 1971.

95. "To all employees at New York University . . . ," May 1970.

96. "We are not alone," May 1971, box 65, folder 3, JHP.

97. Williams Jones, "College and University office staffs have rejected unions, especially District 65," 7 June 1971, box 65, folder 2, JHP.

98. "It's your future, look it over," May 1971.

99. "They Lie Again!," June 1971, box 65, folder 3, JHP.

100. "Vote No Union June 11th," June 1971, box 1, folder Promotional materials issued by No-Union Staff Committee, OGC. I have been able to locate only four people of the thirty-five that are listed as being members of the No-Union Committee. Unfortunately, these four people do not remember anything about the committee. In fact, they do not remember anything about the campaign at all beyond the statement by one lady that "we felt we just didn't need a union."

101. Kleinfield, "Strike Ends; Workers Return Today," 1.

102. Williams Jones, "Better lines of communication between NYU and its employees," 28 May 1971, box 65, folder 2, JHP.

103. Williams Jones, "What you lose if the union wins the election," 3 June 1971, box 65, folder 2, JHP.

104. "Questions and answers about the NYU local," Dec. 1970.

105. "What it's all about," 22 Apr. 1970.

106. "Library workers take first step toward union recognition," March 1970, box 65, folder 3, JHP.

107. "Join Us, We are the NYU Local," 1971, box 65, folder 3, JHP; "The Strike Continues," April 1970, box 65, folder 3, JHP; "Union wins first grievance," May 1970, box 1, folder Promotional of Dist. 65; "Questions and answers about the NYU local," Dec. 1970.

108. "Union wins first grievance," May 1970.

109. *NYU Local News*, 25 July 1970.

110. Jones, "Better lines of communication . . . ," 28 May 1971.

111. Jones, Williams, "The importance of your vote," 10 June 1971, box 65, folder 2, JHP; see also Jones, "Better lines of communication . . . ," 28 May 1971.

112. Jones, "Better lines of communication . . . ," 28 May 1971.
113. Jones, "What you lose . . . ," 3 June 1971.
114. "You can't fool all the people all the time," May 1971, box 65, folder 3, JHP.
115. "A voice in our own affairs," May 1971, box 65, folder 3, JHP.
116. "What it's all about," 22 Apr. 1970.
117. "Can you trust *this* union?," May 1971, box 65, folder 3, JHP.
118. Jones, "Better lines of communication . . . ," 28 May 1971.
119. "Right on with 153," May 1970.
120. JR, an NYU clerical employee, "What Unions do TO You," undated, folder 3, box 65, JHP (emphasis in original).
121. District 65 apparently believed that NYU's nonprofit status should make it less antiunion. Thus, when the university adopted policies the union felt were antiunion, it complained that NYU was acting "like any other private corporation that is trying to keep its employees from organizing themselves." See "Union bustin . . . ," April 1970; and "Who's fooling who?" Sept. 1970, for examples; "On strike—close it down," April 1970, box 65, folder 3, JHP.
122. Lacey Fosburgh, "NYU Law School Is Focusing on Unifying Nationwide Protest," *New York Times,* May 7, 1970, 20.
123. Semeraro, Richard, "New York University's position on District 65's request for recognition," 13 Apr. 1970, box 65, folder 2, JHP.
124. "Union busting . . . ," April 1970; "NYU Library and Placement workers on strike," April 1970, box 65, folder 3, JHP.
125. Williams Jones, "Better lines of communication between NYU and its employees," 28.
126. Jones, "Better lines of communication . . . ," 28 May 1971.

Chapter 6: The Union that Wasn't

1. Mills, *White Collar: The American Middle Classes* (1951, repr. New York: Oxford University Press, 1953), 317.
2. Edward Sargent, "Teachers to Vote Tuesday," *Washington Post,* June 23, 1985, F3.
3. Urban, *Gender, Race, and the National Education Association,* 173.
4. Leo Troy, *The New Unionism in the New Society: Public Sector Unions in the Redistributive State* (Fairfax, Va.: George Mason University Press, 1994), 31–43. See also Freeman and Medoff, *What Do Unions Do?,* 243–44; Bronfenbrenner and Juravich, *Union Organizing in the Public Sector;* and Freeman, "The Effects of Public Sector Labor Laws on Labor Market Institutions and Outcomes."
5. Troy, *The New Unionism in the New Society,* 43–47.
6. "Which One Would You Choose?," 1976, box 6, folder Cincinnati Federation of Teachers Collective Bargaining Campaign, 1976 (hereafter cited as Cincinnati CB), Papers of the AFT Southern Region (unprocessed), Walter Reuther Library, Wayne State University (hereafter cited as PAFTSR).

7. Selden, *The Teacher Rebellion*, 55.

8. For more on the history of the NEA, see Urban, *Gender, Race, and the National Education Association*, quote on page 267.

9. "Know the Challenge," 1980, box 8, folder NEA, PAFTSR.

10. For a history of the AFT see Marjorie Murphy, *Blackboard Unions: The AFT and the NEA, 1900–1980* (Ithaca, N.Y.: Cornell University Press, 1990). For more on the AFT and NEA during the 1980s and 1990s, see Urban, *Gender, Race, and the National Education Association*.

11. *Sarasota Educator*, 1983, box 5, PAFTSR. The AFT's adoption of more professional concerns may be attributable to a number of factors. In part, this shift may have been an attempt by the federation to make itself more attractive to teachers wary of its identification as a union. It may have also resulted from a desire on Shanker's part to strengthen the union's ability to protect its members. The Ocean Hill–Brownsville strike, for which the AFT was responsible, was at heart a dispute over how much control the community should have over the schools versus how much control should be in the hands of teachers and their organizations. In the ideology of professionalism, it is the practitioner that should make the decisions about the proper course of action, not the client. Thus, by advancing the union's claim to being a professional organization, the AFT could strengthen its assertion that it, and not the community, should exercise the greatest control over the schools. Finally, Marjorie Murphy argued that this shift was due to the increased sense of security felt by Shanker. "Shanker's proposals for reform address a world in which the majority of teachers have the protections of collective bargaining. The NEA leadership's caution reflects a basic lack of confidence in the powers of unionism to protect teacher's interests. Shanker's proposal, on the other hand, may reflect an unwarranted confidence in the power of the unions." Murphy, *Blackboard Unions*, 269.

12. Memo from Phil Kugler to Raoul Teilhet, 24 May 1982, box 8, folder NEA, PAFTSR.

13. Memo from Raoul Teilhet to CFT Executive Council, 27 April 1982, box 8, folder NEA, PAFTSR.

14. *Sarasota Educator*, 1983, box 5, PAFTSR.

15. *CFT Newsliner*, 5 Aug. 1976, box 6, folder Cincinnati CB, PAFTSR.

16. "Two responses to the NEA," 1980, box 8, folder NEA, PAFTSR.

17. "Here's what the NEA says about the AFL-CIO," 1980, box 8, folder Fact Booklet, PAFTSR.

18. Selden, *The Teacher Rebellion*, 82.

19. For examples in NEA and AFT literature, see "A more perfect union," 24 Nov. 1976, box 6, folder Cincinnati CB, PAFTSR; and Memo from Phil Kugler to Raoul Teilhet, 24 May 1982. Both Murphy and Urban make use of these linguistic shortcuts to identify the two organizations, as does this study.

20. *The Cincinnati Teacher*, 29 Sept. 1976, box 6, folder Cincinnati CB, PAFTSR; "Which One Would You Choose?," 1976.

21. "Which One Would You Choose?," 1976.

22. "New union for city teachers," *Cincinnati Post,* Dec. 3, 1976, box 6, folder Cincinnati CB, PAFTSR; "Teachers Oust CTA as Agent," *Cincinnati Enquirer,* Dec. 3, 1976, box 6, folder Cincinnati CB, PAFTSR.

23. For Washington, D.C., example see "You've got rights!," 1985, box 8, PAFTSR; for Lake County example, see "One of these unions offers experienced representation right here in Lake County," 1985, box 8, PAFTSR.

24. Urban, *Gender, Race, and the National Education Association,* 269–70.

25. Murphy, *Blackboard Unions,* 223.

26. "You Compare," 1980, box 8, folder Fact Booklet, PAFTSR.

27. "Two responses to the NEA," 1980, box 8, folder NEA, PAFTSR.

28. "Here's what the NEA says about the AFL-CIO," 1980, box 8, folder Fact Booklet, PAFTSR.

29. "Two responses to the NEA," 1980.

30. *Sarasota Educator,* 1983, box 5, PAFTSR.

31. "Which One Would You Choose?," 1976.

32. *Sarasota Educator,* 1983.

33. "Know the Challenge," 1980.

34. "Straight talk about . . . AFL-CIO," 1980, box 8, PAFTSR.

35. "Know the Challenge," 1980.

36. "Here's what the NEA says . . . ," 1980.

37. National Education Association, *Address and Proceedings of the One-Hundred-Tenth Annual Meeting,* 1972, vol. 110, 18.

38. "Two responses to the NEA," 1980.

39. "Straight talk about . . . AFL-CIO," 1980.

40. "Know the Challenge," 1980.

41. "Straight talk about . . . AFL-CIO," 1980.

42. Murphy, *Blackboard Unions,* 268.

43. "The AFL-CIO on Teachers Issues," 1976, box 6, folder Cincinnati CB, PAFTSR.

44. Ibid.; "I fear CFT because . . . ," 1976, box 6, folder Cincinnati CB, PAFTSR.

45. For reference to Dewey, see *Sarasota Educator,* 1983; for reference to Einstein, see "Dear SCTA Members," May 5, 1983, box 5, PAFTSR.

46. "Dear SCTA Members," May 5.

47. Memo from Jerry Byrum to Roger Stephens, 16 Aug. 1976, box 6, folder Cincinnati CB, PAFTSR.

48. *Sarasota Educator,* 1983.

49. "Two responses to the NEA," 1980.

50. "The AFT vs. the NEA," 1980, box 8, folder NEA, PAFTSR.

51. *CFT Newsliner,* Aug. 5, 1976, box 6, folder Cincinnati CB, PAFTSR.

52. "What you don't know about AFT could hurt you," 1985, box 8, PAFTSR.

53. Urban, *Gender, Race, and the National Education Association,* 146.

54. "The Winning Combination," 1976, box 6, folder Cincinnati CB, PAFTSR.

55. "We've made a little list . . . ," 1976, box 6, folder Cincinnati CB, PAFTSR.

56. "Burnout," 1985, box 8, PAFTSR.

57. "Promises . . . Promises . . . Promises," 1976, box 6, folder Cincinnati CB, PAFTSR.

58. *The Cincinnati Teacher,* Oct. 13, 1976, box 6, folder Cincinnati CB, PAFTSR; memo from Charlotte Roe to Walter Waddy, 5 Dec. 1976, box 6, folder Cincinnati CB, PAFTSR; *The Cincinnati Teacher,* Oct. 13, 1976, ; "Publication in one local school by EA supporter," Nov. 29, 1976, box 6, folder Cincinnati CB, PAFTSR; "Local 1520 Could Cost You Plenty," 1976, box 6, folder Cincinnati CB, PAFTSR.

59. "A message for: Vigo County Teachers," 1976, box 7, folder Terre Haute Collective Bargaining Campaign, 1976 (hereafter cited as Terre Haute CB), PAFTSR.

60. "CTA Puts Education First," *Cincinnati Enquirer,* 1976, box 6, folder Cincinnati CB, PAFTSR.

61. *The Cincinnati Teacher,* Oct. 13, 1976; "Local 1520 Could Cost You Plenty," 1976; and "CTA President Ruth Clephane talks with Republican Robert Taft," 1976, box 6, folder Cincinnati CB, PAFTSR.

62. Selden, *The Teacher Rebellion,* 55.

63. Urban, *Gender, Race, and the National Education Association,* 254–55.

64. Allen West, *The National Education Association: The Power Base for Education* (New York: Free Press, 1980), 45.

65. Urban, *Gender, Race, and the National Education Association,* 254–55.

66. Selden, *The Teacher Rebellion,* 55.

67. Ronald Corwin, *Education in Crisis: A Sociological Analysis of Schools and Universities in Transition* (New York: Wiley, 1974), 243.

68. Selden, *The Teacher Rebellion,* 110.

69. For the charge against, see "I'm not in CFT because . . . ," 1976, box 6, folder Cincinnati CB, PAFTSR; for CFT's defense, see "I fear CFT because . . . ," 1976, box 6, folder Cincinnati CB, PAFTSR.

70. Urban, *Gender, Race, and the National Education Association,* 254–55.

71. Corwin, *Education in Crisis,* 235.

72. Memo from Philip Kugler to Vito de Leonardis, 6 Oct. 1976, box 6, folder Cincinnati CB, PAFTSR.

73. Murphy, *Blackboard Unions,* 265.

74. Sam Pizzigati, "She Has a Dream," *NEA Today,* May 1998, 46.

75. Daniel Walkowitz, *Working with Class: Social Workers and the Politics of Middle-Class Identity* (Chapel Hill, N.C.: University of North Carolina Press, 1999).

76. Corwin, *Education in Crisis,* 227.

77. West, *The National Education Association,* 45.

78. "Know the Challenge," 1980.

79. For the first quote, see "I fear CFT because . . . ," 1976; for the second quote, see "Teachers Win Accords in Three Major Cities," 1976, box 6, folder Cincinnati CB, PAFTSR.

80. "Teachers' Federation Files Election Petitions," 1976, box 6, folder Cincinnati CB, PAFTSR.

81. "Dear Colleague," 5 Feb. 1976, box 7, folder Terre Haute CB, PAFTSR; "We are puzzled," 1976, box 7, folder Terre Haute CB, PAFTSR; *Sarasota Educator,* 1983; and "A Strike against fair play," 19 March 1984, box 8, folder PAFTSR.

82. "New union for city teachers," *Cincinnati Post,* Dec. 3, 1976, box 6, folder Cincinnati CB, PAFTSR.

83. Urban, *Gender, Race, and the National Education Association,* 173; and Sargent, "Teachers to Vote Tuesday," F3.

84. "Remember?: The CTA's Record of Failure," 1976, box 6, folder Cincinnati CB, PAFTSR, emphasis added.

85. "No Money??," 1976, box 6, folder Cincinnati CB, PAFTSR.

86. "AFL-CIO Local 1520 Could Cost You Plenty," 1976.

87. "A more perfect union," 24 Nov. 1976, box 6, folder Cincinnati CB, PAFTSR.

88. "Stay with a proven winner," 1976, box 7, folder Terre Haute CB, PAFTSR.

89. *Capital Teachers,* 1985, box 8, PAFTSR; "An open letter to WTU members," 25 Aug. 1984, box 8, PAFTSR; *Capital Teachers,* 1985, box 8, PAFTSR.

90. "An open letter to WTU members," 25 Aug. 1984.

91. "I fear CFT because . . . ," 1976, box 6, folder Cincinnati CB, PAFTSR.

92. "Memo from Charlotte Roe to Walter Waddy," 5 Dec. 1976, box 6, folder Cincinnati CB, PAFTSR.

93. "Looking forward to retirement?," 1976, box 6, folder Cincinnati CB, PAFTSR; "The Association: A Proven Leader in the Legislature," 1976, box 6, folder Cincinnati CB, PAFTSR.

94. *The Cincinnati Teacher,* Aug. 20, 1976, box 6, folder Cincinnati CB, PAFTSR.

95. "CTA President Ruth Clephane talks with Republican Robert Taft," 1976, box 6, folder Cincinnati CB, PAFTSR.

96. "Straight talk about . . . AFL-CIO," 1980.

97. Sidney Peck, *The Rank-and-File Leader* (New Haven, Conn.: College and University Press, 1963), 295; David Halle, *America's Working Man: Work, Home, and Politics among Blue-Collar Property Owners* (Chicago: University of Chicago Press, 1984), 195–97.

98. "How to tell a real issue from a phony," 1976, box 6, folder Cincinnati CB, PAFTSR; "A message for: Vigo County Teachers," 1976, box 7, folder Terre Haute CB, PAFTSR; "NEA AFT (AFL-CIO)," 1976, box 7, folder Terre Haute CB, PAFTSR; *Capital Teachers,* 1985.

99. *Capital Teachers,* 1985.

100. "I'm not in CFT because . . . ," 1976.

101. "-1098-," 1976, box 6, folder Cincinnati CB, PAFTSR; *CFT Newliner,* Oct. 15, 1976, box 6, folder Cincinnati CB, PAFTSR.

102. "What do teachers in 62 districts across the country have in common?," 1976, box 6, folder Cincinnati CB, PAFTSR.

103. "Stay with a proven winner," 1976, box 7, folder Terre Haute CB, PAFTSR.

104. This summary is based on my interview with the president of the local union at DuPont's Deep Water, New Jersey, plant in the summer of 2001. This union is now affiliated with the Paper, Allied Industries, and Chemical Employees (PACE). See also Edward Dent, *Betrayal: Employee Relations at DuPont: 1981–1994* (Lawrenceville, Va.: Brunswick Publishing, 1995).

105. "Know the Challenge," 1980.

106. "Dear Colleague," 29 Nov. 1976.

107 "I fear CFT because . . . ," 1976.

108. "A more perfect union," 24 Nov. 1976.

109. "An open letter to WTU members," 25 Aug. 1984.

110. "You've got rights!," 1985, emphasis added.

111. "Two responses to the NEA," 1980.

112. "Know the Challenge," 1980.

113. "The AFT vs. the NEA," 1980.

114. Urban, *Gender, Race, and the National Education Association*, 269.

115. "Which One Would You Choose?," 1976.

116. "A Strike against fair play," 19 Mar. 1984.

117. "WFT Our Homegrown Organization," 1980, box 8, PAFTSR.

118. "One of these unions offers experienced representation right here in Lake County," 1985, box 8, PAFTSR.

119. "How to save $51.27," 1976, box 6, folder Cincinnati CB, PAFTSR.

120. *The Cincinnati Teacher*, Sept. 29, 1976, box 6, folder Cincinnati CB, PAFTSR.

121. *Action Line*, 1976, box 7, folder Terre Haute CB, PAFTSR.

122. "What Association Dues Dollars Buy," 1976, box 6, folder Cincinnati CB, PAFTSR; "This Professional card will get you $500,000 Occupational Liability Insurance," 1976, box 6, folder Cincinnati CB, PAFTSR; "Locked Out?," 1976, box 6, folder Cincinnati CB, PAFTSR.

123. See "Purdy Collected $7,500," *Retail Clerks Advocate*, Oct. 1954, 5 for an example.

124. See respectively, "Which One Would You Choose?" 1976; and "AFL-CIO Local 1520 Could Cost You Plenty," 1976;

125. "Know the Challenge," 1980.

126. Urban, *Gender, Race, and the National Education Association*, 269–70.

127. "Did you know . . . ," 1985; "An open letter to WTU members," 25 Aug. 1984.

128. *Capital Teachers*, 1985.

129. "What you don't know about AFT . . . ," 1985.

130. Edward Sargent, "Washington Teachers Union Wins Election," *Washington Post*, June 26, 1985, B3.

131. Sargent, "Teachers to Vote Tuesday," F3.

132. State membership figures are from Charlene Haar, Myron Lieberman, and Leo Troy, *The NEA and the AFT: Teacher Unions in Power and Politics* (Rockport,

Mass.: Pro Active Publications, 1994), tbl. 2.1; states where collective bargaining is not permitted is given in Bronfenbrenner and Juravich, *Union Organizing in the Public*, 10.

133. Steven Greenhouse, "Teachers Reject Merger of Unions by Large Margin," *New York Times*, July 6, 1998, 1.

134. Rene Sanchez, "Teachers Union Merger Rejected," *Washington Post*, July 6, 1998, 1.

135. Jolene Franken, "Should NEA and AFT Unite to Form One New Organization?," *NEA Today*, May 1998, 47, emphasis added.

136. Peter Schrag, "Divided They Stand: Merger Mania Hits the Teachers' Unions," *New Republic*, May 25, 1998, 17.

137. See also Urban, *Gender, Race, and the National Education Association*, 269.

Conclusion

1. West, *The National Education Association*, 45.

2. Urban, *Gender, Race, and the National Education Association*, 254–55.

3. Hillman, "The Promise of American Labor," 62.

4. Larry Cohen and Richard Hurd, for instance, argue that workers' aversion to conflict plays a greater role in causing them to oppose unions than their fear for their jobs. Larry Cohen and Richard Hurd, "Fear, Conflict, and Union Organizing," in *Organizing to Win: New Research on Union Strategies*, edited by Kate Bronfenbrenner et al. (Ithaca, N.Y.: ILR Press, 1998).

5. Rogers and Freeman, *What Workers Want* (Ithica, N.Y.: ILR Press, 1999), 142–43.

6. Bronfenbrenner, "Employer Behavior in Certification Elections and First-Contract Campaigns," 89.

7. Rogers and Freeman, *What Workers Want*, 150.

8. Labor Day 2002 poll, AFL-CIO website: http://www.aflcio.org/mediacenter/upload/LaborDay2002Polls.ppt, accessed Dec. 5, 2007.

9. Port Huron Statement, http://coursesa.matrix.msu.edu/hst306/documents/~huron.html, accessed Dec. 12, 2007.

10. Michael Tomasky's article "Party in Search of a Notion," *The American Prospect*, May 2006, 20, generated a good deal of attention during the summer of 2006 and is a good example of this changing emphasis among progressives.

11. Dan Seligman, "In Love with the Teamsters?," *Forbes*, Oct. 6, 1997, 147; Michael Meyer, "Labor's Deliverance?," *Newsweek*, Aug. 25, 1997, 26.

12. John Sweeny, "Time for a New Contract," *Dissent*, Winter 1997, 35.

13. Jane Spencer, "The WTO Protest was only the Beginning," *Nation*, April 24, 2000, 22.

Bibliography

Books and Articles

Adamic, Louis, *Dynamite: The Story of Class Violence in America*, rev. ed. Glouster, Mass.: Peter Smith, 1934.

Allen, Frederick Lewis, *Only Yesterday: An Informal History of the Nineteen-Twenties*. New York: Harper and Brothers, 1931.

Auerbach, James, *Labor and Liberty: The La Follette Committee and the New Deal*. Indianapolis: Bobbs-Merrill, 1966.

Barber, Lucy, *Marching on Washington: The Forging of an American Political Tradition*. Berkeley: University of California Press, 2002.

Becker, Craig, "Democracy in the Workplace: Union Representations and Federal Labor Law," *Minnesota Law Review* (Feb. 1993): 77.

Bell, Daniel, *The Coming of Post-Industrial Society: A Venture in Social Forecasting*. 1973, 1976. New York: Basic Books, 1999.

Bellah, Robert, Richard Madsen, William Sullivan, Ann Swidler, and Steven Tipton, *Habits of the Heart: Individualism and Commitment in American Life*. 1985. Berkeley: University of California Press, 1996.

Bellamy, Edward, *Looking Backward, 2000–1887*. 1888. Cleveland: World Publishing, 1945.

Bernstein, Irving, *The Lean Years: A History of the American Worker, 1920–1933*. Boston: Houghton Mifflin, 1960.

Bernstein, Irving, *Turbulent Years: A History of the American Worker, 1933–1941*. Boston: Houghton Mifflin, 1971.

Berube, Maurice and Marilyn Gittell, eds., *Confrontation at Ocean Hill–Brownsville: The New York School Strikes of 1968*. New York: Praeger, 1969.

Blum, Albert, "Prospects for Organization of White-Collar Workers," *Monthly Labor Review* 87 (Feb. 1964): 125–29.

Bodnar, John, *Immigration and Industrialization: Ethnicity in an American Mill Town, 1870–1940*. Pittsburgh: University of Pittsburgh Press, 1977.

Bodnar, John, *The Transplanted: A History of Immigrants in Urban America*. Bloomington: Indiana University Press, 1985.

Bok, Derek, and John Dunlop, *Labor and the American Community*. New York: Simon and Schuster, 1970.

Brody, David, *Steelworkers in America: The Nonunion Era*. New York: Russell and Russell, 1970.

Brody, David, *Labor Embattled: History, Power, Rights*. Urbana: University of Illinois Press, 2005.

Bronfenbrenner, Kate, and Tom Juravich, *Union Organizing in the Public Sector: An Analysis of State and Local Elections*. Ithaca: ILR Press, 1995.

Bronfenbrenner, Kate, "Employer Behavior in Certification Elections and First-Contract Campaigns: Implications for Labor Law Reform," in *Restoring the Promise of American Labor Law*, 85–111, edited by Sheldon Friedman, Richard Hurd, Rudolph Oswald, and Ribald Seeber, Ithaca: ILR Press, 1994.

Brooks, Robert, *As Steel Goes . . .: Unionism in a Basic Industry*. New Haven: Yale University Press, 1940.

Brotslaw, Irving, "Attitude of Retail Workers Toward Union Organization," *Labor Law Journal* (Mar. 1967): 89–121.

Brown, Cliff, *Racial Conflict and Violence in the Labor Market: Roots in the 1919 Steel Strike*. New York: Garland Publishing, 1998.

Buhle, Paul, Mari-Jo Buhle, and Dan Georgakas, eds., *Encyclopedia of the American Left, 2d ed*. New York: Oxford University Press, 1998.

Clark, Daniel, *Like Night and Day: Unionization in a Southern Mill Town*. Chapel Hill: University of North Carolina Press, 1997.

Cohen, Larry, and Richard Hurd, "Fear, Conflict, and Union Organizing," in *Organizing to Win: New Research on Union Strategies*, 181–96, edited by Kate Bronfenbrenner, et. al., Ithaca: ILR Press, 1998.

Cohen, Lizabeth, *Making a New Deal: Industrial Workers in Chicago, 1919–1939*. New York: Cambridge University Press, 1990.

Cohen, Lizabeth, *A Consumers' Republic: The Politics of Mass Consumption in Postwar America*. 2003. New York: Random House, 2004.

Cohn, Jan, *Creating America: George Horace Lorimer and the* Saturday Evening Post. Pittsburgh: University of Pittsburgh Press, 1989.

Cooper, Laura, "Authorization Cards and Union Representation Election Outcome: An Empirical Assessment of the Assumption Underlying the Supreme Court's *Gissel* Decision," *Northwestern University Law Review* 79 (June 1984): 87–141.

Corwin, Ronald. *Education in Crisis: A Sociological Analysis of Schools and Universities in Transition*. New York: Wiley, 1974.

Craver, Charles, *Can Unions Survive?: The Rejuvenation of the American Labor Movement*. New York: New York University Press, 1993.

Croly, Herbert, *The Promise of American Life*. 1909. Boston: Northeastern University Press, 1989.

Cushman, Barry, *Rethinking the New Deal Court: The Structure of a Constitutional Revolution*. New York; Oxford University Press, 1998.

Daniel, Clete, *Culture of Misfortune: An Interpretive History of Textile Unionism in the United States*. Ithaca: ILR Press, 2001.

Davis, Mike, *Prisoners of the American Dream*. London: Verso Editions, 1986.

De Fleur, Melvin, and Sandra Ball-Rokeach, *Theories of Mass Communication, 3d ed.* 1966, 1970. New York: D. McKay, 1975.

Denning, Michael, *The Cultural Front: The Laboring of American Culture in the Twentieth Century*. London: Verso, 1997.

Dent, Edward, *Betrayal: Employee Relations at DuPont: 1981–1994*. Lawrenceville, Va.: Brunswick Publishing, 1995.

Dubofsky, Melvyn, *The State and Labor in Modern America*. Chapel Hill: University of North Carolina Press, 1994.

Dworkin, James and Marian Extejt, "The Union-Shop Deauthorization Poll: A New Look After 20 Years," *Monthly Labor Review* 102 (Nov. 1979): 36–40.

Englehardt, Tom, *The End of Victory Culture: Cold War America and the Disillusioning of a Generation*. New York: Basic Book, 1995.

Ernst, Daniel, *Lawyers against Labor: From Individual Rights to Corporate Liberalism*. Urbana: University of Illinois Press, 1995.

Farber, Henry, "The Extent of Unionization in the United States," in *Challenges and Choices Facing American Labor*, 15–44, edited by Thomas Kochan. (Cambridge: MIT Press, 1985.

Faue, Elizabeth, *Community of Suffering and Struggle: Women, Men, and the Labor Movement in Minneapolis, 1915–1945*. Chapel Hill: University of North Carolina Press, 1991.

Fine, Sidney, *"Without Blare of Trumpets": Walter Drew, the National Erectors Association, and the Open Shop Movement, 1903–57.* Ann Arbor: University of Michigan Press, 1995.

Fink, Gary, "Labor Law Revision and the End of the Postwar Labor Accord," in *Organized Labor and American Politics, 1894–1994: The Labor-Liberal Alliance*, 239–53, edited by Kevin Boyle. Albany: State University of New York Press, 1998.

Fink, Gary, ed., *Labor Unions*. Westport: Greenwood Press, 1977.

Fink, Leon, and Brian Greenberg, *Upheaval in the Quiet Zone: A History of Hospital Workers' Union, Local 1199*. Urbana: University of Illinois Press, 1989.

Fiorito, Jack, "Human Resource Management Practices and Worker Desires for Union Representation," in *The Future of Private Sector Unionism in the United States*, 205–26, edited by James Bennet and Bruce Kaufman. Armonk, N.Y.: M. E. Sharpe, 2002.

Fones-Wolf, Elizabeth, *Selling Free Enterprise: The Business Assault on Labor and Liberalism, 1945–1960*. Urbana: University of Illinois Press, 1994.

Forbath, William, *Law and the Shaping of the American Labor Movement.* Cambridge: Harvard University Press, 1991.

Foreman, James, *The Making of Black Revolutionaries.* 1972, 1985. Seattle: University of Washington Press, 1997.

Franks, Maurice, *What's Wrong with Our Labor Unions!* Indianapolis: Bobbs-Merrill, 1963.

Fraser, Steve, *Labor Will Rule: Sidney Hillman and the Rise of American Labor.* Ithaca: Cornell University Press, 1991.

Fraser, Steve and Gary Gerstle, *Rise and Fall of the New Deal Order, 1930–1980.* Princeton: Princeton University Press: 1989.

Freeman, Richard, "The Effects of Public Sector Labor Laws on Labor Market Institutions and Outcomes," in *When Public Sector Workers Organize,* 138–71, edited by Richard Freeman and Casey Ichniowski. Chicago: University of Chicago Press, 1988.

Freeman, Richard, "Spurts in Union Growth: Defining Moments and Social Processes," National Bureau of Economic Research, Working Paper 6012, April 1997.

Freeman, Richard, "Why Are Unions Faring Poorly in NLRB Representation Elections?" in *Challenges and Choices Facing American Labor,* 45–65, edited by Thomas Kochan. Cambridge: MIT Press, 1985.

Freeman, Richard, and James Medoff, *What Do Unions Do?* New York: Basic Books, 1984.

Freeman, Joshua, *Working-Class New York: Life and Labor since World War II.* New York: New Press, 2000.

Galbraith, John K., *The Affluent Society.* New York: Mentor Books, 1958.

Galbraith, John Kenneth, *American Capitalism: The Concept of Countervailing Power.* Boston: Houghton Mifflin, 1952.

Gall, Gilbert, *The Politics of Right to Work: The Labor Federations as Special Interests.* New York: Greenwood Press, 1988.

Gallup, George, *The Gallup Poll: Public Opinion, 1935–1971, vol. III.* New York: Random House, 1972.

Gallup, George, *The Gallup Poll: Public Opinion, 1972–1977, vol. I.* Wilmington, Del.: Scholarly Resources, 1978.

Geertz, Clifford, *The Interpretation of Cultures.* New York: Basic Books, 1973.

Gerstle, Gary, *Working-class Americanism: The Politics of Labor in a Textile City, 1914–1960.* New York: Cambridge University Press, 1989.

Gerstle, Gary, *American Crucible: Race and Nation in the Twentieth Century.* Princeton: Princeton University Press, 2001.

Getman, Julius, Stephen Goldberg and Jeanne Herman, *Union Representation Elections: Law and Reality.* New York: Russell Sage Foundation, 1976.

Gitlin, Todd, *The Whole World Is Watching: Mass Media in the Making and Unmaking of the New Left.* Berkeley: University of California Press, 1980.

Goldfield, Michael, *The Decline of Organized Labor in the United States.* Chicago: University of Chicago Press, 1987.

Goldhagen, Daniel, *Hitler's Willing Executioners: Ordinary Germans and the Holocaust.* New York: Vintage Books, 1996.

Goldstein, Bernard, and Bernard Indik, "Unionism as a Social Choice: The Engineers' Case," *Monthly Labor Review* 86 (Apr. 1963): 365–69.

Graham, Hugh Davis, *Civil Rights and the Presidency: Race and Gender in American Politics, 1960–1972.* New York: Oxford University Press, 1992.

Gramsci, Antonio, *The Antonio Gramsci Reader.,* Edited by David Forgacs. New York: New York University Press, 2000.

Griffith, Barbara, *The Crisis of American Labor: Operation Dixie and the Defeat of the CIO.* Philadelphia: Temple University Press, 1988.

Gross, James, *Broken Promise: The Subversion of U.S. Labor Relations Policy, 1947–1994.* Philadelphia: Temple University Press, 1995.

Haar, Charlene, Myron Lieberman, and Leo Troy, *The NEA and the AFT: Teacher Unions in Power and Politics.* Rockport, Mass.: Pro Active Publications, 1994.

Hale, Grace, *Making Whiteness: The Culture of Segregation in the South, 1890–1940.* New York: Pantheon Books, 1998.

Hall, Jacquelyn, James Leloudis, Robert Korstad, Mary Murphy, LuAnn Jones, and Christopher Day, *Like a Family: The Making of a Southern Cotton Mill World.* 1987. New York: W. W. Norton, 1989.

Halle, David, *America's Working Man: Work, Home, and Politics among Blue-Collar Property Owners.* Chicago: University of Chicago Press, 1984.

Halpern, Rick, *Down on the Killing Floor: Black and White Workers in Chicago's Packing Houses, 1904–54.* Urbana: University of Illinois Press, 1997.

Harrington, Michael, *The Other America: Poverty in the United States.* New York: Macmillan, 1962.

Harris, Howell, *The Right to Manage: Industrial Relations Policies of American Business in the 1940's.* Madison: University of Wisconsin Press, 1982.

Harris, Howell, *Bloodless Victories: The Rise and Fall of the Open Shop in the Philadelphia Metal Trades, 1890–1940.* New York: Cambridge University Press, 2000.

Heidenry, John, *Theirs Was the Kingdom: Lila and DeWitt Wallace and the Story of Reader's Digest.* New York: W. W. Norton, 1993.

Higham, John, *Strangers in the Land: Patterns of American Nativism, 1860–1925.* New Brunswick: Rutgers University Press, 1955.

Hirsch, Barry, and Edward Schumacher, "Private Sector Union Density and the Wage Premium: Past, Present, and Future," in *The Future of Private Sector Unionism in the United States,* 92–118, edited by James Bennet and Bruce Kaufman. Armonk, N.Y.: M. E. Sharpe, 2002.

Hobsbawm, Eric, *Age of Revolution, 1789–1848.* 1962. New York: Vintage Books, 1996.

Holland, Dorothy and Debra Skinner, "Prestige and Intimacy: The Cultural Models behind Americans' Talk about Gender Types" in *Cultural Models in Language and Thought*, 88–105, edited by Dorothy Holland and Naomi Quinn. New York: Cambridge University Press, 1987.

Honey, Michael, *Southern Labor and Black Civil Rights: Organizing Memphis Workers*. Urbana: University of Illinois Press, 1993.

Horowitz, Roger, *Negro and White, Unite and Fight!: A Social History of Industrial Unionism in Meatpacking, 1930–90*. Urbana: University Illinois Press, 1997.

Huberman, Leo, *The Truth about Unions*. New York: Pamphlet Press, 1946.

Interchurch World Movement, *Commission of Inquiry, Report on the Steel Strike of 1919*. New York: Harcourt, Brace, and Howe, 1920.

Jacoby, Sanford, *Modern Manors: Welfare Capitalism since the New Deal*. Princeton: Princeton University Press, 1997.

Jacobson, Matthew Frye, *Whiteness of a Different Color: European Immigrants and the Alchemy of Race*. Cambridge: Harvard University Press, 1998.

Kassalow, Everett, "Organization of White-Collar Workers," *Monthly Labor Review* 84 (March 1961): 234–38.

Kazin, Michael, *The Populist Persuasion: An American History*. New York: Basic Books, 1995.)

Kazin, Michael, *Barons of Labor: The San Francisco Building Trades and Union Power in the Progressive Era*. Urbana: University of Illinois Press, 1987.

Keen, Sam, *Faces of the Enemy: Reflections on the Hostile Imagination*. San Francisco: Harper and Row, 1986.

Kessler-Harris, Alice, *In Pursuit of Equity: Men, Women, and the Quest for Economic Citizenship in Twentieth-Century America*. New York: Oxford University Press, 2001.

Klarman, Michael, "Brown, Racial Change, and the Civil Rights Movement," *Virginia Law Review* (Feb. 1994): 7.

Klein, Janice and David Wanger, "The Legal Setting for the Emergence of the Union Avoidance Strategy," in *Challenges and Choices Facing American Labor*, 75–88, edited in Thomas Kochan. Cambridge: MIT Press, 1985.

Kleiner, Morris, "Intensity of Management Resistance: Understanding the Decline of Unionization in the Private Sector," in *The Future of Private Sector Unionism in the United States*, 292–316, edited by James Bennet and Bruce Kaufman. Armonk, N.Y.: M. E. Sharpe, 2002.

Kochan, Thomas, "How American Workers View Labor Unions," *Monthly Labor Review* 102 (Apr. 1979.

Kocka, Jurgen, *White Collar Workers in America, 1890–1940: A Social-Polithite Collar Workers in America, 1890–1940*. London: Sage, 1980.

Korstad, Robert, *Civil Rights Unionism: Tobacco Workers and the Struggle for Democracy in the Mid-Twentieth-Century South*. Chapel Hill: University of North Carolina Press, 2003.

Lears, Jackson, *Fables of Abundance: A Cultural History of Advertising in America.* New York: Basic Books, 1994.

Levison, Andrew, *The Working-Class Majority.* New York: Coward, McCann and Geoghegan, 1974.

Levinson, Edward, *I Break Strikes!: The Technique of Pearl L. Bergoff.* New York: Arno Press, 1969.

Levy, Peter, *The New Left and Labor in the 1960s.* Urbana: University of Illinois Press, 1994.

Lichtenstein, Nelson and Howell John Harris, eds., *Industrial Democracy in America: The Ambiguous Promise.* New York: Cambridge University Press, 1993.

Lichtenstein, Nelson, *The Most Dangerous Man in Detroit: Walter Reuther and the Fate of American Labor.* New York: Basic Books, 1995.

Lichtenstein, Nelson, *State of the Union: A Century of American Labor.* Princeton: University of Princeton Press, 2002.

Lichtenstein, Nelson, *Labor's War at Home: The CIO in World War II.* New York: Cambridge University Press, 1982.

Lippmann, Walter, *Public Opinion.* New York: Harcourt Brace, 1922.

Lippmann, Walter, *Drift and Mastery: An Attempt to Diagnose the Current Unrest.* 1914. Englewood Cliffs, N.J.: Prentice-Hall, 1961.

Lipset, Seymour Martin and William Schneider, *The Confidence Gap: Business, Labor, and Government in the Public Mind.* Baltimore: Johns Hopkins University Press, 1983.

Lipset, Seymour Martin, "The Future of Private Sector Unions in the U.S.," in *The Future of Private Sector Unionism in the United States,* 9–27, edited by James Bennet and Bruce Kaufman. Armonk, N.Y.: M. E. Sharpe, 2002.

Lipset, Seymour Martin, "Labor Unions in the Public Mind," in *Unions in Transition: Entering the Second Century,* 287–320, edited by Seymour Martin Lipset. San Francisco: ICS Press, 1986.

Lipset, Seymour Martin, "North American Labor Movements: A Comparative Perspective," in *Unions in Transition: Entering the Second Century,* 421–54, edited by Seymour Martin Lipset. San Francisco: ICS Press, 1986.

Lipsitz, George, *Rainbow at Midnight: Labor and Culture in the 1940s.* Urbana: University of Illinois Press, 1994.

London, Jack, *War of the Classes.* New York: MacMillan Company, 1905.

Maclean, Nancy, *Behind the Mask of Chivalry: The Making of the Second Ku Klux Klan.* New York: Oxford University Press, 1994.

Manley, Roger and Charles McNichols, "Attitudes of Federal Scientists and Engineers Toward Unions," *Monthly Labor Review* 98 (Apr. 1975): 57–60.

McCartin, Joseph, *Labor's Great War: The Struggle for Industrial Democracy and the Origins of Modern American Labor Relations, 1912–1921.* Chapel Hill: University of North Carolina Press, 1997.

McQuail, Denis, *Mass Communication Theory: An Introduction, 3d. ed.* 1983, 1987. London: Sage, 1994.

Meyer, Stephen, *"Stalin Over Wisconsin": The Making and Unmaking of Militant Unionism, 1900–1950.* New Brunswick, N.J.: Rutgers University Press, 1992.

Mills, C. Wright, *The New Men of Power: America's Labor Leaders.* 1948. Urbana: University of Illinois Press, 2001.

Mills, C. Wright, *White Collar: The American Middle Classes.* 1951. New York: Oxford University Press, 1953.

Mills, C. Wright, *The Power Elite.* 1956. New York: Oxford University Press, 2000.

Mills, C. Wright, "The Trade Union Leader: A Collective Portrait," *Public Opinion Quarterly* 9 (Summer, 1945): 154–81.

Minchin, Timothy, *What Do We Need a Union For: The TWUA in the South, 1945–1955.* Chapel Hill: University of North Carolina Press, 1997.

Minchin, Timothy, *Hiring the Black Worker: The Racial Integration of the Southern Textile Industry, 1960–1980.* Chapel Hill: University of North Carolina Press, 1999.

Minchin, Timothy, *Fighting Against the Odds: A History of Southern Labor Since World War II.* Gainesville: University Press of Florida, 2005.

Minchin, Timothy, *"Don't Sleep With Stevens!:" The J.P. Stevens Campaign and the Struggle to Organize the South, 1963–80.* Gainesville: University Press of Florida, 2005.

Mink, Gwendolyn, *Old Labor and New Immigrants in American Political Development: Union, Party, and State, 1875–1920.* Ithaca: Cornell University Press, 1986.

Mishel, Lawrence, and Paula Voos, *Unions and Economic Competitiveness.* Armonk, N.Y.: M. E. Sharpe, 1992.

Montgomery, David, *The Fall of the House of Labor: The Workplace, the State, and American Labor Activism, 1865–1925.* New York: Cambridge University Press, 1987.

Moody, Kim, *An Injury to All: The Decline of American Unionism.* London: Verso, 1988.

Morawska, Ewa, *For Bread with Butter: The Life-Worlds of East Central Europeans in Johnstown Pennsylvania, 1890–1940.* New York: Cambridge University Press, 1985.

Murphy, Marjorie, *Blackboard Unions: The AFT and the NEA, 1900–1980.* Ithaca: Cornell University Press, 1990.

National Education Association, *Address and Proceedings of the One-Hundred-Tenth Annual Meeting,* vol. 110, 1972.

Niebuhr, Reinhold, *Moral Man and Immoral Society: A Study in Ethics and Politics.* 1932. Louisville: Westminster John Knox Press, 2001.

Norwood, Stephen, *Strikebreaking and Intimidation: Mercenaries and Masculinity in Twentieth-Century America.* Chapel Hill: University of North Carolina Press, 2002.

Parker, Mike, "Industrial Relations Myth and Shop-Floor Reality: The 'Team Concept' in the Auto Industry," in *Industrial Democracy in America: The Ambiguous Promise*, 249–74, edited by Nelson Lichtenstein and Howell John Harris. New York: Cambridge University Press, 1993.

Peck, Sidney, *The Rank-and-File Leader*. New Haven: College and University Press, 1963.

Perse, Elizabeth, *Media Effects and Society*. Mahwah, N.J.: L. Erlbaum, 2001.

Pilat, Oliver, *Pegler: Angry Man of the Press*. Westport, Conn.: Greenwood Press, 1963.

Piore, Michael, and Charles Sabel, *The Second Industrial Divide: Possibilities for Prosperity*. New York: Basic Books, 1984.

Podair, Jerald, *The Strike that Changed New York: Blacks, Whites, and the Ocean Hill–Brownsville Crisis*. New Haven: Yale University Press, 2002.

Potter, Edward, "Labor's Love Lost?: Changes in the U.S. Environment and Declining Private Sector Unionism," in *The Future of Private Sector Unionism in the United States*, 188–204, edited by James Bennet and Bruce Kaufman. Armonk, N.Y.: M. E. Sharpe, 2002.

Preston, William, *Aliens and Dissenters: Federal Suppression of Radicals, 1903–1933*. 1963. Urbana: University of Illinois Press, 1994.

Puette, William, *Through Jaundiced Eyes: How the Media View Organized Labor*. Ithaca: ILR Press, 1992.

Reider, Jonathan, "The Rise of the Silent Majority," in *Rise and Fall of the New Deal Order, 1930–1980*, 246–47, edited by Steve Fraser and Gary Gerstle. Princeton: Princeton University Press, 1989.

Richberg, Donald, *Labor Union Monopoly: A Clear and Present Danger*. Chicago: H. Regnery, 1957.

Riis, Jacob, *How the Other Half Lives: Studies Among the Tenements of New York*. 1890. New York: Penguin Books, 1997.

Roediger, David, *Working Toward Whiteness: How America's Immigrants Became White: The Stange Journey from Ellis Island to the Suburbs*. New York: Basic Books, 2005.

Rogers, Joel, and Richard Freeman, *What Workers Want*. Ithaca: ILR Press, 1999.

Rogers, Joel, "In the Shadow of the Law: Institutional Aspects of Postwar U.S. Union Decline," in *Labor Law in America: Historical and Critical Essays*, 283–302, edited by Christopher Tomlins and Andrew King. Baltimore: Johns Hopkins University Press, 1992.

Ross, Dorothy, *The Origins of American Social Science*. New York: Cambridge University Press, 1991.

Ross, Steven, *Working-Class Hollywood: Silent Film and the Shaping of Class in America*. Princeton: Princeton University Press, 1998.

Rosenzweig, Roy, "Organizing the Unemployed: The Early Years of the Great Depression, 1929–1933," *Radical America* 10, no. 4 (1976): 37–60.

Ryant, Carl, *Profit's Prophet: Garet Garret (1878–1954)*. Selinsgrove, Pa.: Susquehanna University Press, 1989.

Sayles, Leonard, and George Strauss, *The Local Union: Its Place in the Industrial Plant*. New York: Harper, 1953.

Schneider, Eugene, *The Rank-and-File Leader*. New Haven: College and University Press, 1963.

Schneider, David, *American Kinship: A Cultural Account*. Chicago: University of Chicago Press, 1980.

Seidman, Harold, *Labor Czars: A History of Labor Racketeering*. New York: Liveright Publishing, 1938.

Selden, David, *The Teacher Rebellion*. Washington, D.C.: Howard University Press, 1985).

Sitkoff, Harvard, *A New Deal for Blacks: The Emergence of Civil Rights as a National Issue: The Depression Decade*. New York: Oxford University Press, 1978.

Smith, Robert Michael, *From Blackjacks to Briefcases: A History of Commercialized Strikebreaking and Unionbusting in the United States*. Athens: Ohio University Press, 2003.

Stein, Judith, *Running Steel, Running America: Race, Economic Policy, and the Decline of Liberalism*. Chapel Hill: University of North Carolina Press, 1998.

Strauss, George, "Dilemma for Engineers: Union or Professional Society?" *Monthly Labor Review* 87 (Aug. 1964): 1026–28.

Stromquist, Shelton, *Reinventing "The People": The Progressive Movement, the Class Problem, and the Origins of Modern Liberalism*. Urbana: University of Illinois Press, 2006.

Susman, Warren, *Culture as History: The Transformation of American Society in the Twentieth Century*. New York: Pantheon Books, 1984.)

Swanberg, W. A., *Luce and His Empire*. New York: Scribner, 1972.

Thompson, E. P., *The Making of the English Working Class*. New York: Vintage Books, 1963.

Tomlins, Christopher, *Law, Labor, and Ideology in the Early American Republic*. New York: Cambridge University Press, 1993.

Tomlins, Christopher, *The State and the Unions: Labor Relations, Law, and the Organized Labor Movement, 1880–1960*. New York: Cambridge University Press, 1985.

Troy, Leo, "Twilight for Organized Labor," in *The Future of Private Sector Unionism in the United States*, 59–76, edited by James Bennet and Bruce Kaufman. Armonk, N.Y.: M. E. Sharpe, 2002.

Troy, Leo, *The New Unionism in the New Society: Public Sector Unions in the Redistributive State*. Fairfax, Va.: George Mason University Press, 1994.

Tugwell, Rexford, *The Brains Trust*. New York: Viking Press, 1968.

Urban, Wayne, *Gender, Race, and the National Education Association: Professionalism and Its Limitations*. New York: RoutledgeFalmer, 2000.

Veblen, Thorstein, *Engineers and the Price System*. New York: B. W. Huebsch, 1921.

Walkowitz, Daniel, *Working with Class: Social Workers and the Politics of Middle-Class Identity*. Chapel Hill: University of North Carolina Press, 1999.

Waring, Stephen, *Taylorism Transformed: Scientific Management Theory since 1945*. Chapel Hill: University of North Carolina Press, 1991.

Weiler, Paul, "Promises to Keep: Securing Workers' Rights to Self-Organization under the NLRA," *Harvard Law Review* 96 (June 1983): 1760–85.

Witwer, David, *Corruption and Reform in the Teamsters Union*. Urbana: University of Illinois Press, 2003.

West, Allen, *The National Education Association: The Power Base for Education*. New York: Free Press, 1980.

Whyte, William, *The Organization Man*. 1956. Philadelphia: University of Pennsylvania Press, 2002.

Witwer, David, *Corruption and Reform in the Teamsters Union*. Urbana: University of Illinois Press, 2003.

Wood, James Paysted, *The Curtis Magazines*. New York: Ronald Press, 1971.

Zahavi, Gerald, *Workers, Managers, and Welfare Capitalism: The Shoeworkers and Tanners of Endicott Johnson, 1890–1950*. Urbana: University of Illinois Press, 1988.

Zaniello, Tom, *Working Stiffs, Union Maids, Reds and Riffraff: An Organized Guide to Films about Labor*. Ithaca: Cornell University Press, 1996.

Zieger, Robert, "From Primordial Folk to Redundant Workers: Southern Textile Workers and Social Observers, 1920–1990," in *Southern Labor in Transition, 1940–1995*, 273–94, edited by Robert Zieger. Knoxville: University of Tennessee Press, 1997.

Zieger, Robert, *The CIO, 1935–1955*. Chapel Hill: University of North Carolina Press, 1995.

Papers and Archives

Papers of the Amalgamated Clothing and Textile Workers of America (unprocessed), Kheel Center, Cornell University.

Papers of Frank Ix & Sons, Inc. (unprocessed), Special Collections, University of Virginia.

James Hester Papers, NYU Archives.

Office of the General Counsel, NYU Archives.

Papers of the AFT Southern Region (unprocessed), Walter Reuther Library, Wayne State University.

Index

LAWRENCE RICHARDS
earned his Ph.D. from the
University of Virginia.

Worker City, Company Town: Iron and Cotton-Worker Protest in Troy and Cohoes, New York, 1855–84 *Daniel J. Walkowitz*

Life, Work, and Rebellion in the Coal Fields: The Southern West Virginia Miners, 1880–1922 *David Alan Corbin*

Women and American Socialism, 1870–1920 *Mari Jo Buhle*

Lives of Their Own: Blacks, Italians, and Poles in Pittsburgh, 1900–1960 *John Bodnar, Roger Simon, and Michael P. Weber*

Working-Class America: Essays on Labor, Community, and American Society *Edited by Michael H. Frisch and Daniel J. Walkowitz*

Eugene V. Debs: Citizen and Socialist *Nick Salvatore*

American Labor and Immigration History, 1877–1920s: Recent European Research *Edited by Dirk Hoerder*

Workingmen's Democracy: The Knights of Labor and American Politics *Leon Fink*

The Electrical Workers: A History of Labor at General Electric and Westinghouse, 1923–60 *Ronald W. Schatz*

The Mechanics of Baltimore: Workers and Politics in the Age of Revolution, 1763–1812 *Charles G. Steffen*

The Practice of Solidarity: American Hat Finishers in the Nineteenth Century *David Bensman*

The Labor History Reader *Edited by Daniel J. Leab*

Solidarity and Fragmentation: Working People and Class Consciousness in Detroit, 1875–1900 *Richard Oestreicher*

Counter Cultures: Saleswomen, Managers, and Customers in American Department Stores, 1890–1940 *Susan Porter Benson*

The New England Working Class and the New Labor History *Edited by Herbert G. Gutman and Donald H. Bell*

Labor Leaders in America *Edited by Melvyn Dubofsky and Warren Van Tine*

Barons of Labor: The San Francisco Building Trades and Union Power in the Progressive Era *Michael Kazin*

Gender at Work: The Dynamics of Job Segregation by Sex during World War II *Ruth Milkman*

Once a Cigar Maker: Men, Women, and Work Culture in American Cigar Factories, 1900–1919 *Patricia A. Cooper*

A Generation of Boomers: The Pattern of Railroad Labor Conflict in Nineteenth-Century America *Shelton Stromquist*

Work and Community in the Jungle: Chicago's Packinghouse Workers, 1894–1922 *James R. Barrett*

Workers, Managers, and Welfare Capitalism: The Shoeworkers and Tanners of Endicott Johnson, 1890–1950 *Gerald Zahavi*

Men, Women, and Work: Class, Gender, and Protest in the New England Shoe Industry, 1780–1910 *Mary Blewett*

Marching Together: Women of the Brotherhood of Sleeping Car Porters
  Melinda Chateauvert
Down on the Killing Floor: Black and White Workers in Chicago's Packinghouses,
  1904–54   *Rick Halpern*
Labor and Urban Politics: Class Conflict and the Origins of Modern Liberalism in
  Chicago, 1864–97   *Richard Schneirov*
All That Glitters: Class, Conflict, and Community in Cripple Creek
  Elizabeth Jameson
Waterfront Workers: New Perspectives on Race and Class   *Edited by Calvin Winslow*
Labor Histories: Class, Politics, and the Working-Class Experience   *Edited by*
  Eric Arnesen, Julie Greene, and Bruce Laurie
The Pullman Strike and the Crisis of the 1890s: Essays on Labor and Politics
  Edited by Richard Schneirov, Shelton Stromquist, and Nick Salvatore
AlabamaNorth: African-American Migrants, Community, and Working-Class
  Activism in Cleveland, 1914–45   *Kimberley L. Phillips*
Imagining Internationalism in American and British Labor, 1939–49   *Victor Silverman*
William Z. Foster and the Tragedy of American Radicalism   *James R. Barrett*
Colliers across the Sea: A Comparative Study of Class Formation in Scotland and the
  American Midwest, 1830–1924   *John H. M. Laslett*
"Rights, Not Roses": Unions and the Rise of Working-Class Feminism, 1945–80
  Dennis A. Deslippe
Testing the New Deal: The General Textile Strike of 1934 in the American South
  Janet Irons
Hard Work: The Making of Labor History   *Melvyn Dubofsky*
Southern Workers and the Search for Community: Spartanburg County,
  South Carolina   *G. C. Waldrep III*
We Shall Be All: A History of the Industrial Workers of the World (abridged edition)
  Melvyn Dubofsky, ed. Joseph A. McCartin
Race, Class, and Power in the Alabama Coalfields, 1908–21   *Brian Kelly*
Duquesne and the Rise of Steel Unionism   *James D. Rose*
Anaconda: Labor, Community, and Culture in Montana's Smelter City   *Laurie Mercier*
Bridgeport's Socialist New Deal, 1915–36   *Cecelia Bucki*
Indispensable Outcasts: Hobo Workers and Community in the American Midwest,
  1880–1930   *Frank Tobias Higbie*
After the Strike: A Century of Labor Struggle at Pullman   *Susan Eleanor Hirsch*
Corruption and Reform in the Teamsters Union   *David Witwer*
Waterfront Revolts: New York and London Dockworkers, 1946–61   *Colin J. Davis*
Black Workers' Struggle for Equality in Birmingham   *Horace Huntley and*
  David Montgomery
The Tribe of Black Ulysses: African American Men in the Industrial South
  William P. Jones
City of Clerks: Office and Sales Workers in Philadelphia, 1870–1920
  Jerome P. Bjelopera

The University of Illinois Press
is a founding member of the
Association of American University Presses.

Composed in 10.5/13 Adobe Minion Pro
with FF Meta display
by Jim Proefrock
at the University of Illinois Press
Manufactured by Thomson-Shore, Inc.

University of Illinois Press
1325 South Oak Street
Champaign, IL 61820-6903
www.press.uillinois.edu

DATE DUE